This beautifully cr[illegible]ographically and sociologically at th[illegible]bution to Visual Sociology, it teache[illegible] techniques at the same time as it sho[illegible]ly and aesthetically by working wi[illegible]

Caroline Knowl[illegible]*mmunity Research, Goldsmiths, University of London*

This is the 'go to' book for visual researchers. Terence Heng brings together a wealth of practical know-how with a comprehensive methodological knowledge of visual ethnography. Written in an accessible, engaging and dynamic narrative style, this insightful text will be an invaluable resource for novice and experienced researchers across the arts, humanities and social sciences.

Elaine Campbell, *Professor of Criminology, Newcastle University*

A well-written, practical resource, Heng guides the social scientist through the technical and social processes required to create meaningful, impactful photographs.

Helen Lomax, *Professor of Health and Wellbeing, University of Northampton*

Visual Methods in the Field

The use of images, particularly photography, has been steadily gaining popularity in academia, but there has not yet been a book that deals with the act and process of photo-taking in the field. Drawing upon 21 years of photographic experience and sociological research, Terence Heng's immersive and narrative style will:

1. introduce photography as a qualitative method;
2. discuss the intricacies of, challenges in and opportunities for using a camera in the field;
3. explore common themes and topics in social science research, including photographing rituals, space, people and objects;
4. advise on navigating the always evolving technological landscapes of traditional, digital and mobile photography.

Visual Methods in the Field: Photography for the Social Sciences is a photography guide written for researchers by a researcher. Using in-depth ethnographic case studies from research done in various urban environments, this book will act as a crucial bridge for students in geography, sociology, education, media studies and other social sciences to incorporate photography into their research repertoire.

Terence Heng is an Assistant Professor at the Singapore Institute of Technology, and received his PhD in Visual Sociology from Goldsmiths, University of London. Working on the intersections between creative practice and sociological research, Terence investigates the making of ethnic identities amongst Chinese individuals through everyday rituals and geographies, and was the inaugural winner of the International Visual Sociology Association's Prosser Award in 2015. His research has been featured in journals like *The Sociological Review*, *Geographical Review*, *Cultural Geographies* and *Visual Communication.*

Visual Methods in the Field

Photography for the Social Sciences

Terence Heng

Routledge
Taylor & Francis Group
LONDON AND NEW YORK

First published 2017
by Routledge
2 Park Square, Milton Park, Abingdon, Oxon OX14 4RN

and by Routledge
711 Third Avenue, New York, NY 10017

Routledge is an imprint of the Taylor & Francis Group, an informa business

British Library Cataloguing in Publication Data
A catalogue record for this book is available from the British Library

Library of Congress Cataloging in Publication Data
Names: Heng, Terence, 1978- author.
Title: Visual methods in the field : photography for the social sciences / by Terence Heng.
Description: 1 Edition. | New York : Routledge, 2016.
Identifiers: LCCN 2016018289| ISBN 9781138810327 (hardback) | ISBN 9781138810334 (pbk.) | ISBN 9781315749594 (ebook)
Subjects: LCSH: Social sciences—Research. | Photography in the social sciences. | Qualitative research.
Classification: LCC H62 .H377 2016 | DDC 300.72/1—dc23
LC record available at https://lccn.loc.gov/2016018289

ISBN: 978-1-138-81032-7 (hbk)
ISBN: 978-1-138-81033-4 (pbk)
ISBN: 978-1-315-74959-4 (ebk)

Typeset in Bembo
by RefineCatch Limited, Bungay, Suffolk

Printed and bound in Great Britain
by Bell and Bain Ltd, Glasgow

MIX
Paper from responsible sources
FSC® C007785

For E-Ping

Contents

Thematic list of contents

The thematic list of contents lists selected topics in this book in a more traditional sequence when teaching photography.

Figures

Tables

Acknowledgements

Special thanks to my teachers, lecturers, professors and mentors over the years who have influenced my academic journey. Most importantly, Caroline Knowles at Goldsmiths who saw me through all the ups and downs of my PhD in Visual Sociology. Wyn Morgan at Nottingham who started me on the path of academia. Sue Dopson at Oxford, who first planted in me the idea of photography as a way to do research. Les Back and Paul Halliday at Goldsmiths, Miri Song at Kent, Liew Kai Khiun at Nanyang Technological. Deepest thanks too to Hui Yew-Foong at Hong Kong Shue Yan, who gave me the opportunity to be part of the Bukit Brown Documentary Project, and whose advice about academia and publishing proved invaluable. Thanks, too, to my colleagues at my current university, the Singapore Institute of Technology, and especially Provost Loh Han Tong who chose to take a chance on me. Karen Hong, Mervyn Tan, Charles Carroll, Jiow Hee Jhee and Jeanette Ng for their support and encouragement.

I would also like to thank individuals at UniSIM and the UniSIM Centre for Chinese Studies (UCCS) – Foo Tee Tuan, Tan Soo Yean and Linda Chiu, who all in one way or another contributed to the creation of this book – especially through the UCCS Small Research Grants programme and travel grants programme that allowed me to continue my research even as an adjunct. Thanks as well to Gerhard Boomgaarden and Alyson Claffey at Routledge, who have worked to give this book a home and have guided me over the last two years to its completion.

My deepest thanks to my family – my wife E-Ping, who has endured all the late nights, vacations and weekends spent writing and researching. My sister Deborah and her family – Lutfey, Aaryan and Ishaan, my parents-in-law Ngoh Bah and Emily, my mother Jenny, and my late father Ivan, who all have shaped and continue to shape my meandering paths. And, of course, to God for courage and comfort.

Finally, thanks to my informants and collaborators in the field, who are too many to be named exhaustively, but some I must specially mention. All the couples who allowed me to be both photographer and researcher at their weddings and Ng Chin Leng from Singaporebrides.com who started me on my professional path. Angela Goh, Martina Yeo and Ip Pik Ching from the Bukit Brown Documentary Project. Victor Yue, Nicholas Fu, Kervin, Lim Kim Hui, Jonathan, Bosheng, Joseph, Jave Wu and the worshippers at *Xuan Jiang Dian, Fu Tian Dian, Shan Wei Tan* and *Bao De Gong* for their incredible patience and tolerance.

chapter 1

Introduction: photography in the field

Introduction

In 2012 I was asked by Dr Hui Yew-Foong, an anthropologist working in Singapore to assist in the visual documentation of Bukit Brown Cemetery, commonly called Bukit Brown for short. Long forgotten as a municipal cemetery in the 1970s, Bukit Brown is now symbolic of the tensions between conservation and progress in the nation-state of Singapore. Sited on prime land near ultra-expensive landed properties, it was announced in 2008 that the cemetery would first be cut in half by a four-lane road connecting the North of Singapore to its central motorway, and then in another 20 years be terraformed into more housing with more property. The state, realising a surge in demand for heritage and notions of the past, commissioned a three-year study to document and record not only the affected graves, but also the social and cultural life of the cemetery.

It was during the latter in which I first realised a need for this book. As a photographer trained in Sociology (and not the other way around), I focussed on visually engaging with the rituals, individuals and artefacts of Bukit Brown, whilst Yew-Foong both spoke to our informants and photographed when he could. I carried the equipment I would normally use on professional shoots, whilst Yew-Foong and other research assistants used smaller all-in-one cameras. In perfect lighting conditions, our images had similar levels of sharpness and detail – good samples of visual data documenting everyday objects in a cemetery. The problems began to occur when we started photographing in different and often difficult conditions. Grave exhumations were often carried out at night, with little artificial light. Covered in primary tropical rainforest, we were layered in a blanket of darkness – and the only photographs (and some videos) that we could use as data became mine.

As much as the anecdote sounds like a call for larger budgets for equipment (and admittedly good, professional-grade gear does make a research project easier), it is not. With 20 years of experience first as a commercial photographer, then as a social researcher who employs visual methods, I knew how to use my camera to its maximum potential. Even while trying to ensure that I had developed a nuanced understanding of the rituals I was observing, my mind was constantly assessing the situation and deciding on aperture and metering modes, while monitoring shutter speeds to prevent blurriness from camera shake. I observed and composed, then observed again through my camera's lens, using it as a fulcrum of interaction between me and my informants. In other words, I was, as Edward Weston (1965) puts it, "seeing photographically."

Although a number of social researchers work regularly and successfully with photographers (Knowles 2006; Knowles and Harper 2009), we are more likely to see scholars taking up a camera to record their own observations, especially certain social science disciplines, such as Anthropology (Banks 2001; Pinney 1997; Pink 2008), Sociology (Harper 2012), Human Geography (Comaroff 2007) and Education (Prosser and Schwartz 1998).

In recent years there has been a marked increase in interest in visual methods, but often the response to this interest has been to consider the post-photographed photograph, rather than the photograph that has yet to be photographed. In her very excellent book *Visual Methodologies* (2006), Gillian Rose sets out the aim of the book, which is to "provide a basic introduction to a range of methods that can be used to interpret visual images, and (the book) . . . provides enough references for (the reader) to develop more detailed methods if (the reader) need(s) to." (Rose 2006:xiv). Rose, drawing from Hall (1997), points out that there is no one true meaning or interpretation of an image, and therefore, in order to have one's meaning deemed acceptable, one must be able to justify that meaning, hence the need for a robust and rigorous *visual* methodology, a way to develop theories of the visual.

Rose's book is exemplary of the texts available to social researchers interested in the broad topic of "visual methods." Most students will also have read Sarah Pink's *Doing Visual Ethnography* (2007), which introduced me and many of my peers to the idea that one *could* use a camera in the field. Other useful books in this genre include those by Banks

(2001), Collier and Collier (1986), Mitchell (2011) and Spencer (2011). Whilst such volumes were and still are invaluable to theorising, understanding and using visual images as part of one's research, many fail to recognise, or minimise, the aspect of creating the photographs that are to be read.

For example, in *Visual Methodologies*, Rose does devote an entire chapter to the act of making photographs as part of one's research project (Rose 2006:237). Creating two broad categories, the use of photographs to *support* and *supplement* social science research, Rose explores the various ways in which photographs are used and created by researchers. However, little attention is paid to the "creation" aspect. She discusses the act of photo-documentation, in particular Suchar's (2004) project on documenting gentrifying neighbourhoods and how he chooses to use a "shooting script" – a series of sub-questions about his chosen space – to link the kinds of photographs taken with his research question. But in doing so she only addresses the "how-to" from a non-technical, social science perspective (i.e. a shooting script might tell a researcher how to focus his or her attention on particular spaces, objects or people, but does not say how such photographs should be created, or what the challenges of creating these photos are). Likewise, in Douglas Harper's also-excellent guide to Visual Sociology, entitled *Visual Sociology* (2012), Harper takes the reader on a journey of documenting the social using visual means, particularly photography. However, Harper's focus is also on the sociological techniques of research, i.e. what should be included in a photograph. Harper does include a small section towards the end of the book that discusses the technical aspects of the methods he introduces, including aperture, shutter speed and so on, but this is fleeting compared to the much more in-depth discussions of photography-related subjects.

In other words, although there are a number of very well-written guides in the social science literature on *what* to photo-document and how to *read, interpret* and *use* the created photograph, there is a lack of information and guidance on *how* the photographs should be created from a *technical* point of view. Although some will argue that this niche is filled by technical manuals or photography classes, I propose that such approaches ignore the needs of social science researchers and the fields in which we do our work. Through this book, I will argue for the need for an awareness and fluency in "photographic grammar," that while all photographs are useful and hold ethnographic value (Pink 2008), there is much potential for social researchers to "add ethnographic value" by creating more impactful, detailed or expressive images that support their arguments, inspire social change or simply make social research *look better* or, as Barthes (1981) would put it, for us to code *studium* into our images. In the rest of this chapter I will first map out what I mean by photographic grammar, framing it within well-known thought-pieces by Sontag (1977), Barthes (1981), Weston (1965) and others – I will show through examples how, all things being equal, a strong photograph helps communicate data more powerfully than a weak one. I will then introduce the rest of the book chapters, showing how, through case studies in the field, one can develop one's own version of photographic grammar.

Developing a photographic grammar

In an increasingly globalised academic landscape, albeit one that is still prejudiced towards works in English, command of the English language is a valuable scholarly trait. However, with widening participation in publishing and submissions, publishers often encounter writers whose first language is not English submitting their work. This is evidenced, for example, in Taylor & Francis's website for author services,[1] where various videos have been posted in Mandarin, Arabic, Japanese and Korean offering advice to potential authors, along with suggestions and links to external, third-party companies who can assist with writing style and grammar. Such services suggest that a well-written, clearly argued and fluent book or journal article appears more likely to be well-received than one that is not.

The Oxford dictionary[2] defines grammar as "The whole system and structure of a language or of languages in general, usually taken as consisting of syntax and morphology (including inflections) and sometimes also phonology and semantics." It also considers the term "grammar" to imply "the basic elements of an area of knowledge or skill," as well as "a set of actual or presumed prescriptive notions about (the) correct use of a language." Good grammar, therefore, implies the ability to follow a prescribed set of rules regarding a language or skill in order to demonstrate mastery of said language or skill. To have good grammar, especially in the case of language, may not necessarily mean the user is an effective communicator, but it does suggest that the user has some ability pertaining to the medium. While it is not in the purview of this book to discuss the theories of effective communication (or the skills necessary to be an effective communicator), I want to propose that, for the purpose of this analogy, we accept that good grammar is an important contributor to the development of skills and eventual mastery in a particular area of knowledge.

From a photographic point of view, mastery is a crucial aspect of a photographer's toolkit. Whilst many social researchers approximate adequate competency with a camera to be similar to that of a voice recorder (i.e. if you can use it and turn it on, that's good enough), photographers have more exacting expectations. In her book *The Photography Reader* (2003), Liz Wells included a short but exceptional essay by Edward Weston (1886–1958), a twentieth-century American photographer best known for his work on nudes, still life and landscapes. Weston was also the first photographer to be awarded a Guggenheim Fellowship, and his work remains archived at the University of California: Santa Cruz and the Smithsonian Museum. Weston's essay, *Seeing Photographically* (1965), was written in 1943, when photography was becoming increasingly popular, but significantly before the explosion of personal imaging devices that we see in mobile technology today. However, what Weston wrote about the act of photography remains as pertinent now as it was in 1943.

> *It is learning to see photographically – that is, learning to see his subject matter in terms of the capacities of his tools and processes, so that he can instantaneously translate the elements and values in a scene before him into the photograph he wants to make.*
>
> (Weston 1965:173)

One of Weston's main arguments in his essay was that photographers of his age had not yet achieved a level of technical mastery that allowed them to photograph instinctively, to express their intention or tell their story with the camera as an extension of themselves. Instead, Weston points out that ". . . few photographers master their medium. Instead they allow the medium to master them and go on an endless squirrel cage chase from new lens to new paper to new developer to new gadget . . . becoming lost in a maze of technical information" (1965:173). Whilst Weston seemed to advocate a minimalist approach to equipment, he was also telling photographers to master their "tools" and "processes" (1965:174).

How does one achieve that mastery in the context of social science research? The majority of us are, after all, not professionally trained photographers who have spent many years honing their craft in the same way we hone our theoretical and methodological minds in graduate school. But in the same way we practise and refine (hopefully) our grammar of language when performing academic writing, I argue that we need to do the same when creating visual images. If we hold ourselves to high standards of grammar and language when writing, so too should we apply those same standards to the creation of data – quantitative, qualitative, visual or otherwise. We are often quick to determine and judge the quality of both quantitative data – p-values, R^2, chi-squared and so on – and qualitative data, from the number of individuals one might have interviewed to the length of time one is involved in a participant observation study. Such standards have taken much time and effort to construct, and this introduction is only the beginning of the development of photographic grammar. But for the purpose of this book, I will propose a few things that will frame the rest of the chapters in creating "good" (however subjective) photographic data.

What might constitute good photographic grammar? Again, from a technical perspective, many photographers would point to various rules that are taught as basics to beginners – "correct" exposure, the rules of thirds, framing, leading lines and so on (Cross (2014) calls it a technical-aesthetic). Whilst these rules are useful and indeed should not be ignored, they are not the only aspect we should be concerned with. As social researchers, we are in the business of communicating the social conditions, relationships, values, opinions and circumstances of our informants, collaborators or interlocutors. Although many photographers (especially documentary photographers) seek to do the same, our photographs, especially those we choose to present as important data, need to be encoded to be as, if not more, useful than textual descriptions, quotes from our informants, or bar graphs from survey results.

In other words, our photographs need to invite readers to *study* them so as to inform their understanding of our argument. I propose that Barthes's (1981) concept of *studium* is useful here. As Houlihan (2004) notes, "the studium speaks of the interest which we show in a photograph, the desire to study and understand what the meanings are in a photograph, to explore the relationship between the meanings and our own subjectivities." La Grange (2005) further elaborates on this by outlining the five functions of studium – "to inform, to represent, to surprise, to cause to signify, to provoke desire" (Barthes 1981:28). For the purpose of developing a photographic grammar in social research, I propose that three of these functions are the most relevant – to inform, to surprise and to provoke desire. I will deal with each of these in turn.

To inform

In Barthes's framework, the photograph is the subject of three things – the operator (the photographer who photographs), the spectum (the referent or the thing that is photographed) and the spectator (the individual who views and consumes the photograph). The act of *informing*, according to Barthes, lies in the detailed definition of a photograph, the same kind of mechanical fidelity that Weston (1965) writes about in his article on seeing photographically. Barthes's vision of the photograph is that it shows details – and through these details the photograph transmits knowledge of the referent to the spectator. For a mundane photograph that is taken "as is" (straight-on angle, 50mm lens mimicking the human eye's field of vision, perfectly flat lighting conditions), this function tends to be accurate – the photograph is a source of information and knowledge. For social researchers looking to develop cultural inventories of their informants' lives, photographs can potentially tell a more nuanced story than a textual description. But this idea of information is simplistic and needs to be extended – information about details, about mundane elements, only reveals part of the social data that we strive to capture and present. Instead, a photograph can "inform" us of a great number of other things (Banks 2001) – emotion, ambience, and other sensorial aspects of the referent.

In my own visual research (Heng 2014), I often use a sensorial approach (Pink 2008) in my fieldwork, taking on the role of a wandering ghost during the 7th Chinese lunar calendar month, also known as the Hungry Ghost Festival. As part of this approach I wandered the urban neighbourhood late at night, photographing makeshift altars and offerings that were part of rituals for the festival. The photographs I chose to curate and eventually publish (Heng 2014, 2015) did more than just show evidence of altars during a particular period of time, they demonstrated the way altars influenced the spaces they were placed in, creating a secondspace (Soja 1996) of spirituality that overlaid carefully planned and arranged firstspaces set out by the state.

In Figure 1.1, a Singapore hawker (colloquial term for a small business owner often selling food, groceries or sundries) from the adjacent market and food centre gingerly places an offering on a well-manicured grass patch. Here, there were two ways of photographing my subject. I could approach him and ask him to repeat what he just did whilst photographing him straight on. In order to ensure that that I documented the

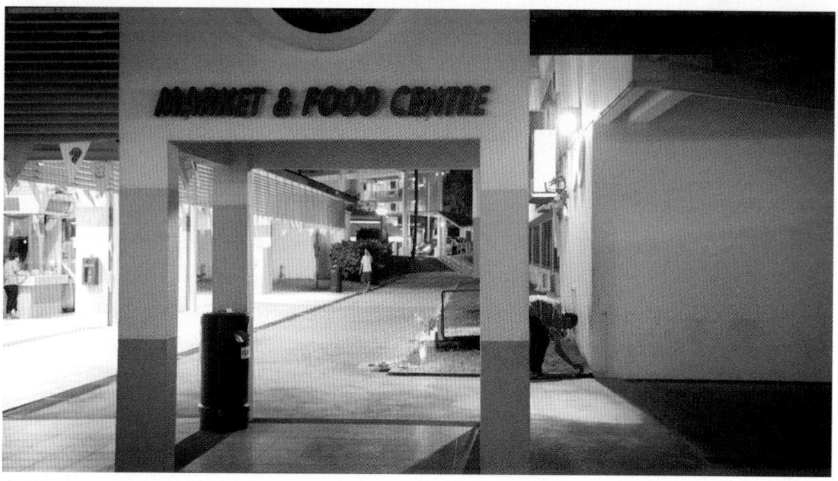

Figure 1.1 Hawker planting makeshift altar in Singapore.

entire ritual, I would take many photographs in sequence, from the same angle, probably also using some source of artificial light (e.g. camera flash) to ensure sharpness and detail.

Such an approach would certainly achieve an intention to show place-making (Crang 1998) in a particular space. It would also prove to be a useful way of understanding everyday life in Singapore at a particular point of time. However, I would argue that such photographs are too easily replaceable by textual descriptions or a video clip. They only "inform" us of the individual and his actions, not the context, circumstances, environment or other factors that texture his everyday life (Lefebvre 1996) and his identifications. Even as they reveal what he is doing, they hide many other things that could tell us more about the man himself and the ritual.

Instead, I chose to take a wider approach, framing him between pillar and wall (partly also to suggest the constrictions of identity politics by the state), using the signpost as an informational foreground, and contrasting his act against the right-angled straight lines on the ground that demarcated one area from another.

To surprise

The term surprise often implies a sense of suddenness and/or shock (pleasant or unpleasant). But in this section I argue that the surprise we can incorporate into our photographs is more about the unexpected epiphanic insights that a photograph can grant that textual observations are unable to do. Barthes notes that when a photograph surprises, it is through one of five means. One, the "exoticity" of the referent (how rare it is in relation to the spectator – one might argue that this is an important feature in both anthropological and mass media images of "distant" tribes). Two, revealing something that the human eye is incapable of viewing (like freeze-framing the spinning blades of a moving helicopter, as noted by Zhang (2012)). Three, including the display of "prowess" – which could mean either the photographic achievement of something extremely difficult, or perseverance in a particular photographic project. (Barthes used the example of Harold Edgerton's Milk Drop Coronet photograph (1936).) Four, the "contortions of technique" that distort an individual's assumption of what the human eye perceives – Peter Jackson's use of forced perspective in the *Lord of the Rings* and *The Hobbit* trilogies are very good examples of this (see Allain 2012). Finally, the "lucky find," a juxtaposition or positioning of elements in a photograph not often expected in everyday life.

Whilst these five means are useful in understanding how a photograph works to surprise, not all of them are equally feasible to all researchers in all research projects. For instance, one's field of study may or may not be seen as rare or exotic, depending on who the audience might be. The "lucky find," when "found," is an extremely powerful tool, but unreliable in that one leaves much of it to chance, rather than creating opportunities for that chance to occur. However, we can distil these five means into a few simplified guidelines to create "surprising" photographs. The first is the *inclusion of secondary elements that provide new interpretations, contrasts, juxtapositions and insights not necessarily intended by the photographer.* Doing this increases the chances that we create, rather than stumble upon, a "lucky find," and we display a certain "prowess" in combining disparate elements into a coherent photographic narrative. The second is to acknowledge that in a series of photographs, "mundane" and descriptive images are only part of any particular visual data set.

In Figure 1.2, we see the culmination of pre-exhumation rituals in Bukit Brown Cemetery. *Bai Ku Qian* 白库钱 (or White Gold Money) are effigies of silver pieces thrown into the air to pay spirits for safe passage for the living (in this case, the grave diggers and grave claimants). Surrounding the three main actors in the photograph (claimant, priest and gravedigger) are friends of the claimant to the right, two conservation activists on either side of the image recording the rituals for posterity, and in the centre far background a curious European family who are on-lookers on a weekend walk (the cemetery is located close to a large expatriate community).

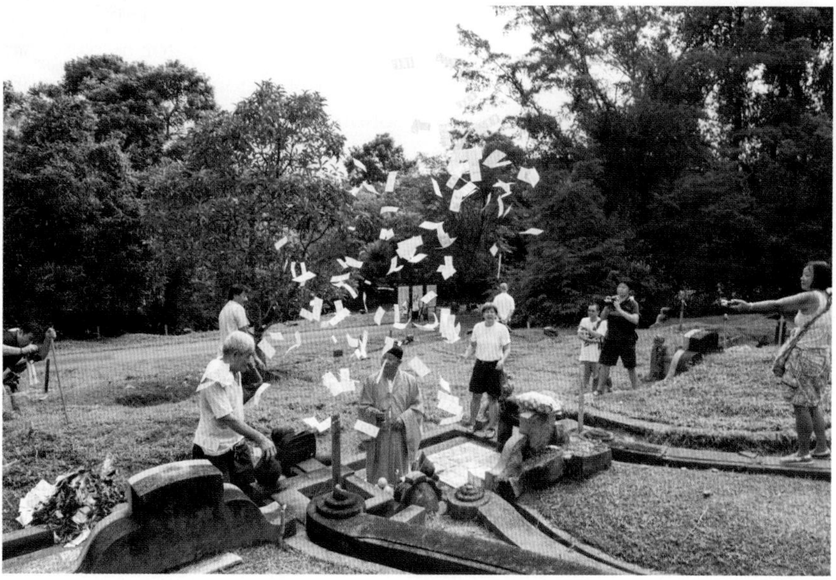

Figure 1.2 Juxtaposition and surprise.

Like the hawker in Figure 1.1, the scene again presented several ways in which I could have photographed it. I could have zoomed into the shot to focus on the Taoist priest and gravedigger, or I could have rotated my camera to create a portrait-oriented photograph to maximise the throw of *Bai Ku Qian*, effectively capturing the central third of the photograph. However, I again chose to stand back and shoot wide. Upon reviewing my photograph, I realised that I had unwittingly included the two activists as framing points. In doing so I had added to the photograph. Not only was this a mundane documentation of a ritual, but it was now narrative of the multiple personal, social and political journeys of the state, individual and civil society that textured Bukit Brown's development, and of how much of a public spectacle the space had since become.

To signify

This creation of an unexpected (and sometimes unintended) narrative within a particular photograph also suggests the third and perhaps most important feature of a photograph with good grammar – it can signify a meaning beyond the literal and descriptive presentation of its subject. Barthes explains this feature by referring to masks – that photographs cannot "aim at generality" (Barthes 1981:34) unless they take on a mask. In his example of Richard Avedon's *William Casby, Born in Slavery* (1963), Barthes talks of literal masks, that the portrait of William Casby – a photograph of his face – is not only a portrait of Casby but also "the project of society and its history," with "the essence of slavery laid bare: the mask is the meaning." (ibid. 34). In this case the mask becomes a proxy for a sociological imagination (Mills 2000), a way for us to see an expression of the wider social and cultural implications that surround it.

Barthes's argument about a good photograph, as la Grange (2005) explains, makes us think and reflect. It makes us see the photograph as not just a photograph of something, but a photograph of the many things that our research tries to express and explain to the reader. This book is not about reading a photograph, as that topic has been well covered in the analysis and understanding of visual materials, nor is it about attempting to "encode" a photograph with specific meaning (although many photographers do do that). What this book *is* about is how one can produce meaningful, powerful, and evocative photographs that speak to the reader and have an ethnographic richness to them. To do this, we need to be fluent with a photographic grammar, and to have this fluency, we need to show some mastery over our medium.

In this rest of this book I will be showing specific situations in which social researchers might find themselves, and how they can make use of photography to develop visual material. I will be dealing with basic techniques that can be applied to a wide range of cameras, although the technical quality of a photograph can and will vary based on one's camera and lens of choice.

Contents of this volume

Immediately following this chapter I will deal with equipment, and how researchers might ready themselves for being visual researchers in the field. (In this book, I will refer to visual researchers as social researchers who conduct their research through visual means.) At the time of writing, digital photography is evolving at a rapid rate, with smartphones becoming increasingly popular as a tool for vernacular photography by both amateurs and professionals. As visual researchers in this period, we are faced with an increasingly myriad number of choices to make when starting out – Digital Single-Lens Reflex cameras, compacts, mirrorless Interchangeable-Lens Cameras and of course smartphone cameras. What size, shape, brand or type of camera should one purchase? Should they be obtrusive for credibility or unobtrusive for non-confrontational image-making? Faced with these options, I will propose a framework of 3Fs – Field Presence, Final Delivered Image and Features (and Flexibility). Through these three factors one can judge the most appropriate eqiupment to bring to the field, and also see how different kinds of ethical, practical and theoretical considerations texture one's choice of camera. Rather than looking at exact models, I will consider different general categories of camera sizes and capabilities, and how they can be best exploited in the field to create photographic data.

The process of photography does not end with the capturing of an image onto a roll of film or memory card. Instead, post-processing is becoming increasingly important to a wider range of individuals, who now have easier access to digital darkrooms than to their chemical predecessors. As such, visual researchers need to be aware of the processes of editing, storing and disseminating digital images after they have been created in the camera. In Chapter 3 I will discuss some pre-shoot workflows *prior* to entering the field. What precautions and preparations should one make when preparing to shoot? I will consider some basic settings that researchers should be aware of when capturing images, like file formats for easier processing post-shoot and for dissemination as part of one's scholarly output. Because data is also often stored for periods of time before it is analysed (or in this case processed), it is also important to consider the ways in which it can and should be safely stored in mechanical, optical or solid-state options. At the same time, other pieces of equipment can help a visual researcher maximise their time in the field. Although an increase in photography as a "lifestyle" has led to a confusing market of products and add-ons that promise to improve one's photographs, some recent developments in the way cameras are carried and handled can prove to be useful for quick-access and movement in the field.

Oftentimes when entering the field, our first encounter is with space and place. Chapter 4 deals with the challenges of photographing the urban environment and the challenges of documenting social and cultural landscapes. I will propose that certain theoretical and methodological frameworks are useful for engaging with the photography of space – particularly that of Tim Ingold's concept of dwelling (Ingold 2000), Edward Soja's framework of first, second and thirdspace (Soja 1996), and Sarah Pink's take on sensory ethnography (Pink 2008). I will consider technical issues related to creating both wide-open cityscape images and portraits of more intimate spaces in urban neighbourhoods and apartment blocks, looking at composition techniques using wide-angled lenses, colour contrast for working with mixed lighting (especially in urban environments with artificial street lighting) and ISO speed.

Chapters 5 and 6 consider the photography of everyday life. Everyday life is an increasingly important concept in understanding how individuals and social groups make sense of their existence (Lefebvre 1996), and social researchers often find themselves positioned as observers of, and sometimes participants in, the everyday lives of their informants. This puts them in an excellent position to photograph their observations, but how one should go about doing so both effectively and ethically (from a technical perspective) is not often discussed. I will propose in these chapters that, using a framework of symbolic interactionism (Goffman 1969), a documentary / photojournalistic approach (Knowles and Sweetman 2004) to photographing everyday life is advantageous in creating photographic data useful for qualitative analysis. Chapter 5 begins by looking at acts of consumption – how does the researcher photograph the tapestries of a consumption-focussed society or event? Using a case study of weddings (Heng 2012) as a compressed event of sociality, I will show how certain compositional techniques can be used to highlight consumptive practices. In particular, I will consider such practices from the perspective of action and interaction, utilising techniques such as focus lock and the rule-of-thirds. Chapter 6 takes one step further and considers how rituals can be photographed. Unlike the occasional unpredictability of everyday life, however mundane, rituals are repetitive by nature, allowing for the social researcher to engage with some experimentation when documenting them over and over again. I will propose here that rituals can be photographed as both a literal and an expressive record (Edwards 1997) of everyday life.

Other scholars like Collier and Collier (1986) have shown the usefulness of photographing a cultural inventory – i.e. the exhaustive documentation of artefacts in the field, but *how* could these objects be photographed better to support the stories we tell? In Chapter 7 I will examine the challenges and opportunities in photographing objects as part of research. Taking a case study of ritualistic found objects in the Hungry Ghost Festival (Teiser 1996), I will explain how objects in themselves need not simply be documented for the sake of documentation, but can act as central points of discussion and interpretation of social events and practices. Chapter 8 interrogates the process of photographing people, both formally (as portraits) and informally (as candids). Visual researchers have long considered the human element as important in showing social interaction, but many of these "people-images" are mundane and matter-of-fact. Although this cannot be avoided in certain situations (see Pinney 1997), I will argue in Chapter 8 that, where possible, we should work to create portraits that both illustrate our observations and arguments and offer additional insights to the person or interaction that text alone could not achieve. Furthermore, I will also show how even when photographing *without* human faces we could tell stories of human interaction. Chapter 9 takes a specialised look into photography in difficult lighting conditions, for example in the night. Oftentimes night photography is characterised by the use of tripods or a steady control of artificial light. However, these options are not always available to a social researcher, and here I will demonstrate the techniques for photographing in low-light situations using equipment similar to what one might have in daylight conditions. Whilst low-light photography can sometimes call for specialised equipment, there are simple techniques available to ameliorate the need to purchase more gear.

In Chapter 10, I will consider an increasingly popular form of visual documentation – smartphone photography. Given the pace of development in smartphone technology, particularly in the area of software (which can be updated by a manufacturer multiple times within a year), it is difficult to develop a fixed set of guidelines for shooting with a smartphone. In particular, new algorithms make post-processing on a phone much easier, sometimes eliminating the need for additional software. But other aspects of a smartphone remain more consistent – its shape for example, which allows us to look at best practices for handling and photographing. Other issues that will be considered in this chapter include the limitations of smartphones, such as their low-light capability, resolution and ISO ratings.

Chapter 11 looks at what happens post-photography. Post-processing is increasingly important in the photographic (and videographic) process. The digital darkroom is where errors are corrected, colours enhanced and stories (or lies, depending on one's perspective) are told. While post-processing's efficacy has its limits, especially in the context of visual ethics in social research (see Chapter 12), it is a crucial tool in the development of photographs, transferring power from the hands of a processing lab to that of the photographer. This chapter will look at the typical workflow of a visual researcher, from transferring images, to editing them on a photo editor like Photoshop, to storing them for posterity, to preparing them for print and web circulation.

Chapter 12 looks at the technical aspects of photographic ethics for visual researchers. Prior to this chapter, I will have touched on various aspects of general photographic etiquette in the field, but this chapter will summarise the various ethical issues we may encounter when engaging with our subjects in the field, particularly in the area of photography. Drawing from previous work done by other visual scholars, like Pink (2007) and Wiles et al. (2012), we will discuss the issues of consent, anonymity and privacy. The book concludes with some final remarks and an annotated photo essay showing the technical details of each image.

Conclusion: three case studies underpinning this book

This book is not about how to better read photographs as part of an interpretive process, nor is it about how to theorise an image from any particular social science discipline. There are many books, journal articles and websites that do this thoroughly and excellently (see in particular Rose (2006) and Harper (2012)). This book is meant to be read in tandem with such books, asking how, if one wanted to create images to read, interpret, theorise or use as part of the wider research process, how then would such images be created? That said, it is also not a purely technical "how-to" book, because such books also exist in sizeable quantities. This book positions technical knowledge *within* the context of fieldwork in social research. It aims to teach researchers how to use a camera proficiently and effectively within their capacities as social researchers, and not as professional photographers. As such, the book is framed in two particular ways. The first is that technical knowledge is deliberately streamlined to ensure a researcher knows *enough*, but not *everything* that is to know about a particular topic. For example, whilst a single chapter (Chapter 11) is dedicated to Photoshop / digital post-processing here, one could read or write an entire book about the possibilities and limitations of the software. Instead, I will show the specific techniques and shortcuts that allow useful and impactful images to be created.

The second way in which this book is framed is through the use of sociological and ethnographic case studies, based on my own experience in conducting social research in the field, particularly that of the Southeast

Asian nation-state of Singapore. An ex-British and Japanese colony, Singapore has undergone rapid urbanisation and modernisation in the last 100 years, and now is reputed to be a hyper-modern, consumptive global-city (Sassen-Koob 1990). Remaining as one of the few nation-states where Chinese migrants now comprise the majority host-society (Cohen 1997), Singapore has contended with various issues related to space, politics and the formation of ethnic identities (Kong 1993). Much of my research since 2005 has been to understand the ways in which Chinese diasporic identity is formed and performed through the use of material artefacts, ritual and spatial practices. This book draws from my use of visual methods in the field to show the various photographic techniques used to document and research Singaporean Chineseness (Heng 2011). The first few chapters of this book will also sequentially introduce the three case studies and give a broader overview of the context in which my visual research took place. At the beginning of each chapter, there will also be a tag denoting which case study is being used to illustrate the photographic techniques being covered in the chapter. But for now I will briefly outline these case studies.

The first case study surrounds the social and cultural documentation of Bukit Brown Cemetery. Situated in the centre of Singapore, the cemetery is home to more than 100,000 graves, and is considered one of the largest Chinese cemeteries outside of China. In 2008, the state declared that the cemetery would be demolished to make way for residential housing, starting with the introduction of an eight-lane highway bisecting it. As part of a state-funded research project, I was tasked with photographing the social and cultural landscape of Bukit Brown Cemetery – including exhumation and re-interment rituals, grave-cleaning rituals and other activities carried out by various religious groups throughout the year. The project lasted three years and resulted in more than 30,000 images, some of which will be shown here as examples of photographic techniques.

The second case study follows from the first, and is a wider visual study into the practices of Chinese religion devotees. Chinese religion is a syncretic and hybridic belief system that combines elements of Taoism, Buddhism and Folk religion (DeBernardi 2012; Tong and Kong 2000), and is often practised by individuals in China or who are part of the Chinese diaspora. Although diminishing in numbers statistically, Chinese religion devotees still form an important part of Singaporean Chineseness. I will use examples and photographs ranging from the everyday life of Chinese religion practitioners to the special rituals and events in the religious calendar, including the Hungry Ghost Festival, Nine Emperor Gods Festival and the Winter Clothing Festival. I will also bring a special focus on spirit mediums or *Tang-ki*. These are individuals who enter into a trance and channel particular deities from the Taoist or Buddhist pantheon (DeBernardi 2012). *Tang-ki* are a significant aspect of Chinese religion, evidence of transported cultural forms (Gilroy 1993) from China to other parts of the world, particularly in South-East Asian diasporic communities like Singapore.

The third case study is also concerned with Singaporean Chineseness, but looks at a particular significant life event in the form of weddings. Between 2004 and 2011 I conducted a deep participant observation study into the ways wedding rituals and artefacts were consumed by Chinese individuals in Singapore through the lens of diasporic ethnicity. My fieldwork involved an extensive stint as a professional wedding photographer, tasked with documenting and narrating day-long wedding rituals that took place in a variety of locations, from bridal bedrooms to 900-seat banquet halls. The project resulted in an observation of 69 weddings, producing about 80,000 photographs, and the use of numerous photographic and post-processing techniques in concentrated bursts of activity.

It is hoped that through the narrative of case studies and easy-to-follow technical guidelines, this book will contribute to better interdisciplinary connections between photographic practice and social research. Many photographers see the value of research and many researchers see the value of photography, and this mutual respect has spawned important collaborations in the social sciences (see, for example, Knowles 2014). However, little has been done to encourage social researchers to pick up the camera and allow themselves to make the ethnographic and meaning-laden images that their trained eye can see. This book aims to make that encouragement a bit more palatable.

Notes

1 http://journalauthors.tandf.co.uk/benefits/resources.asp#link3. Retrieved 27 Feb 2016.

2 http://www.oxforddictionaries.com/definition/english/grammar.

chapter 2

Equipping yourself in the field

Introduction

In her seminal text *On Photography*, Susan Sontag wrote that "the camera is the ideal arm of consciousness in its acquisitive mood" (1977:2). Cameras are an extension of a visual researcher. They are more than just tools, and work as non-human actors (Callon, Law and Rip 1986) in developing (and sometimes interfering in) the intentions, interpretations and observations of their users. Amongst professional photographers, the choice of camera and lens often comes after many years of practice, where this choice lies as much in personal preferences as the technological constraints of the their time (especially amongst early photographers like Eugene Atget) as the demands of their genre. According to Crawford (2015),[1] many famous documentary photographers used a combination of rangefinders (Henri Cartier-Bresson, Robert Frank, W. Eugene Smith) and Single-Lens Reflex Cameras, or SLRs (Dorothea Lange, James Natchwey, Sebastião Salgado), likely for their speed, versatility and portability.

Many enthusiast photographers will often concern themselves with the type, brand and model of camera used to capture good photographs, appropriating as much credit to the camera/lens as to the ability of the photographer. "What camera/lens did you use?" has subsequently given rise to the conventional advice that "it's not the camera, it's the photographer." Both of these viewpoints contain some levels of truth – technology is optimised in the hands of those that know how to use it, but the same technology also creates opportunities and affordances in particular situations for its users. There are practical and important reasons as to why one would choose a DSLR over a large, tripod-mounted medium-format film camera, over a smartphone camera.

If you are starting out in visual research and are thinking about purchasing a camera, there are a plethora of websites, magazine, superstores and enthusiast friends who would be more than happy to offer advice. In a consumption society, the purchase of a piece of technology is met with the ferocity of connoisseurship, enthusiasm and social emulation, with some brands entering the luxury segment of conspicuous consumption, as evidenced in cameras like the Hasselblad Lunar (West 2012).[2] Rather than discussing the absolute values of megapixels, focussing speed, or other specifications, this chapter instead considers the purchase of gear within the context of a researcher working in the field. This is different from writing about the "best camera to buy," because such a camera only exists in enthusiast spreadsheets, technical reviews and marketing brochures. Instead, this chapter will consider the typical needs of the visual researcher in the field, and what kinds of cameras and lenses that are best suited to fulfil those needs.

When deciding on a camera, researchers should first think about their own *needs* – both in creating the image in the field and how the image will be used in the future. To this extent, I propose that camera choice can be framed in three "F"s – field presence, final delivered image and features. I will deal with each of these in the rest of the chapter, but before that, I will very briefly explain the main camera typologies.[3] For the purpose of this book, I will be focussing on *digital* rather than film cameras, owing to their ubiquity and streamlined workflows, which I shall also discuss in Chapter 3.

The 3Fs – field presence, final delivered image, features

Field presence

Field presence is defined in this book as the degree to which one's camera causes a disturbance in one's field of study, and by disturbance I mean an externality in which one's informants will behave differently from if the camera had not been noticed. Whilst many researchers will argue that their presence alone is a form of disturbance, it is important to realise that cameras can affect the relationship between researcher and informant in both positive and negative ways. For example, a camera may work in favour of the researcher in that it becomes a talking point in a community, but a large DSLR might lead to the researcher being rejected access to the field, as was the case of Lewis Hine in the 1920s. As such, this section examines the possible implications of carrying different kinds of camera

Table 2.1 Field presence scale

Inconspicuous		*Noticeable*			*Very noticeable*
Smartphone	Compact All-in-ones Smartphones with attached lenses	ILC (4/3)	DSLR with small lens	DSLR with short zoom lens ILC (4/3) with telephoto lens	DSLR with telephoto lens

when doing visual research, and how this might affect a researcher's role and relationship with his or her informant and/or field.

Field presence is about not just the size of the camera, but also the social roles that individuals *tend* to associate with certain kinds of cameras. For example, large, dark-coloured cameras with long lenses are often associated with photojournalists or sports photographers, and more often than not the person carrying the camera is assumed to be a professional, someone whose presence then implies an institutional connection. In a field where informants are suspicious or even hostile to institutions such as newspapers or state agencies, these cameras may harm both relationships and the photographer. In contrast, cameras associated with casual or amateur use will arouse fewer suspicions and attract less attention, and are well-suited for situations in which photography is allowed but not encouraged. Smartphones are the most inconspicuous of cameras because they are not *primarily* cameras but communication devices. In other words, one could be assumed to be doing other activities – texting, calling, etc. – when raising a smartphone to eye-level, which reduces the risk of confrontation. Finally, because cultural norms in many societies with high levels of smartphone use are already aligning to a saturation of amateur smartphone photography, individuals in these societies are less likely to feel uncomfortable with a smartphone pointed in their direction.

In thinking about social norms and the role of the researcher as photographer, I propose that Junker's (1960) typology of roles in participant observation is a good way to frame field presence in practice. In this typology, researchers are placed along a spectrum of participation and observation – ranging from a complete observer to a fully-embedded participant playing a central role in the field. I will consider three cardinal points in this spectrum, the two aforementioned full-observer and

Table 2.2 Suggested uses of different cameras based on field presence and role

	Full participant	*Participant-observer*	*Full observer*
Camera is central to role	DSLR (Pro) DLSR (Ent)	DSLR (Pro) DLSR (Ent) ILC (4/3)	DSLR (Pro) DLSR (Ent)
Camera is peripheral to role	Smartphone Compact		DLSR (Ent) ILC (4/3)

full-participant roles as well as the midpoint of participant-observer. In each of these cardinal points, one can assess the suitability of a particular type of camera.

In Table 2.2 I have placed a number of suggested camera choices based on field presence and roles. Note that these are only suggestions, and the choice of camera may change even when the researcher is in the field, owing to the fluidity of circumstances and field relationships. When working as full and passive observer, a researcher's presence is accepted by informants. During the Bukit Brown Cemetery Documentation Project, I was tasked to document the social and cultural life of the cemetery, but not necessarily participate in that life. To do this, I was attached to various families who were exhuming the remains of their ancestors, and to follow the process and ritual of exhumation and re-interment. I also visited the cemetery at various times of the year, particularly during certain special periods like *Qing Ming*, a Chinese version of All-Saints Day, and the Hungry Ghost Festival, or "7th Month" (so termed after the 7th month of the Chinese lunar calendar, see Chapter 4). At any point where I met individuals or groups engaged in rituals, I was introduced to them as an academic involved in documentation, and hence a passive observer.

In this project, I allowed myself the luxury of carrying any and all equipment I felt was necessary. This involved two professional DSLRs, one with a short zoom lens and another with a long telephoto lens, one slung on each shoulder. I also carried a large camera bag that held additional lenses, a flashgun and memory cards. This, of course, increased my field presence but also allowed me unhindered access whilst observing some rituals because it established my role as an official documentarian representing a government agency (as opposed to some activists who were present at the invitation of the families but were restricted access by officials who were overseeing the safety of the ritual).

In contrast to this, my research in weddings brought me to the other side of the spectrum as a wedding photographer, wherein I was a full and active participant, taking photographs as a professional deliverable. I was also deeply involved in each ritual, sometimes being called upon as the "wedding expert" to give advice or orchestrate the movements of the bride and groom. At this point the camera was central to my role, and in order to properly perform my role as a professional, I had to give assessment signals (Lampe, Ellison and Steinfield 2007) of my competence and experience. These assessment signals were manifest in the field presence of my DSLR, where a smaller camera that was capable of delivering similar results would not have contributed to my credibility. On the other hand, had I been present in another professional role, perhaps that of a wedding planner, I would have had to carry a much smaller camera that contributed to my comportment.

Final delivered image

When assessing a camera, many reviewers will focus on the "quality" of the image that the camera produces. This is not to be confused with the ethnographic or aesthetic quality of an image, but rather its technical aspects – sharpness, clarity, resolution and noise interference. In the past, film cameras were largely black boxes; what determined image quality was the type of film used and the lens attached to that camera. With the introduction of digital cameras and the immobility of digital sensors (film's replacement), it is now important to consider the camera itself when considering image quality. In general, image quality is influenced by the size of the sensor in a camera.

One would often come across a camera advertised with a particular image resolution, measured in megapixels. In the mid-2000s camera manufacturers engaged in what was known popularly as a megapixel-war, advertising the number of megapixels as a proxy for the quality of a camera (more being better). However, recent advances have meant that megapixels are no longer the only indication of a digital image's quality (also known as the Megapixel Myth). Rather, it is the *size* of the megapixel relative to the size of the camera's sensor that determines quality. Larger pixels on a larger sensor tend to deliver better images,[4] as they are able to capture more light and thus more information about the scene.

Sensor size often correlates positively to the size of the device that houses it. In other words, the larger the camera, the larger the sensor tends to be, and the better the quality of image in terms of sharpness, brightness, contrast and "cleanness." A clean image is one that is faithful to the actual scene, without digital artefacts or electronic noise to "muddy" it (see Chapter 11). As Shu (2013)[5] notes, camera manufacturers measure the sensors in their cameras differently, either by height–width or diagonally. There are a myriad number of categories of sensors (Full-Frame, APS-C, APS-H, Four-Thirds and Micro Four-Thirds), but suffice to say at this point that the size of the sensor is important to our choices for the reasons of camera size (field presence) and image quality. In Chapter 3 we will consider how a sensor size also affects the focal length of a lens (popularly known as a crop factor).

The quality of a final delivered image will both limit and afford what we can use it for in our research outcomes. Perhaps one of the more difficult factors to consider when preparing to enter the field with a camera is what the eventual image will be used for. As projects build and develop, our aims and objectives for our data can vary immensely. Furthermore, one could simply argue that the safest approach would be to choose a format and camera that can deliver images suitable for all forms of media – printed books, online channels and even large-format exhibition prints. However, in conjunction with the other two "F"s – field presence and features (and flexibility), a camera that is able to generate such images is not always feasible in the field. Indeed, the highest-resolution models in the market, medium-format digital cameras, are far more bulky and cumbersome, owing to the need to house larger digital sensors. In other words, one needs to balance trade-offs in field presence and features with the final delivered image. Because of their size and portability, mobile phones have tended to give lower image quality than even compact cameras, but with the introduction of better software algorithms, in the right lighting conditions, provide prints comparable to much larger digital cameras. More importantly, one should keep in mind a number of questions when deciding on what camera to bring into the field with regards to image "quality." Two questions might emerge.

The first is "What is the most likely channel / medium through which my images will be viewed?" From a social science research viewpoint, we can think of the answers in terms of typical research outcomes – an online journal, a more traditional mainstream print journal article or book and a more art/design/visually focussed print outcome (which may be a journal article, book or print exhibition). Online-only journals often require the smallest resolutions, owing to viewer screen variations, storage and download-speed restrictions. In this case, screenshots of videos are also usable, allowing one to use a wide variety of cameras to achieve an intended outcome. In the online-only peer-reviewed journal *Sociological Research Online*, images need only be 600 pixels in width (an iPhone 6's maximum image width in contrast was more than 2000 pixels in 2014). Traditional print journals and book publishers in the social sciences, for now, also appear to have a greater tolerance for image quality – as the image printed is often black and white, and text is still the primary concern.

The issue of image quality becomes a serious concern when we consider journals, book publishers and other mediums that expect the highest possible quality, or when the image is central to our analysis. An additional question also arises here – how does one typically present one's images? In traditional mainstream print journal articles, images are typically presented in a certain way, in-line with the journal's house style, which is often in black and white, and either as a paragraph on its own or in an appendix. Other journals like *Visual Communication* or *Visual Communication Quarterly* are far more fluid in their approach, sometimes employing graphic designers to create interesting layouts that generate or expand on the aesthetic quality of an image. In these cases images might be cropped, expanded, used as backgrounds and more, meaning that a high image-quality will create more opportunities for artistic expression as well as avenues to more layers of ethnographic richness. Furthermore, should one's images be printed for large-scale exhibitions, the ability for an image to be enlarged then becomes much more important than if it had stayed within an A4-sized journal article.

Features (and flexibility)

The final "F" is actually two interrelated "F"s. Although they could have been considered separately, it makes sense to discuss them together because one tends to imply the other. Cameras with more *features* have a tendency to be more *flexible* in adapting to different situations, and vice-versa. Again, the market has diversified so much over the last 10 years that general rules of thumb about different categories of cameras and their features no longer hold true. For example, it was not easily possible to fine-tune a smartphone's light meter or exposure setting in 2005, but professional-level apps allow for a simulacrum of these adjustments typically found in DSLRs. In this section I will consider three aspects of features and flexibility – one, the ability to change lenses; two, adaptability in different lighting conditions; and three, the ability to fine-tune settings in an efficient manner. I will deal with each of these in turn.

Ability to change lenses

The ability to swap between different lenses was a major advantage of SLRs and DSLRs over compact cameras in the 1980s and 1990s. This not only allowed one to use a wide lens (for small and cramped areas) or telephoto lens (when standing far away from a subject), it also created affordances for the use of high-quality lenses that could potentially improve image quality tremendously. In this case, DSLRs have an advantage over other cameras considered in this chapter in the sheer number of options available to each camera body. Major manufacturers like Canon and Nikon produce a wide number of lenses at different price points and quality to suit different users (these are known as marque lenses), and are also supported by other manufacturers like Sigma and

Tamron who produce lenses of equivalent specification but often at a lower price point (these are known as third-party lenses).

The ability to change lenses also means that one can alter one's field presence to a limited extent. Attaching a small unobtrusive lens onto a DSLR can make the camera no larger than a large four-thirds camera or compact. Conversely, fitting a large, professional-grade zoom lens onto a DSLR creates a different aesthetic to the researcher, comporting oneself as a professional, or at least professional-like, photographer. We will consider lenses further in Chapter 3.

Flexibility in different lighting and environmental situations

Around 2011, before it was sold to Microsoft and dissolved as a brand, the Finnish mobile phone company Nokia attempted to launch a flagship smartphone called the Lumia 9000. Central to its marketing and advertising campaign in the United Kingdom was the phone's ability to photograph in difficult lighting conditions – something that Nokia trumpeted when making direct comparisons to Apple's iPhone. The reason for this was that like the iPhone, many smartphones struggled to create good, usable images in lighting conditions other than bright light, owing to limitations in their image capturing sensors. The iPhone, for example, defaults to as low as possible an ISO speed (more on this in Chapter 3) in order to achieve the least amount of electronic noise in an image, thus optimising image quality. The Nokia Lumia 9000 succeeded to a certain extent, but because camera quality was not the only determinant in a smartphone's success, it remains only a minor player in the smartphone market.

If one were to conduct research in only optimal lighting conditions, a smartphone might be sufficient, but this then creates a kind of methodological inflexibility, where technology becomes an impediment to creating compelling visual data (although I am cognizant of other restrictions like role and acceptance within the field). Again, professional grade DSLRs tend to have the greatest flexibility when dealing with different lighting conditions – although many compacts and mirrorless ILCs have been steadily improving as well. The ability to change lenses for different conditions also contributes to further flexibility. My point in this section is that like image quality, not all cameras create the same deliverables, and the results can vary quite dramatically even if compensated by a skilful photographer.

But what about using artificial light like a built-in flash or the LED xenon light in a smartphone? This is, of course, an option, particularly when detail is important and a number of photographers have embedded the use of flashguns into their aesthetic. However, artificial light has a tendency to increase one's field presence tremendously (see Chapter 9), making its use feasible only in certain circumstances and within certain roles that one might take in the field. Also, artificial light often removes much of the "found" quality in the image, imposing the photographer into the image – which we will discuss more again throughout the book.

Ease of manual override

This last factor tends to scale with the skill and/or experience of a photographer, especially one who fine-tunes his or her camera settings on the fly, something that I have increasingly done the more practice I get. Whilst more and more cameras are allowing users to customise exposure settings (even smartphones have an app to simulate this), it is not always easily done. In enthusiast or compact cameras, these things are often done through a software menu, requiring a number of button presses or steps. In semi-professional and professional grade cameras, they are present in dedicated buttons and dials. Whilst this factor may seem frivolous – a researcher can be patient – it is important when working in a field that is characterised by a fast-paced environment. If one is photographing a static landscape or cityscape, changing settings can be done at one's discretion. However, in a more events-based situation, like a wedding, festival, sporting event, or even just on a street, the ability to quickly adapt to the light and subject are crucial.

Camera typologies and the 3Fs

Digital Single-Lens Reflex cameras

Digital Single-Lens Reflex cameras, or DSLRs for short, are the typical cameras carried by professional photographers, especially in the photojournalism, sports, social and editorial photography sectors. For the longest time, DSLRs and their film compatriot, SLRs, were defined by their mechanical operation – an internal mirror and prism that allowed the user to "see" almost exactly what the camera was seeing through an optical viewfinder. Light travelled through the lens, was reflected by the mirror in the camera and refracted through the prism into the viewfinder (see Figure 2.1). In other words, the user saw an optical reflection of the scene. This was considered an advantage over compact film cameras, which had a separate viewfinder, thus not giving a WYSIWYG (what-you-see-is-what-you-get) effect. To an average consumer choosing between a film SLR and a compact, another advantage was the ability to change lenses to suit different situations and subject matter.

DSLRs can be further sub-divided into four general categories – Professional, Semi-Professional, Serious Amateur / Enthusiast and

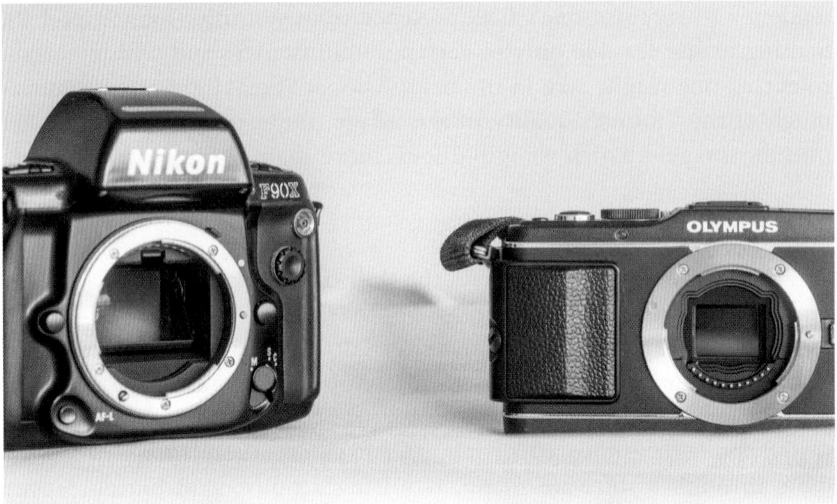

Figure 2.1 On the left is a film Single-Lens Reflex camera, which operates in the same way as its digital cousin. A mirror sits between the film/sensor that bounces light from the lens up into the prism before it is viewed through the viewfinder. In contrast to this, mirrorless Interchangeable-Lens Cameras (ILCs), smartphones, digital compacts and digital rangefinders all do not have a mirror, with light passing directly through the lens onto the sensor, which is then streamed to a photographer on the LCD screen behind.

Amateur / Enthusiast. Major camera manufacturers like Canon and Nikon will produce cameras across these categories, while other smaller manufacturers like Samsung, Olympus and Panasonic will focus their efforts on one or more categories. The categories are divided along the lines of features, price and build quality (durability, etc.).

> Useful tip: Features in DSLR camera models are not exclusive to each model. Very often technology "trickles-down" from professional grade cameras to their cheaper counterparts. If you are on a budget, it pays to read up on the different features of cameras. For example, in 2015 the Nikon D600 serious enthusiast camera, retailing for about £1199, carried the same sensor as the professional grade Nikon D4s selling at £4299, meaning, ceteris paribus, the quality of the image would not differ dramatically.

Apart from the lens interchangeability and the ability to use a WYSIWYG optical viewfinder, DSLRs also tend to have the most features that allow a user to fine-tune their exposure settings and the way a photo is taken. As a general rule of thumb, professional grade DSLRs have the most features, are the priciest and have the most durable build quality. They also tend to have more dials and movable parts that allow professionals to change particular settings on the fly, rather than go through a time-consuming software menu. However, these cameras also tend to be the heaviest and bulkiest of the ones we are considering, and thus may not be appropriate, depending on one's role in the field.

Mirrorless Interchangeable-Lens Cameras

One of the main technological breakthroughs of the last 10 years has been the introduction of mirrorless Interchangeable-Lens Cameras (or mirrorless ILCs). Unlike DSLRs, mirrorless ILCs do not have a mirror to reflect an image into an optical viewfinder. Instead, a video-feed is transmitted from the lens to an *electronic* viewfinder or screen (the same principle applies to digital compact cameras and smartphones). Electronic viewfinders were not initially popular because the image presented in the viewfinder did not have the fidelity of an optical image (i.e. it was like looking at a poor-quality video), and some cameras also lagged when a user was trying to track a moving subject. However, in the past five years, technology has improved tremendously to the point that the electronic image, or "live-view" as some manufacturers term it, has started to become a viable alternative to the optical viewfinder.

As such, mirrorless ILCs are now the growth-area for enthusiast photographers. They offer similar features to DSLRs but come in a smaller and lighter package, owing to the removal of the mirror and prism necessary in an optical WYSIWYG viewfinder. As the name implies, it is also possible to swap lenses like DSLRs on mirrorless ILCs. The downside for many enthusiast grade mirrorless ILCs is that in order to make them smaller, the sensor size was also reduced by about a third. This is known as the micro four-thirds (4/3) system, pioneered by the camera manufacturer Olympus. The 4/3 sensor is smaller and thus has a lower pixel count – reducing the maximum theoretical size of print enlargements. Other factors like increased noise sensitivity (which we will further examine in Chapter 9 on low-light photography) also need to be considered. Well-known examples of mirrorless ILCs currently on the market include Sony's Alpha 7 range, Olympus's PEN (consumer) and OM (enthusiast and professional) range and Fujifilm's X-T and X-E series of cameras.

Useful tip: To most researchers, the image quality difference between a DLSR and mirrorless ILC is increasingly negligible, especially with advances in camera sensors. Full-frame mirrorless ILCs are also increasingly available, but their size and weight make them comparable to some medium sized DSLRs, negating their portability and field presence advantage (more on this later).

Smartphones

If this book had been released in 2006, this section would not have existed. Although smartphones have existed since the first Blackberry in 1999, imaging technology in smartphones only became viable as a documentation tool with the introduction of Apple's iPhone and Google's Android Operating System (OS) smartphones. The term "iPhoneography," or the act of photography using an iPhone, only emerged around 2006 with the introduction of the iPhone 2, featuring a 2 megapixel camera. With the introduction of Instagram and other social media channels, where photographs were disseminated online rather than in print, lower resolution images gradually became more acceptable as bona-fide pieces of visual documentation. In the last few years, smartphones have begun to replace compact cameras as the casual photographer's camera of choice.

Smartphones are likely to play a very important role in visual research in the coming years. Not only does technology afford increasing opportunities for detailed and effective ways of photographic documentation, video documentation is also more viable with every new model that is released. In this book we will see how smartphones can be used effectively in certain environmental situations and circumstances, but it is also important to understand that the average smartphone still experiences significant technical limitations.

Useful tip: Not all smartphone cameras are made the same, the algorithms in each smartphone operating system also playing a part in the eventual image created.

Compact cameras / fixed lens compacts

In the 1990s, one would typically choose between a compact camera and an SLR, starting with the former and then 'upgrading' to the latter as one's interest and experience grew. Compact cameras were the tool of choice for casual and amateur photographers – individuals seeking to make simple images to remember experiences (Sontag 1977). They were all-in-one devices, simple cameras that had fixed, non-changeable lenses and limited features. With the introduction and improvement of smartphones, compact cameras are often relegated in the popular imagination – their falling average retail prices also an informal indication of their decreasing popularity.

However, some manufacturers have noted that their size, weight and simplicity were attractive to enthusiasts and professionals who were looking for a simple and reliable back up option. Today, compact cameras are also sub-divided along similar lines to DSLRs – professional, enthusiast and casual. Professional grade compact cameras allow for full manual override options as well as high quality lenses and sensors, sometimes costing more than an entry-level DSLR. Examples include Sony's RX-series, Panasonic's GH-series, and Fujifilm's X100 range of cameras. Enthusiast models like Canon's G-series of prosumer (professional consumer) cameras were introduced as early as 2002, and continue to be refreshed every one to two years. In the right hands, these cameras tend to deliver better and clearer results than smartphones.

Useful tip: Even if one was to own a smartphone, a good compact camera could prove to be very useful in the field. Look for models with the ability to manually override settings and good image quality results.

Other emerging devices

An entire book could be dedicated to the myriad number of other specialist choices available to photographers – digital rangefinders, medium-format cameras with digital backs, double-frame panoramic film cameras and ultra-high-definition video cameras capable of photographic stills all exist on the equipment landscape. These all potentially serve the needs of different research projects, especially digital rangefinders, which share similar characteristics to mirrorless ILCs, but for the purpose of the book we will focus on the most commonly used devices that are available to as wide a demographic of researchers as possible.

Lens typologies

Although digital sensors in cameras are now increasingly important for the quality of an image, the lens that is used to capture that image remains equally important, and is one of the reasons for the wide range of price and variance in lenses, from simple "kit lenses" (those sold in a package with a camera, usually an entry-level DSLR) to professional quality lenses. Lenses vary widely in their use and features, and while many of us in the field make use of the more common kinds, there are also specialised lenses designed for specific purposes – medical, portrait, close-up and architectural photography, for example. As you progress through your own photographic journey you may find yourself using some of these, potentially when photographing small artefacts (see Chapter 7), but in this section I will be considering some of the more common kinds of lenses you will encounter when starting out. However, to avoid lengthy explanations, I have included a table below (Table 2.3) with a quick glossary of lens nomenclature.

In an extended article explaining the human eye, perceived vision, cone of visual attention and camera lenses, Roger Cicala (2012)[6] explains the differences between what one sees and what a camera sees through a lens based on its focal length. The focal length of a lens can be defined as "distance in millimetres from the optical centre of a lens to the imaging sensor when the lens is focused at infinity" (Hawkins 2015).[7] Practically speaking, the focal length of lens determines its angle of view, or how much of any particular scene a camera can take in. The shorter the focal length, the wider the angle of view and vice-versa.

Cicala notes that there are persistent debates about what focal length approximates to that of the human eye, and whilst conventional wisdom often points to a focal length of 50mm, it is closer to 43mm. That said, many photographers begin their journey with the purchase of a lens that is either 50mm or has a short zoom-range that includes the 50mm focal length (often from a wide-angle to short telephoto), also known as a standard zoom lens. The former is bought because high-quality prime

Table 2.3 Types of lenses

Name	*Definition*
Fixed / prime lens	Lens that is of a single focal length and cannot change
Zoom lens	Lens that covers a range of focal lengths
Wide-angle lens	Lens that covers focal lengths of less than 50mm
Standard lens	Lens that is 50mm in focal length
Telephoto lens	Lens that covers focal lengths of more than 50mm
Marque lens	Lens manufactured by camera manufacturers (Nikon, Canon, Leica, etc.)
3rd-party lens	Lens manufactured by companies that do not primarily make cameras (Tamron, Sigma, Tokina, Samyang)
Kit lens	Lens that is typically sold as a bundle with entry-level DSLRs or ILCs. Typically smaller and less expensive, but of a lower quality in comparison to professional lenses
Professional lens	Higher-quality lens that is made for professional standards, often has a wider maximum aperture (see Chapter 3) compared with kit or non-professional lenses

lenses with 50mm tend to be relatively inexpensive and offer excellent value-for-money, and the latter because many entry-level DLSRs and ILCs come bundled with a kit zoom-lens that includes this focal length, usually the equivalent of 28–80mm.

In the field, you will often find that a standard zoom lens is useful for many situations, especially when you are a researcher in or near the scene you are observing and/or participating in. In my own practice, I have found myself using a 24–70mm zoom lens for most of my photography, sometimes carrying just this one lens during my fieldwork. But the choice of lens / lenses to carry and use comes down to many factors, including personal preference, role, budget, the context of the field and so on. My own preference stems not just from how I position myself in the field (close but not too close to my subjects), or the conditions of the field itself (individual's reaction to the act of photography, from which distance photographs can be taken, spatial restrictions like small rooms), but also from years of experimentation in which I determined what my personal "style" of photography entailed. I found that I preferred to situate my subject within his/her/its environment, creating context and additional layers of meaning and understanding. At the same time, I would also include photographs of smaller details to reinforce particular observations made in my fieldwork. As such, having a lens that could zoom out to the former (24mm) and then zoom in to do the latter (70mm) proved to be very effective. In Table 2.4, I have also summarised some suggestions for lens focal length in fieldwork, and will also discuss the type of lenses used in different situations throughout this book.

Table 2.4 Lens use recommendations

Approximate lens focal length	*Field circumstances*	*Researcher's role*	*Type of research*
Very wide- to wide-angles (22mm – 35mm)	• Small and enclosed spaces • Little room to manoeuvre or to position oneself • Versatile for many different spaces and circumstances	• Deeply embedded role, where the participants are comfortable with your photographing them at a close distance	• Landscapes / cityscapes (Chapter 4) • Studies of space and spatialities (Chapter 4) • Ritual action (Chapter 6) • Environmental portraits (Chapter 8) • Social and cultural inventories (Chapter 7) • Everyday action and interaction (Chapter 5) • Low-light photography (Chapter 9)

(*Continued*)

Table 2.4 Continued

Approximate lens focal length	*Field circumstances*	*Researcher's role*	*Type of research*
Wide to standard (35mm – 55mm)	• Medium-sized spaces that may require some zooming-in • Versatile for many different spaces and circumstances	• Mix of observer and participant, able to move both closer and further away from subject	• Environmental portraits (Chapter 8) • Social and cultural inventories (Chapter 7) • Studies of space and spatialities (Chapter 4) • Everyday action and interaction (Chapter 5) • Ritual action (Chapter 6) • Low-light photography (Chapter 9)
Short to medium telephotos (55mm – 180mm)	• Medium to wide open spaces that need zooming in without having to reposition oneself	• More passive role, keeping further away from subject	• Close-up portraits (Chapter 8) • Details of artefacts (Chapter 7) • Details of rituals (Chapter 6) • Everyday action and interaction (Chapter 5)
Medium to long telephotos (180mm and above)	• Wide open spaces where access and proximity to subject may be limited	• Role that is distant from the subject, surreptitious photographer (allowed but not encouraged to photograph)	• Everyday action and interaction (Chapter 5) • Details of rituals (Chapter 6) • Candid portraits (Chapter 8)

Conclusion: so what should I buy?

Despite the multiple possibilities of camera, lens, sensor type, size and more, most individuals who start out and who want a camera for general photography in a wide variety of situations will begin with an entry-level DSLR for three important reasons. One, the ability to change lenses means that specialist lenses can be bought to complement existing gear without having to buy another camera. Two, entry-level DSLRs are value-for-money, sacrificing a bit of portability (and some would also say style) to give the greatest number of features to a photographer wanting to learn how different settings and customisations work in photography. Three, such settings and features are often the best way to learn photography, as most DSLRs allow for easy ways to manually override settings to let a photographer experiment.

When buying an entry-level DLSR you will also likely be buying a kit lens that comes bundled with the body. These lenses are usually sufficient for most general photography, though the next lens most beginners would buy would usually be a telephoto zoom, commonly either 80–200mm or 70–300mm. Purchases after that would then depend on the nature of one's work. If you are photographing many small objects for their details, a macro lens of 60, 90 or 105mm would be very useful. However if you are photographing the everyday life of your informants in their homes, a wider lens of 24mm and below for environmental portraits or social/cultural inventories would be more appropriate.

However, it is important not to be caught up in a vicious cycle of upgrading equipment, in the technologically deterministic belief that the next camera will immediately transform the quality of one's photograph. Even as early as the 1950s, Edward Weston was already pointing out the follies of those who would prize *ownership* of equipment over *understanding* of equipment. Of course there are exceptions, for example in difficult conditions where a particular feature of a camera, like high ISO capabilities can mean the difference between a noisy image and a clean image (see Chapters 3 and 9). In the next chapter, I will consider the basic concepts of photography and how they relate to practice in the field.

Chapter exercises

Experimenting with different field presences

If you have the opportunity to use or borrow different kinds of cameras and lenses, try bringing them out into a public area to see how people react to your presence as a photographer. Specifically, try shooting the same area and same things at the same time, wearing the same outfit, with cameras of differing field presence. You can try:

- a DSLR with a standard zoom lens;
- a DSLR with a long telephoto zoom lens;
- a mirrorless ILC with a standard zoom lens;
- whatever smartphone you can get your hands on.

You will find, depending on where you try this experiment, that individuals will perceive and react to you in different ways, though, depending on the situation, such changes may be subtle.

Notes

1 http://precise-moment.com/2015/02/09/top-25-famous-photographers-cameras/. Retrieved 18 Feb 2016.

2 http://www.gadgethelpline.com/photokina-2012-hasselblad-shows-ludicrously-expensive-lunar-mirrorless-camera/. Retrieved 19 Feb 2016.

3 It is important also to remember that over the past 10 years, camera technologies have changed dramatically. What were once neat categories of camera types in the 1970s–1990s have now had their boundaries blurred by hybrid cameras that could very well be considered in more than one category. The overview of camera types is for us to better understand the broad categories of cameras and their assorted affordances and limitations.

4 Some camera manufacturers also employ algorithms and processes including interpolation and resampling to improve the appearance of images. With technology changing and improving every 6 months, it would not be prudent to explain every procedure, expect that one needs to be aware that not all cameras are equal, even if they are advertised as being so.

5 http://www.digitaltrends.com/photography/image-sensor-size-matters/. Retrieved 18 Feb 2016.

6 http://petapixel.com/2012/11/17/the-camera-versus-the-human-eye/. Retrieved 18 Feb 2016.

7 http://www.digitalcameraworld.com/2015/10/15/what-is-focal-length-camera-photography/. Retrieved 18 Feb 2016.

chapter 3

The visual researcher's workflow – pre-fieldwork

Key technical concepts

- Exposure triangle
- Aperture, shutter speed, ISO rating
- Camera exposure modes
- A visual researcher's comportment
- Camera file formats
- Memory cards and batteries

Introduction

Before one steps out into the field to do visual research, one also needs to prepare in ways other than choosing a camera. Although a camera is principally the tool with which one captures data, there are other factors that should be anticipated. Although there is no end to what could be considered preparation, I will cover three important aspects. Firstly, what are the general settings on a DSLR to ensure a flexible enough level of photography without having to constantly make adjustments? Secondly, how does the carrying of a camera or cameras affect one's comportment in the field? Thirdly, what mundane aspects of visual methods do we need to take into consideration to ensure that the images we work with are usable and effective in conveying our insights and observations? But before we think about these issues, we need to understand the fundamental process of exposure in a camera, and how adjusting three important settings tends to affect how an image is produced.

The exposure triangle

In his book on the fundamentals of creative photography, David Prakel (2010) shows Philip Lange's *Toast*, a photographic piece of art that represents the various ways in which an image may be under, "correctly," or over-exposed. The more brown a piece of toast, the more light has fallen onto it, causing exposure. If we take this analogy further and compare a camera to a toaster, we can see how the *process* of exposure is better explained. Most toasters have three settings that determine the degree of brownness in a slice of toast. One, the time for which the toast stays in the toaster, under the heating element. Two, the intensity of the heating element. And three, the thickness of the bread that is being toasted. These three factors can be expressed as a triangle showing their inter-relatedness.

If one were to desire a certain level of brownness of toast, this could be achieved through any number of combinations of the three factors – for

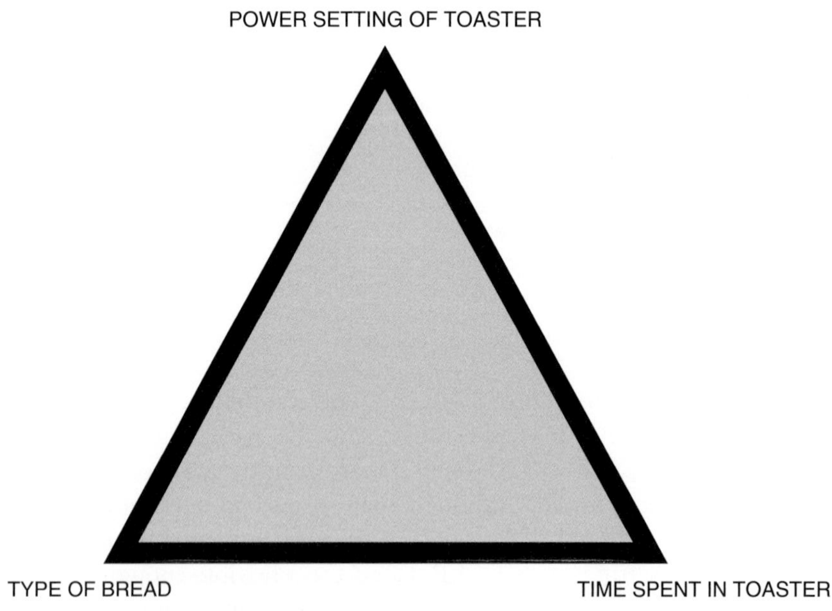

Figure 3.1 Three factors that influence the brownness on a slice of toast.

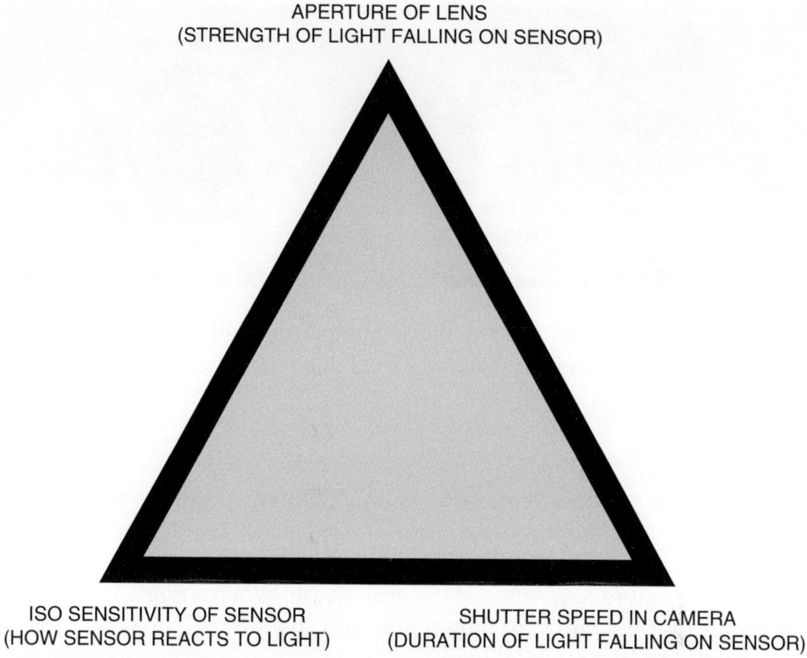

Figure 3.2 An exposure triangle showing the equivalent factors to toasting bread.

example thinner bread with less heat or thicker bread with a longer time spent in the toaster. Prakel (2010:26) notes this to be congruent to the law of reciprocity, "which states that the total light energy (exposure) is the product of light intensity and exposure time." These three factors can be mapped onto three key features in any typical camera – the aperture, shutter speed and ISO sensitivity (of either a roll of film or digital sensor). Like a toaster and a slice of bread, these three factors are balanced against each other in order to achieve a particular exposure. I will deal with each of these in turn.

Aperture

The aperture is commonly referred to as the "hole" in a camera's lens that allows light to pass through. The larger the aperture, the more light passes through the lens and falls onto the camera's sensor, and vice-versa. The size of the hole is measured in f-stops, also known as an Exposure Value (EV) unit. The majority of lenses on the market today use a standard f-stop scale, which is an increasing scale of numbers based on powers to the square root of 2 (practically speaking, knowing this is not necessary) – thus giving us typical f-stop values of 2.8, 3.5, 4, 5.6, 8, 11, 16 and 22. The smaller the number, the larger the hole and the more light that passes through.

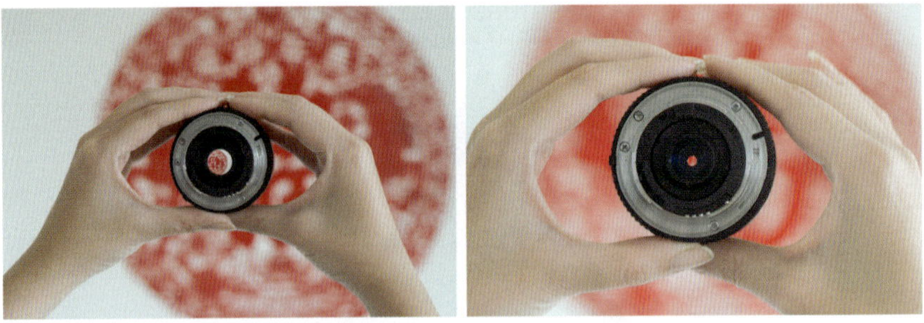

Figure 3.3 The image on the left shows an aperture fully open at f/2.8; the image on the right shows the aperture closed down to f/11.

Useful tip: Lenses have a maximum and minimum aperture – this information is usually found on the front of the lens as a ratio, e.g. 1:2.8 or 1:3.5–5.6. When a single number is shown, it means that the lens has a constant aperture regardless of its focal length. When a range is shown, it means that the lens's maximum aperture changes as it changes from its shortest to longest focal length. Constant apertures on zoom lenses are preferred by professionals, and tend to be larger in size.

Adjusting the aperture also affects the depth-of-field of an image, something that we will discuss in Chapter 7 (Photographing objects) and Chapter 8 (Photographing people). For now, it is important to understand the depth-of-field as the degree to which the distance within an image is sharp, and that it explains why a typical portrait photograph has a blurred background, and a typical landscape photograph is sharp throughout from foreground to background. Generally speaking, the smaller the f-stop number, the shallower the depth-of-field, and vice-versa.

Shutter speed

A camera's shutter is typically a set of interlocking panels that open and close like window blinds. Shutter speed commonly means the rate at which the shutter opens and closes to allow light to pass through the lens onto the camera's sensor. It is typically measured in seconds (1, 2, 30) and fractions of seconds (1/100, 1/250, 1/500th of a second). The longer the shutter is open (i.e. the slower the shutter speed), the more light falls onto the sensor, creating what is known as a "longer exposure".

The shutter speed is important for two reasons. The first is that when handholding a camera (as most of us would do in the field), there are general minimum speeds that need to be adhered to in order to prevent

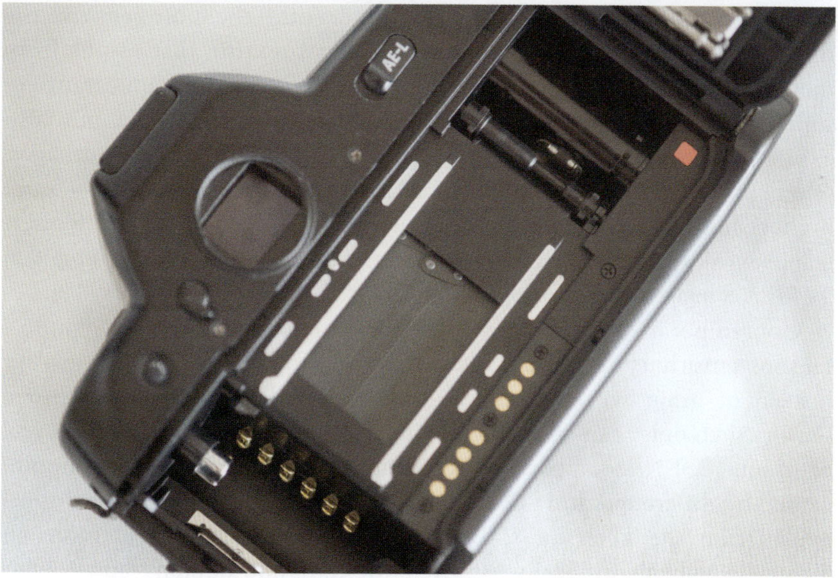

Figure 3.4 An old film SLR from the late 1990s, opened at the back to show the interlocking leaves of a shutter.

a photograph from becoming blurry through camera shake. This will be covered in Chapter 9 on low-light photography. The second is that adjusting the shutter speed allows one to freeze or blur moving objects. All things being equal, slower shutter speeds tend to create a blur on moving subjects and faster shutter speeds tend to freeze moving objects (of course, this depends on the speed of the subject).

Useful tip: As you get more experienced, you can tell the speed of a shutter just by listening carefully to the sound of the shutter opening and closing. This gives you more time to compose your images rather than constantly worrying about your settings.

ISO sensitivity

Older readers will remember a time when buying film from a store, we would typically choose from boxes with numbers of 200, 400 or 800. These numbers corresponded to the ISO (International Standards Organisation) sensitivity of the film, or as some would call film speed or ISO rating. The higher the ISO rating, the more sensitive the film is to light, allowing for faster shutter speeds and/or smaller apertures. However, this higher sensitivity also came with a trade-off – the more sensitive the film, the larger the grain. Grain is an optical texture that results from metallic particulate in processed film. Large grain gives the appearance of softer images, sometimes resembling the dots on a golf ball. Grain also explains the texture often seen in old war and photojournalism images, where photographers had to use high-ISO speed film in order to ensure higher shutter speeds in difficult situations. See, for example, Robert Capa's work on the Normandy Invasion, like *France. Normandy. June 6th, 1944. US troops assault Omaha Beach during the D-Day landings* (1944).

Contemporary digital cameras use the same ISO numbers to denote a sensor's sensitivity to light. This works in a similar way to film, except instead of grain we experience noise – digital interference within a sensor. Such noise can affect the colour fidelity, sharpness and overall feel of an image. To see samples of photographs with varying degrees of noise caused by differences in ISO ratings, see Brady (2015), or for a technical explanation see Peterson (2011:24). We will discuss noise more in Chapter 9, when considering issues in low-light photography, and how to reduce it in post-processing in Chapter 11. Suffice it to say for now, the lower the ISO speed on a digital camera, the sharper and cleaner the image quality.[1] That said, ISO sensitivity appears to be improving at exponential rates in contemporary digital cameras, but like much of this technology, the best performances come at a price.

Under, over and "correct" exposure

The combination of these three factors – aperture, shutter speed and ISO – make what is known as an "exposure," i.e. the exposure of light onto a camera's film or digital sensor. Exposing a sensor to light enables the camera to create a photograph, but like bread, a photograph can be over-exposed, underexposed or have a "correct" exposure. When a photograph is overexposed, it appears brighter than the amount of light actually falling on the scene or subject that one was photographing. When a photograph is underexposed, it appears darker than the amount of light actually falling on the scene or subject that one was photographing. Overexposed photographs tend to be exceedingly bright, with highlight details (the brightest parts of any particular image) missing or "over-blown." Underexposed photographs tend to appear "muddy" or "murky," with very marked underexposure casting a grey pall over an image.

I have chosen to denote "correct" exposure with quotes because whilst there is something technically known as a "correct" exposure (an accurate technical representation of the amount of light falling on a photographed subject, object or scene – see also Chapter 11 on histograms and clipped images), what is "correct" is also a subjective and fluid category. Some

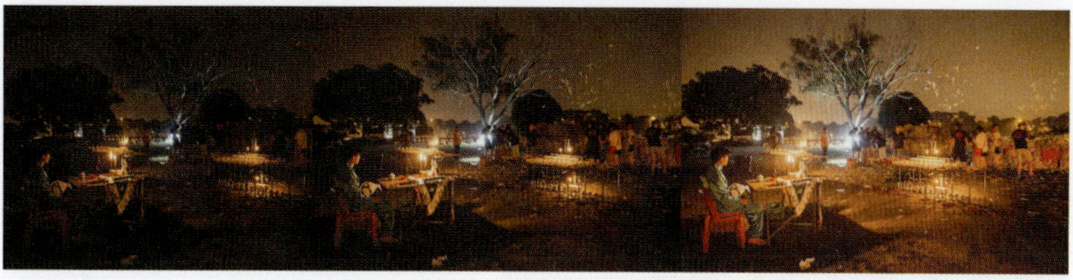

Figure 3.5 A spirit medium oversees the scattering of *Bai Ku Qian* into the air during a ritual at a cemetery in the west of Singapore. The three images show various levels of exposure, with the one in the middle closest to what would be considered "correct". However, I would have chosen the photograph on the left, deliberately underexposing to give a sense of moodiness and quiet in the cemetery.

photographers have been known to studiously and obsessively check their camera's histogram to ensure a smooth level of exposure across an image, but I would argue that this is not necessary unless one requires the highest of details. Part of incorporating *studium* into an image is to evoke emotion, and there are many times when playing around with the level of exposure can contribute to different emotional reactions. Of course, this is not to say that one should not have *any* control over exposure in a camera.

The "green mode," PASM and picture modes

A camera's mode determines the way it adjusts its aperture, shutter speed and (in some modes) ISO sensitivity. Many DSLRs, even semi-professional ones, will include a fully automatic mode that is represented by a green rectangle, "auto" or camera icon. In this mode the camera has full control over all settings, and creates an exposure that would be considered technically uniform (i.e. the "correct" exposure). Similarly, "P" mode refers to programme mode, a fully automatic mode that does allow for a certain degree of override by the user. Other typical modes are seen in Table 3.1.

Of the modes listed in Table 3.1, visual researchers would tend to use either programme or aperture-priority, as these offer the most flexibility and guarantee of a usable image. Advanced users would use shutter-priority and manual mode situationally, the latter when lighting conditions on subjects are consistent and do not require constant recalibration. Pre-set modes like portrait, landscape and sport tend to be legacy settings from the 1980s, and while they are useful, they also adhere to "dominant narratives" of what a portrait or landscape photograph looks like, and thus do not allow for the full creativity of an individual photographer to be utilised. In my own work, I overwhelmingly leave the camera on aperture-priority, and adjust other related settings (mostly the camera's light meter, exposure compensation and ISO speed) independently.

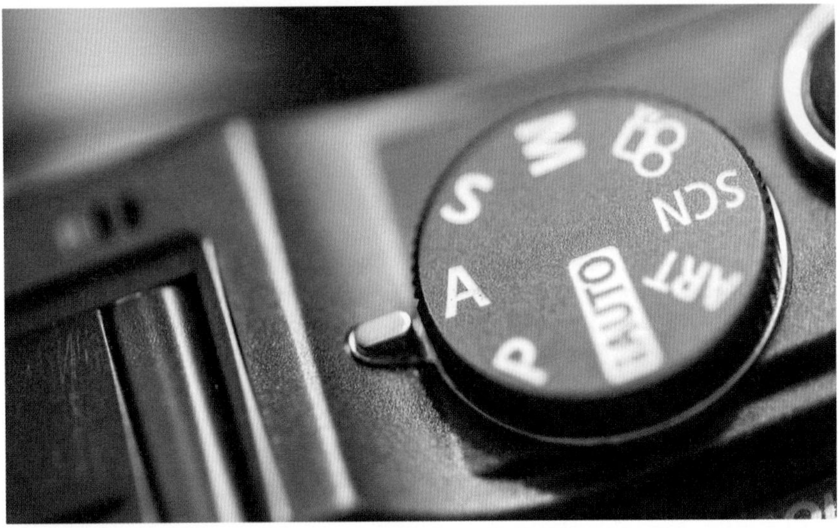

Figure 3.6 Many cameras have a "mode wheel" that allows you to select from various degrees of manual override (none to full). The photograph shows the controls of an Olympus mirrorless ILC, where full-auto is depicted by their own branded iAUTO mode.

Table 3.1 Typical camera modes

Mode	*Typical symbols on camera*	*What it does*
Programme	P	Fully automatic with some manual override, like turning off the camera's flash or setting its ISO speed
Aperture-priority	A, Av	User sets the aperture and camera sets a corresponding shutter speed to get a "correct" exposure
Shutter-priority	S, Tv	User sets the shutter speed and camera sets a corresponding aperture to get a "correct" exposure
Manual	M	User sets shutter speed and aperture
Portrait	Icon of an individual	Camera sets as large an aperture as possible to create a blurred background
Landscape	Icon of mountains	Camera sets as small an aperture as possible to create a sharp background
Sport	Icon of person running	Camera sets as high a shutter speed as possible to freeze moving objects

Comporting yourself as a visual researcher in the field

In Chapter 2 we discussed how the size and/or type of camera can affect the way informants and collaborators interact with you in the field, in accordance with the field presence of a camera. A large and conspicuous DSLR could affect the way individuals behave, or in some cases cause harm to the photographer. In addition to field presence, I propose that there are three important and intertwined factors to consider when approaching the field visually. One, the expected role of the visual researcher in relation to the act of photography. Two, the existing relationship of the researcher to other participants. And three, the mode in which the image is captured.

As noted in other books on visual (Pink 2007) and non-visual ethnography (Hammersley and Atkinson 2007), the role of the researcher in the field is important. It is even more important when deciding to bring a camera, particularly a conspicuous one, to photograph informants, their spaces and their belongings. In my own research on Singaporean Chinese wedding rituals (Heng 2011, 2012), I took on the role of a professional wedding photographer, so I was *expected* to carry a camera and to take not just photographs of the bride and groom, but also candid images of guests, rituals and objects. It also helped that prior to the wedding, I had established my reputation as a wedding photographer who shoots from a photojournalistic perspective, ensuring that the images I produced (and thus the way I interacted with guests at the wedding) were not seen as inconsistent with my role. At the same time, my role dictated the use of a camera that made me look like a professional – a DSLR, sometimes with an extra flashgun attached, completed my comportment as a wedding photographer.

This suggests that it is important to attempt to establish roles in which carrying a camera is the norm, even if that camera is small and unobtrusive. When working with community groups, I find that offering free photography services in exchange for using the photographs as part of my research is often an amenable exchange, a kind of barter trade. To effect this role, it is also important to be proficient in photography that your informants are willing to trade access for. This is usually some form of event or portrait photography – simple but efficient photos that can create official documents of your informants.

Useful tip: It is not just the kind of camera you carry, but the *way* you carry it as well. Enthusiastic photographers, experienced or otherwise, sometimes "over-gear" themselves, carrying several camera bodies, extra lenses, large camera bags and tripods. Whilst this may give the appearance of readiness, it often creates unnecessary bulk and impedes movement. Simplifying one's equipment allows for a more fluid process of photography. Once I have established sufficient knowledge of the field, I carry just one camera and lens, backed-up with a smartphone should the camera fail.

Existing relationships between visual researcher and informant are also important and affect the kinds of cameras that can be or are used. Before her book, *In the Kitchen* (2009) was published, Dona Schwartz presented photographs of her project aimed at documenting the everyday life of her family in their home's kitchen. Schwartz explained her technical approach, a large DSLR with a flashgun, shooting with a wide to standard zoom in the confined space of the kitchen. Schwartz noted that the reason that she was able to use such equipment was because of her role as mother and relationship to the rest of her subjects, who gave her unimpeded access to their lives and themselves. Conversely, Lewis Hine, in what would have been an early version of a covert visual ethnography, regularly posed as anything but his role as investigator for the National Child Labour Committee (Cade 2013). The "existing relationship" between him and the gatekeepers of his potential subjects (exploited children) was obviously fraught with obstacles and even danger. He found roles that necessitated a camera, like that of a fire inspector, in order to continue with his visual documentation. Whilst this would probably not be feasible within the current climate of social science ethics (we will discuss this more in Chapter 12), Hine's experience is a valuable example of role and comportment in the field.

Finally, it is important to think about the *way* in which the subject is photographed. By this I do not mean the technical considerations, which we shall visit in the proceeding chapters, but the social interaction in which the camera captures an image. Visual researchers need to be mindful of the context in which they photograph, as well as the way they use the camera as a fulcrum of interaction between them and their informants. Again, role and relationships do play a part, but regardless of these two factors, our behaviour as photographers making photographs is also crucial.

Photographing our subjects can vary in the degree of obtrusiveness and/or intrusiveness. For example, for research on bodily inscriptions and tattoos, Back (2007) set up a large-format camera, mounted on a tripod in the street, and offered to take portraits of passers-by and their tattoos. The process was both public and private, asking individuals for their intimate stories in an open context. Other visual work involves simultaneous observation and documentation, like that of Sarah Pink's work on female bullfighters in Spain (Pink 1997), where as part of her ethnographic work she also photographed bullfights, a very public spectacle. In both instances, the camera was obvious and part of the public domain, and the subjects were approached in the context of themselves as individuals performing in a public arena. Likewise, in my case study of transient aesthetic markers in neighbourhoods (Heng 2015), I had chanced upon a ritual being carried out in the amphitheatre of a town centre, surrounded by on-lookers and passers-by. The priest and devotees were visibly involved in the ritual, but were making no attempts to hide what they were doing. In this sense, my camera did not add to nor detract from their performance, nor was my presence as a photographer taken as intrusive or even noticeable.

This becomes more complicated when photographing subjects whose performances are not public, or who are not entirely comfortable with being photographed, but not entirely *uncomfortable* either. This is a liminal area of tense and delicate relationships, where over-reaching one's boundaries by taking a picture at the wrong time and/or in the wrong circumstances can lead to a deterioration in relationships and opportunities for more photographs. Photographers who get over-excited can also become over-involved – stepping into personal spaces or breaching the established norms of behaviour in that particular field. In this case, careful use of a camera, keeping in mind the noises it can make (especially shutters in DSLRs) and lights it emits (not just a flash, but many DSLRs also use an additional lamp to help in focussing) helps to minimise intrusions and irritations.

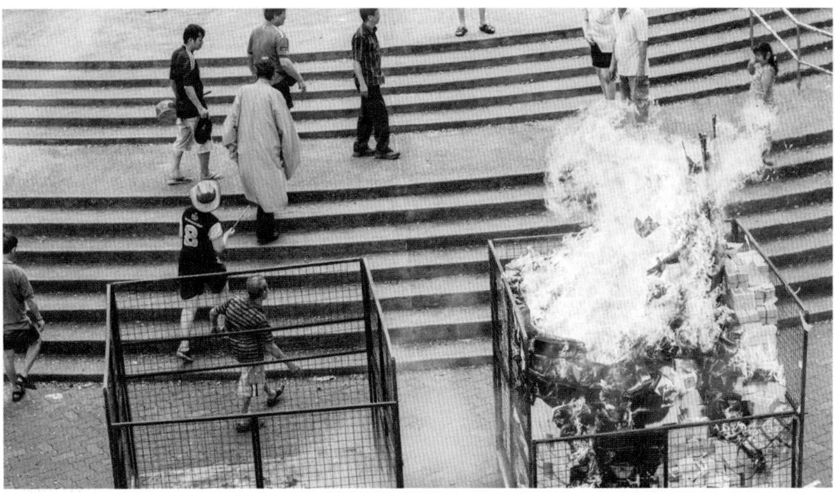

Figure 3.7 Shooting from a bird's eye view on an overhead pedestrian bridge, I documented the ritual without entering the personal spaces of the participants.

Useful tip: Smartphones and compact cameras are great for remaining unobtrusive, and some cameras also use an electronic shutter, eliminating the noise of a mechanical shutter opening and closing. However, as mentioned in Chapter 2, there is a trade-off in quality. If you know how to operate your camera with the minimum of activity, you can appear almost invisible to your subjects.

File formats

DSLRs typically capture images in one or more of three file formats – JPEG, TIFF and a proprietary Raw format unique to each camera manufacturer. For the purpose of this chapter I will be focussing on the two most commonly used formats – JPEG and Raw, as TIFF files are easily derived from Raw files (see Chapter 11 on post-production for more information). Most of us would be familiar with a JPEG, this being the standard type of file for photographs on the internet and in our smartphones. JPEGs have the advantage of being relatively small in terms of file size, and easily read in a variety of devices and platforms; they also give a good trade-off in terms of size and quality. Most DSLRs and other digital cameras will also use the JPEG format by default.

Cameras will also usually allow a user to choose the quality of JPEG captured, often denoted in two or three sizes (depending on the manufacturer, one will see settings such as Normal, Fine, or Basic). The main point here is the trade-off between image size (width and height) and file size (megabytes). Choosing a smaller JPEG size will result in one being able to store more images, but less able to enlarge the photograph when printing, editing or cropping.

However, I would argue that instead of JPEG, a researcher should, as much as possible, use the Raw setting on her camera. A Raw image is an unprocessed file that retains as much information captured by the camera's sensor as possible. (The term "Raw" relates to the lack of processing done within the camera.) JPEGs in contrast are processed and compressed by the camera, resulting in smaller file sizes but less information. Raw files come in a variety of proprietary formats. Nikon uses .NEF, Canon uses .CR2 and Olympus uses .ORF. Whilst these files are easily viewed in the camera in which they are captured, they require either special software or a plug-in on most computers to be viewed and/or edited. We will consider these factors in Chapter 11 when discussing post-production.

Despite this reduced universality in file formats, Raw files are still the preferred option for photographers, largely because of the amount of information they retain. This information is not just simple dates or times, but also the multitude of exposures and gradations relevant to the scene that the camera's sensor captured. This means that Raw files not only have a greater latitude for errors in exposure (one can correct the brightness of a Raw file in many more degrees than a JPEG), but they also have a better quality of tones and colours, which reduces issues like banding (uneven changes in tone) when printing a photograph. Finally, Raw (and TIFF) files are lossless, unlike JPEGs, which are known as lossy. Lossy files degrade very slightly every time they are opened, edited and re-saved. Although this is not noticeable for a vast majority of users (not even to me, admittedly), Raw and TIFF files are still the best format for long-term storage and archiving.[2]

Useful tip: Given the ever-decreasing price of memory cards, it is advisable to use the highest possible setting of JPEG if shooting in the format. Many cameras allow for one to capture in both Raw and JPEG simultaneously for convenience – e.g. quick sharing of images with others. However, this does tend to use up memory card space at a greater rate.

Other practical advice

Carrying your camera

Whilst it may seem to be an obvious point that one would need a bag and camera strap to carry a camera, the *choice* of bag and strap can extend or shorten your focus in the field. Camera straps have not evolved much for the last 20–30 years, until recently. In the 1990s, the furthest innovation was a padded neoprene strap that would help distribute the weight of a heavy camera more evenly, allowing for less discomfort. However, this meant that the camera was still often slung across one's neck, causing, from my own experience, neck strain and tiredness. In the last few years, camera strap manufacturers have started experimenting with different ways of carrying a camera, particularly a DSLR. Two methods are worth mentioning, a cross-body strap that employs the use of a carabiner to hook to the bottom of a camera via its tripod bush, allowing for a smoother action in bringing the camera to one's eye, and a waist-mounted solution that allows a camera to be holstered to one's waist. Both give a military-feel to carrying a rifle or handgun, but operate on two important principles. The first is an attempt to take the weight of the camera *off* the neck completely, rather than just reducing the weight. This tends to reduce fatigue, and helps a photographer to retain focus in the field. The second is the ease of access of the camera. If a camera is slung on one's shoulder, it sometimes takes a few seconds for a photographer to deploy it, during which the photographic moment may be lost.

Useful tip: These two principles are useful in informing one's choice of strap, but it does not mean one needs to buy a new camera handling device. If you are using a typical camera strap, sling the camera onto your shoulder with the lens facing *inwards*, rather than outwards. This allows you to smoothly bring the camera to your eye, and also protects the lens (usually the most delicate part of a DSLR) from unintended knocks and shocks.

When carrying a camera, some photographers choose purpose-built bags with padding and ballistic nylon, and others simply place the camera in whichever bag they are carrying with their field notes and other accessories. Although using a purpose-built bag often extends the lifespan of one's camera, it can also attract unwanted attention in the field, especially with bags that are large, rectangular, and look like they are meant to carry audio-visual equipment. Camera bags also affect one's comportment – large camera bags or knapsacks give the illusion of either enthusiasm or expertise, but again can affect one's relationship with one's subjects in the field, both in their perception of you as a photographer, and also in your *kinaesthetic* movement within a field environment. In my own experience, large bags make me less agile and able to manoeuvre myself to document my subjects, such that when I am doing research at weddings, I will often leave my bag in the corner. This tends to work, except that my bag sometimes finds its way into many of my photographs!

It is thus important to remember that the bag is an extension of how you want to be perceived as a photographer, and how much you want to ensure that your camera is protected. Bag manufacturers are becoming increasingly aware of this, and have begun manufacturing camera bags that do not look like camera bags, albeit at a premium price. Artisan bag makers, using leather and canvas rather than nylon, are also increasingly populating the shelves of specialist photography stores and websites.

Useful tip: For the majority of us, some degree of padding in any bag would suffice to protect a camera. There are smaller padded cases that could be inserted into bags to afford protection, although a dedicated bag is still useful. If you typically reside in a humid country, remember not to store your camera in your bag for long periods of time, as this can sometimes promote the growth of fungus in lenses.

Memory cards

Older books and magazines on photography would often include a section on film buying, handling, usage and storing. Film was an important part of a non-digital SLR, because its character would in part determine the colour, detail and grain of the final photograph. With digital SLRs film has been replaced by sensors that cannot be swapped out of a camera body. Instead of film, we need to take memory cards into consideration. Most digital cameras will use either a CompactFlash card, some variant of a Secure Digital (SD) card (SD or MicroSD), or a combination of the two. Memory cards are often differentiated by their writing speed, capacity and brand, with some like Sandisk, Kingston and Lexar being the more recognisable of manufacturers.

Write speed is defined as the rate at which a camera can record images to the card. The faster the write speed, the faster the image is recorded, and the less likely it is that the camera will lag when one is taking photographs. Write speeds are often advertised either in megabytes per second (mb/s) or in multiples of "x" (233x, 300x), but the Secure Digital Card Association has created a standardised system for easy recognition, denoted as classes. There are two main categories, speed class and UHS speed class, the latter denoting ultra-high write speeds for high-definition video (SD Association 2015).[3] Speed class can range from 2 to 10, denoting the minimum serial data in megabytes per second, i.e. Class 10 denotes a minimal write speed of 10mb/s. UHS classes are currently 1 and 3, denoting minimum serial data in multiples of 10, i.e. UHS-3 denotes a minimal write speed of 30mb/s.

In general, it is advisable to purchase either Class 10 or UHS-1 SD cards, as these tend to give the most flexibility in the field, and allow one to either record video or take photographs. The megapixel-count of your digital camera is also a factor, as the larger the megapixel count, the larger the file size of each photograph, and the longer it takes to write to a card. Although, most DSLRs have a buffer that allows a certain number of photographs to be taken in rapid succession, faster cards ensure that a camera is ready to be used more quickly after a preceding image is captured, all other things being equal. However, after a certain point, a faster card will not deliver any additional benefits (and cards are always getting faster).

Batteries

Like digital cameras, battery technology is also constantly improving, although it has been noted that development is far less rapid than other technologies. With the introduction of digital cameras, batteries are now more important than ever. With manual, mechanical cameras, batteries were only necessary to operate the camera's meter, meaning that a picture could still be taken with no battery life. This is not the case with digital cameras, and it is important to keep an eye on your camera's battery life.

The two greatest drains at the moment on a camera's battery are the on-camera flash, and increasingly the camera's LCD/LED screen, particularly cameras that rely on such screens to frame and compose images. As we saw in Chapter 2, DSLRs still retain an optical viewfinder, which is still used as the primary way to compose when shooting. Other cameras like compacts or smartphones use an LCD/LED screen exclusively. The longer the screen remains active, the faster the battery drain.

If you are using a camera that does not have an optical viewfinder, or if you rely on the LCD/LED screen for most of your photographs, then there are a number of ways in which battery life can be maximised. One, reduce the brightness of the LCD/LED screen in your camera menu. Like smartphones and laptops, brightness is positively correlated to battery life. Two, some cameras have power-saving modes that put the camera to sleep after a certain period of inactivity. However, whilst this may conserve battery power, it means that the camera will take longer than normal to capture a photograph, meaning that there is a greater chance of missing a moment (another reason why I still prefer to work with DSLRs). Three, focus on capturing photographs rather than videos, as the processing power needed to capture video drains battery life more than still photographs. Four (and this applies to all cameras), reduce the use of the on-camera flash – as this tends to drain battery life when used frequently (in the following chapters I will show how flash can be used strategically rather than indiscriminately). Finally, and this also applies to all cameras, it is useful to invest in a spare battery or two, depending on your usage. Batteries are inexpensive relative to the price of a camera, and are useful when one is spending long periods of time away from power sources. It is also advisable to carry a battery charger when travelling rather than just a spare fully charged battery, as this reduces the risk of running out of power in the field (especially with cameras that use proprietary batteries and chargers).

Conclusion

This chapter served as an introduction to the basics of exposure and how to prepare oneself to conduct visual research in the field. Apart from comportment, the key point of this chapter is to remind the reader that very mundane aspects (dressing, memory cards, batteries) of visual methods need to be taken into consideration for a successful journey into the field. Throughout the rest of this book, I will be touching on various aspects mentioned in this chapter, especially aperture, shutter speed, ISO and exposure, as there are a number of techniques and effects directly related to adjusting these variables.

Chapter exercises

Getting to grips with exposure

The key aspect to learn in Chapter 3 is about exposure, and what under, over and correct exposures are meant to look like. By understanding this you will be able to tell with a glance at your LCD screen whether you need to further adjust a setting to balance your exposure. To practise, try these steps:

1. Set your camera on full manual mode, usually the M setting in the exposure dial or menu.
2. Keeping your aperture and ISO speed constant (say f/5.6 and ISO 200), photograph a scene in daylight whilst changing only your shutter speed.
   a. Try a variety of speeds, but to see the extremes of exposure, set one to 5 seconds and another to the fastest possible speed your camera can be set to.
   b. On either extreme you are likely to get a completely white photograph in the former (total overexposure) and a completely black photograph (total underexposure).
3. Keeping your shutter speed and ISO constant (try 1/200 sec and ISO 200), photograph a scene in daylight experimenting with changes in your aperture.
   a. Again, try a variety of apertures to see how it can affect the exposure while keeping all other things constant – you may not be able to achieve a completely white or black photograph, but the differences in exposure will be apparent

Notes

1 Not all cameras deal with sensor sensitivity in an equal way. In general, the smaller the sensor, the worse the levels of noise as ISO speeds increase. Full-frame, professional cameras typically handle high ISO speeds best, but because of the variation in cameras, it is always good to check out professional camera review websites if photographing at high ISO speed is important to you.

2 Raw files do have disadvantages other than their proprietary format. They tend to be much larger than JPEGs (sometimes 4 to 5 times as much) and thus take up more space on both one's computers and one's camera memory cards. Some cameras allow one to shoot in "compressed" Raw format, reducing file sizes to more manageable levels.

3 https://www.sdcard.org/developers/overview/speed_class/. Retrieved 8 July 2015.

chapter 4

Photographing space and "scapes"

Key technical concepts

- Avoiding ubiquitous photographs of space
- Structure and subject
- Vantage points
- Straight lines
- Juxtaposition
- Multiple images and angles

Case study keywords: Chinese religion in urban Singapore, Teck Ghee Court

Introduction

In this section, I will explain some important techniques for photographing urban spaces. When trying to understand a social group, institution or individual, researchers often also seek out the spaces which they inhabit and dwell in (Ingold 2000), for through that dwelling they shape and are shaped by this space. Spaces can give us clues into the social life of communities, potentially revealing their ethnic identities (Soja 1989) or aspects of their everyday life (Harper 2012). For example,

Harper's project of a piazza in Italy was to sociologically interrogate the mundane movements of its inhabitants, so as to better understand what role the piazza played in the life of the town. In other words, it was not just about creating portraits of people and society, it was also about creating portraits of space and developing informed, ethnographic narratives from these portraits. Much of the social science research on space using visual methods comes from works of sociologists, geographers and anthropologists. In addition to his images of the piazza, Harper also photographed scenes of Hong Kong using a specialist panoramic camera, capturing a wide array of spatial arrangements and interaction (Knowles and Harper 2009). Likewise, Simpson (2012) makes use of wide-angles as well as time-lapse techniques in his photography to document the place-making actions of street performances in Bath in the United Kingdom. On the other hand, Hoffman's (2012) work on miners in Mayengema combines and juxtaposes images of space with studies of the body in an effort to understand the intersections of labour, the environment and the individual.

Photography of space and place is thus an important aspect of telling the social story, and photographic surveys and overviews of the spaces of our informants are useful in revealing the cartographical ways in which they lead their lives. For example, in Sebastião Salgado's seminal book, *Workers* (Salgado et al. 1993), he includes a top-down photograph of gold miners toiling in a large manmade hole in the ground. Titled *Serra Pelada Gold Mine* (1986), the photograph gives a sense of the immense scale of human labour involved in the extraction of resources in Brazil, and of the anonymising effect of the work entailed by the workers' density and numbers. Earlier work by Berenice Abbott (1939) also shows the power of spatial photography – her work of New York City in the 1930s takes a macro-look at the systems and structures of the city. Her photographs are more than just architectural documentations of space. Rather, they interrogate, often through the play of light and shadow cast by buildings and other structures, the material culture of the city, paying tribute to the work of Eugene Atget. Photographers in Asia also continue with this tradition – Darren Soh's study of the geometric stacked-ness of Singapore's high-rise buildings is a hypnotic reminder of the vertical arrangements by way of which one of the most densely-populated nation-states in the world operates. For example, *20 Geylang Lorong 3* is a study in the lines and intersections that criss-cross and intersect within our everyday lives, arranging and being arranged by the individuals who dwell within and modify them (Soh 2014). It is in this highly planned environment that I will be situating this chapter.

Introducing Teck Ghee Court and the Hungry Ghost Festival

Teck Ghee Court was the first urban neighbourhood I photographed in earnest, in an attempt to document the place as part of a research project on the Hungry Ghost Festival. Teck Ghee Court is a small suburban area in the north of Singapore in a larger town called Ang Mo Kio. Ang Mo Kio is typical of what Singaporeans would call the "heartlands" – high-density, high-rise, state-subsidised flats built from the 1960s onwards. For every district of flats there exists a "town centre" of amenities like a wet market (butcher, fishmonger, vegetable sellers, etc.), hawker centre (a collection of sole-proprietor food stalls), *kopitiams* (literally, coffee shop – a Singaporean version of a pub) and other small retails shops selling sundries, religious goods and other everyday necessities.

The Hungry Ghost Festival is a major event in the Singaporean Chinese religious calendar. Occurring in the seventh month of the Chinese lunar calendar (sometime in August or September), it is believed that the spirits of the dead are released from their netherworld dwelling to roam the physical world for 30 days (Teiser 1996). During this time, they require both sustenance and entertainment. Devotees and adherents will perform a variety of rituals to appease these ghosts. Most of the time this involves placing roadside and itinerant altars on the ground with food and other offerings so that the spirits may nourish themselves; the staging of travelling roadshows (known as *getai*, 歌台) for the entertainment of both the living and the dead; and the burning of *kim zua*, 金纸 (gold money) as effigies of currency meant to be used in the netherworld.

My photo documentation of roadside and itinerant altars in Teck Ghee Court was an attempt to understand the different ways in which Singaporean Chinese individuals made sense of their spiritual spaces in the context of highly planned and regulated public spaces set out by the Singaporean state, and in doing so performed their own understanding of what it means to be Chinese (Heng 2014, 2015). As others (Kong 1993; Kong and Yeoh 2003) have noted, Singapore's public spaces are decidedly planned and regulated, with "official" religious spaces being closely controlled and distributed in the form of competitively auctioned land parcels (Kong 1993). Singaporeans' ethnic identities are equally planned and regulated (Kong and Yeoh 2003; PuruShotam 1998), and a combination of these two means that most public space is secularised and homogenised.

But it is during rituals like the Hungry Ghost Festival that we see such regulations temporarily subverted and undermined. Itinerant altars can be as simple as a few incense sticks stuck to the ground with some offerings of food, or as elaborate as tables with embroidered cloths mimicking an altar, laden with all sorts of food and gifts for ghosts. The planned spaces were thus re-imagined into spiritual spaces, in which human and ghost intermingled freely. Through my photography, I sought to create a visual narrative of these changed and fleeting spiritualised spaces. But how could I make my photography different? In the next section I will discuss some basic ideas for making photographs of space more meaningful.

Avoiding ubiquitous photographs of space

Along with people, objects, animals and food, spaces and places are amongst the most often-photographed topics. Because of this, there exists an enormous collection of photographs, many online, that depict all sorts of spaces and places around the world – whether it is the intimate spaces of home, or very public landscapes and cityscapes, individuals are generating these images at an exponentially increasing rate. In other words, quotidian depictions of space and place are numerous and ubiquitous (see Chapter 8 for a similar problem when photographing individuals). The challenge then for those doing visual research in the social sciences is how to transcend this vernacular style of spatial photography to make our photographs interesting and meaningful to our research and our audience. To do this, we must first understand how such ubiquitous photographs are created and what they constitute.

Photographers sometimes differentiate between a "snapshot" and a "photograph," arguing that snapshots are taken without consideration of composition, subject or other technical aspects (see Beasley 2015). Although this bifurcation is simplistic, it is a useful way for us to understand the difference between photographs with and without aspects of *studium*. Snapshots are said to be mundane and casual, lacking the ability to *significantly* inform, surprise or signify. This inability, I propose, comes from the fact that individuals are used to seeing such photographs on an everyday basis. If we deconstruct these snapshots, three common issues tend to arise with them – the angle from which the photograph was taken, the lack of a focal point from which a reader makes inferences, and the lack of compositional techniques that lead the reader's eye through a narrative within the photograph. I will deal with each of these in turn.

The angle from which a photograph of a particular space or place is taken is important, as it sets the tone for the rest of the photograph. Such an angle exists from two perspectives. One is on a vertical plane, that is, the position of the camera from the level at which the photograph was taken (top down, eye level, waist level, bottom-up). The other is on a horizontal plane, that is, the position of the camera at the level at which the photograph was taken (straight on, slightly off-centre, very off-centre). Many snapshots tend to be taken at eye-level with a slightly downward tilt, on an off-centre to slightly off-centre axis. Whilst this may sound overly specific, reflecting on one's practice reveals such an angle to happen more often than not.

The second is a lack of focal points – this often occurs in much wider spaces where a photographer is trying to show a layout or some form of large space, like a plaza, field, or town square. Given the scale of such spaces, one is tempted to simply photograph the space at the point of entry, using it as an introductory photograph to the rest of the space. This type of snapshot simply shows the space without something for a reader to consider, and ignores the nuances of the space (however wide), revealing little more than the scale (assuming there are objects with which to compare it). Focal points do not have to be major structures or objects, for they could also be individuals, patterns, lines or smaller objects, but their presence aids in guiding a reader's eye *around* that space. Related to this is the third aspect, that is, a lack of compositional

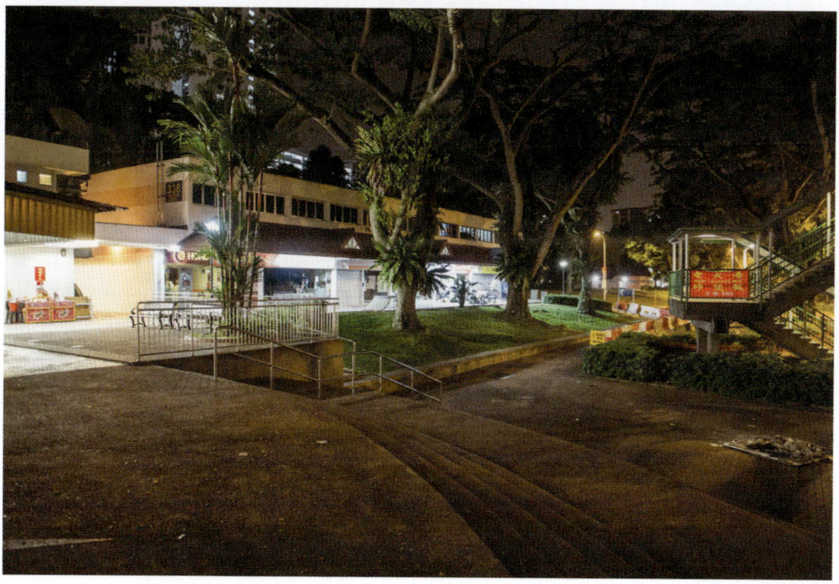

Figure 4.1 Upon entering my field of study, Teck Ghee Court, I wanted to give an overview of the amphitheatre, altar on the left and zinc sheet of ashes of *kim zua* on the right. However, there is little to commend about this image. Shooting at eye level (I am about 6 foot tall), I have produced a photograph that is unexciting and ubiquitous, something that any passer-by might shoot out of curiosity. There lacks any focal point to draw the reader's eye into the photograph. This composition would have worked better as a panorama (see Chapter 10).

techniques that do similar work of assisting, encouraging and tempting the reader to visually explore the photograph. Such techniques, which I will cover in this chapter and the rest of the book, are ways in which photographers make use of the scene, angles and their cameras to create considered images. Snapshots appear to present a space "as is" – ignoring the need to develop aspects within the photograph that make the photograph more interesting or intriguing.

Useful tip: This comparison of "snapshot" and "photograph" almost sounds as if every photograph must be planned and executed with precision. That is not true. "Snapshots" are useful in that they provide a quick way of generating visual data for future reference, like field notes, but are less useful in making a convincing visual argument. As one practises with a camera, compositional techniques often become almost second nature.

Photographing structure and subject

To create more considered photographs of space it is important to understand what we are photographing. Space, particularly urban space, is rarely completely empty or devoid of decoration or markers. When photographing space we need to realise that we are not just showing the viewer what the space looks like, but what stories the space tells us about the ways individuals live, the ways the space is used and so on. As such, it is important to first be cognizant of two aspects of space pertinent to social analysis – structure and subject. Structure is defined here as the shape and overall feel of the space. These could be horizontal, circular and vertical lines of buildings, different shadows and highlights cast by lamps, fires or sunlight, patterns and textures formed by grass, trees or tiles. Such "structural" elements come together to create an architectural identity for space and, photographed on its own, allows a social researcher to develop the "look" of a particular space.

Subject is defined here as the objects, markers, artefacts, individuals or actions that add character to a particular space. In my study of transient aesthetic markers, I make reference to scholars such as Soja (1989) who discuss the use of aesthetic markers that give places a "look" of ethnic occupation. These aesthetic markers might be shopfronts or signboards that individuals attribute to certain ethnic identities, and that thus create an identity for the space in which these shopfronts or signboards exist. My included subjects in this chapter are overwhelmingly the spiritual objects that are scattered and placed in mundane locations during the

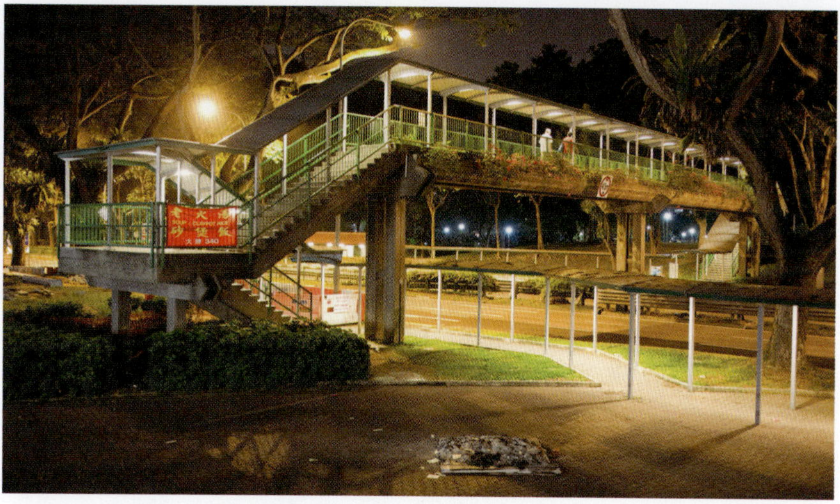

Figure 4.2 Another photograph of the central amphitheatre of Teck Ghee Court from a different perspective, this time emphasising the overhead pedestrian bridge leading to Bishan Park. The structure here is the leading and diagonal lines of the bridge, which draw the viewer's eyes around the image, and give a sense of scale and depth to the primary subject, which is a makeshift zinc sheet in the foreground, holding burnt ashes of paper effigies of "Hell Money" – burnt for the consumption of wandering spirits.

Hungry Ghost Festival. But when photographing any space, it is useful to keep an eye out for subjects that create a narrative of the way individuals live and dwell in these spaces.

Focal points and straight-on perspectives

A key aspect when photographing space is to first think either about the subject, and where this subject might be placed within a photograph, or the structure, and how this structure is best presented photographically, or both. Having a subject within a spatial photograph is useful as it creates an opportunity for at least one focal point within your image. In Figure 4.2 we see two possible focal points. The most obvious, in the foreground is a pile of ashes of burnt *kim zua* on a zinc sheet as a subject. The second is the bridge as a structure. The first helps to establish the photograph's topic, which is offerings made during the Hungry Ghost month. The second helps to establish the general structural and architectural feel of the space – what it looks like, how it might feel in the physical world, and so on.

Comparing Figures 4.1 and 4.2, I took a slightly different approach to the way I angled my camera. In Figure 4.1 I had photographed from a slightly off-centre position (on a horizontal axis), and pointing my camera slightly downwards from eye-level (I was standing up without kneeling, squatting or bending). In Figure 4.2 I kept the camera level and positioned myself such that my primary subject (the pile of ashes from burnt *kim zua*) was almost straight-on or directly in front of my camera. This slight change in the way the camera is aimed at a space can (but not always) affect the way we understand the photographed space, and while they may appear subtle and/or insignificant, these differences are the nuances that help to make photographs more meaningful and interesting. In the rest of this chapter, I will be considering other compositional techniques that I employed during my study of Teck Ghee Court that helped me better depict the spaces that I was studying.

Vantage points

Typical camera settings: Wide-angled lenses, 14–28mm. Smaller apertures of f/5.6 – f/16 to maximise depth-of-field.

For initial photographs of space, one approach is to create wide-angled, sweeping views of the landscape. This not only allows you to contextualise

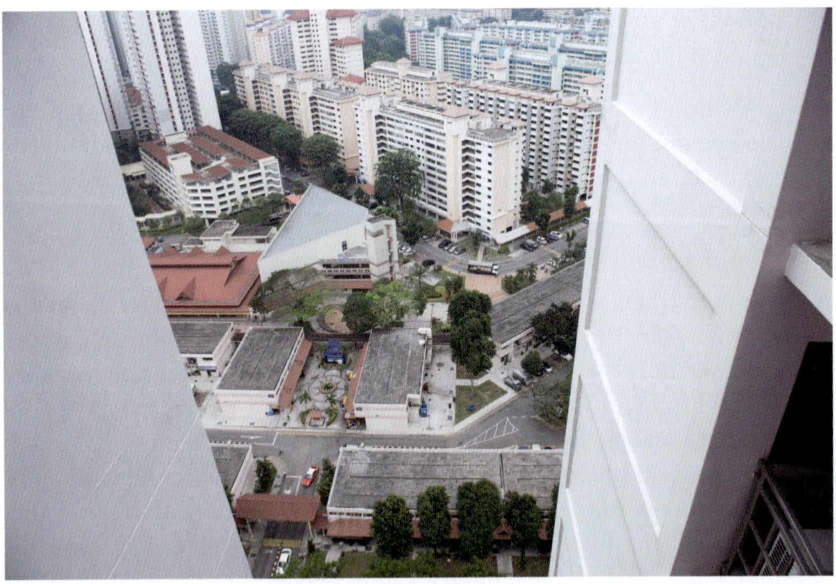

Figure 4.3 Overview of the main vehicular entrance to Teck Ghee Court and the town council headquarters (triangular roof), 30 storeys up, photographed from a common area of an apartment block. Note how the block's walls are used to frame the landscape, but also to emphasise the verticality of space in the surrounding neighbourhood.

the space for your viewers, but also to plan future visits and focus on particular areas. *Vantage points* are useful here – in Teck Ghee Court the town centre is bounded by high-rise flats, locally known as HDB (Housing Development Board) flats. Where once built to four to nine storeys, contemporary HDB flats now tower up to 50 storeys, eschewing their predecessors' modernist architecture. In Figure 4.3, we can see how a photograph from a high vantage point achieves three effects – an "aerial" survey of Teck Ghee Court showing the layout of the wet market and shops, a sense of boundedness using the walls of a newly-built high-rise HDB flat as a framing device, and a contextualisation of Teck Ghee Court as a "mature estate," showcasing older HDB flats in the background.

Vantage points do not always have to be at the highest point in a space, or even a high point. In Chapter 2 (see Table 2.4), I discussed how the intrusiveness of a photographer could be mitigated by the use of a longer lens and a degree of respectful distance (see Chapter 2 – field presence, and Chapter 4 – looking professional). This meant also positioning myself away from (and above) the centre of attention, which was a burning ritual taking place in Teck Ghee Court's amphitheatre. I noted that an overhead pedestrian bridge near the amphitheatre allowed

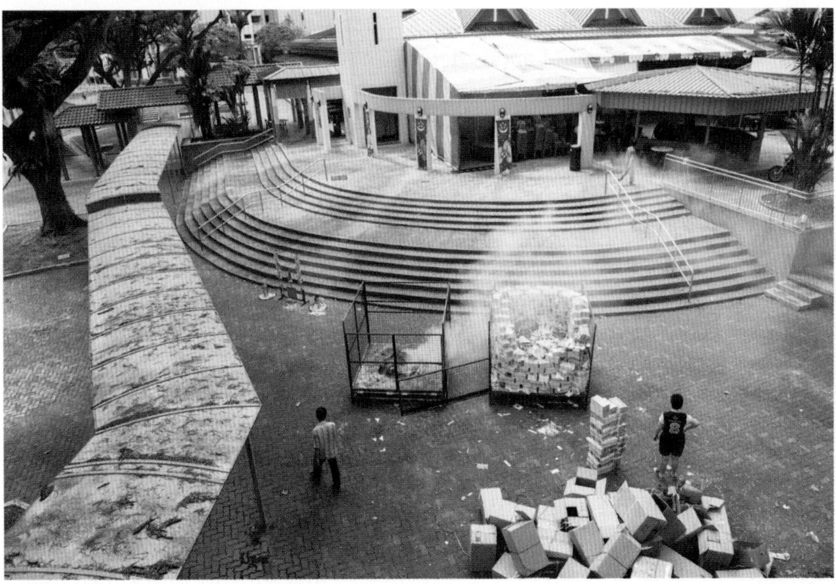

Figure 4.4 High vantage point – many photographers are tempted to photograph social interactions from an eye-level perspective. Even from afar the instinctive reaction is to use a telephoto lens to isolate particular emotions or interactions (i.e. to "zoom in" on the action). Detaching oneself momentarily and photographing the social space allows for a more contextualised approach.

me to photograph the ritual in an unobtrusive manner. Although it was tempting to simply photograph individual actions using a telephoto lens, I also chose to first photograph the general area of social activity in which the ritual was taking place. So I chose to use a wide lens, similar to the one I used in Figure 4.1, and created a one-image story of the ritual.

I have also chosen to use low vantage points to show a sense of scale and verticality in my images. Teck Ghee Court is surrounded by high-rise flats, which, when compared to the itinerant altars and offerings, dwarf the efforts of individuals, creating a parable of state and individual constructs. To show this I often chose to photograph not just altars and offerings in isolation, but also the space in which they existed and where they interacted with other individuals, imagined or otherwise. In Figure 4.5 I photographed a set of offerings in two ways. One was to show the way the offerings were scattered around, and their temporary nature as compared to more permanent, structural altars. The second was to show how these offerings worked in relation to the wider structures of Teck Ghee Court. To do this, I positioned the offerings at the bottom third of the image and used a wide, 17mm lens to incorporate the background landscape of high-rise flats.

When photographing landscapes from vantage points, a deep depth-of-field, achieved through a combination of the use of aperture and focal lengths, is important to capture as much detail as possible. As mentioned in Chapter 3, the aperture of a lens determines the depth-of-field of a photograph, meaning how sharp and detailed the foreground and background of an image is. The higher the aperture number (smaller the aperture), and the shorter the focal length of the lens, the deeper the depth-of-field. In order to create a sense of the spaces in which individuals and groups operate and interact, I would choose to use a small aperture to capture as much detail as possible. In Figure 4.3, the photograph shows not just the entrance to Teck Ghee Court (in the foreground) but also the shape, structure and design of HDB flats in the background, from staircases to detailing on the roof. With a wide focal length of 24mm, I was able to achieve this image with an aperture of f/5, but to gain more detail it is often recommended to photograph between f/8 and f/16.

Using such aperture settings in broad daylight (and an appropriate ISO setting) often means that it is possible to photograph such scenes using only one's hands. But in more challenging lighting conditions, perhaps at night, towards the evening or early in the morning, a lack of available light will limit shutter speeds for small aperture settings. This is why many landscape photographers will rely on a tripod to photograph landscapes because small apertures often mean slower shutter speeds (less light is being let into the camera) and potentially blurry photographs.

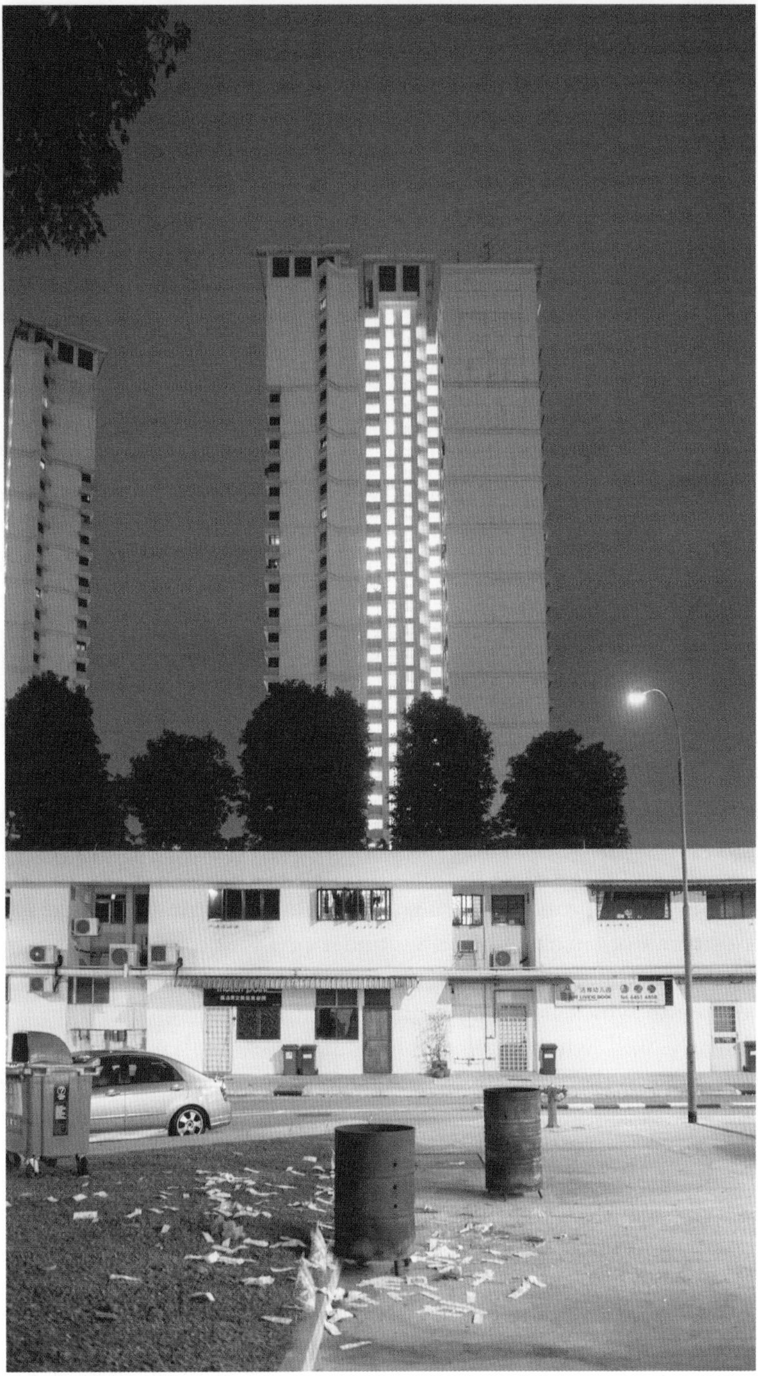

Figure 4.5 Incorporating the principle of a rule-of-thirds (see Chapter 5), I tried to show the tensions of structured and unstructured, official and unofficial, state and individual, order and disorder in the form of buildings and offerings.

Useful tip: Landscape photographers also tend to prefer lower ISO speeds, as this will usually result in cleaner, less noisy images that reveal finer details. Low ISO speeds also correspond to lower shutter speeds, hence again the necessity for a tripod.

Straight lines

Typical camera settings: No specific focal lengths, aperture or shutter speeds, but issue is most prevalent when a horizon is prevalent, usually with wide-angled lenses.

Professional landscape photographers will often point out that a common mistake when photographing landscapes is the presence of unlevelled horizons, that is, a line that should typically be horizontal, or is assumed to be horizontal, is crooked or misaligned. Examples include a tilting horizon of the floor (assumed to be level) or more obviously, the sea or ocean. There are, of course, technological reasons for some of these effects – barrel distortion inherent in some lenses is one good example. But more often than not, unlevelled horizons can be exacerbated when one takes a photograph, perhaps because time did not permit a considered composition, the subject being photographed was moving, or there was some degree of parallax error.

Unlevelled horizons can be corrected fairly easily in post-processing software, but the issue can also be minimised whilst out in the field and using a camera. The first way is to use the gridlines of a camera or a smartphone when composing. Gridlines are a series of interconnecting lines that appear on a camera's or smartphone's viewfinder or LCD screen. By aligning a particular horizon, ceiling edge or floor to these gridlines, one can minimise the degree to which horizons are unlevelled in a photograph. This works particularly well when photographing static scenes, i.e. spaces without moving subjects that allow one the time to compose and align an image.

Useful tip: Gridlines are not always set on by default, but can quite easily be activated. They are commonly activated through the camera's menu, often under options similar to "Framing Guides" or "Framing Guidelines." Some cameras give several options, including the number of lines present (creating either a 9 square grid of 3 by 3 lines, or a 24 square grid of 4 by 6 lines).

At the same time, one needs to be mindful about positioning the camera in relation to the space to maintain straight lines. Perspective distortion,

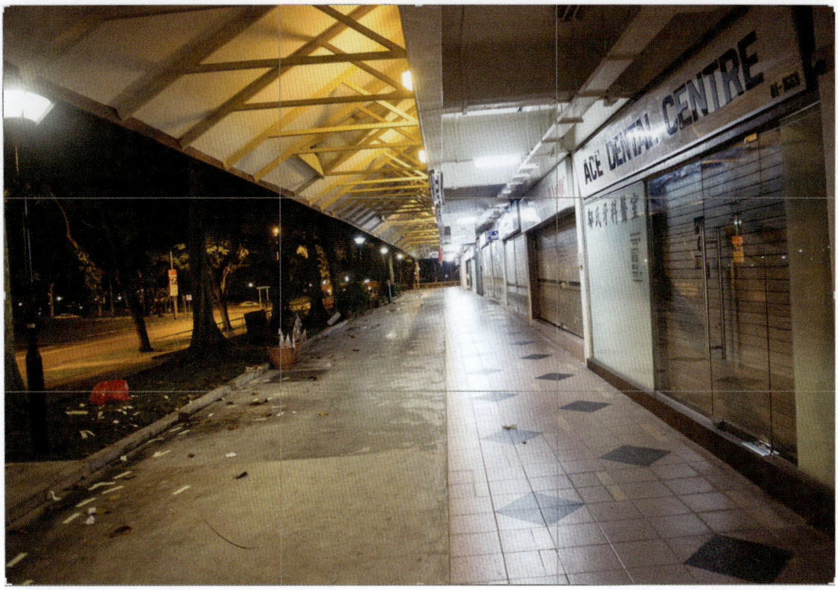

Figure 4.6 Using Photoshop's grid lines, I can replicate what one might see in a 3 × 3 grid overlay in a camera. This photograph has been deliberately tilted to the left to show a misalignment between the gridline and horizon. By tilting the camera towards the right and aligning the end of the corridor in the distance to the grid, one can minimise uneven horizons even before they are post-processed.

the effect that occurs when a camera is angled too high or low in relation to a subject, can cause vertical lines to converge either upwards or downwards (also known as converging verticals). This effect is most noticeable if one tries to photograph a tall building or tower while standing at the base of the structure, where the building sides will then appear to lean towards each other (as is the case in Figure 4.3, when I photographed downwards). While this may be a desired effect amongst some photographers, and unavoidable for other photographs, it is sometimes desirable to ensure that both horizontal and vertical lines are kept straight. That said, converging verticals can sometimes add a sense of drama to the image.

Figure 4.7 shows one such example of the need to level a horizon, even in an urban environment.

Useful tip: Post-processing software is making the process of straightening vertical and horizontal lines easier and more automated. Adobe's Lightroom, for example, has a crop and straighten tool. See Kost (n.d.) for a 30 min tutorial on the principles of post-processing straightening.

Juxtaposition

Typical camera settings: No particular focal length, aperture or shutter speed.

In Figures 4.5, 4.6 and 4.7 one can notice that there is a juxtaposition of not just tones, but elements in each photograph. In Figure 4.5 it was the low-rise flats in the mid-ground against the high-rise versions in the background, along with the chaos of strewn offerings against the rigidity of state-planning. In Figure 4.6 such fluidity against rigidity showed up again, this time in the bare smooth concrete of one walkway against the geometric tiles of the other, the offerings and itinerant altars conspicuously kept to the left, almost as if they were deliberately occupying that fluid space. In Figure 4.7 that juxtaposition is between the mundane everyday objects of Teck Ghee Court (letterbox, plastic chairs, telephone box) and the sacred itinerant altar set up for the festival.

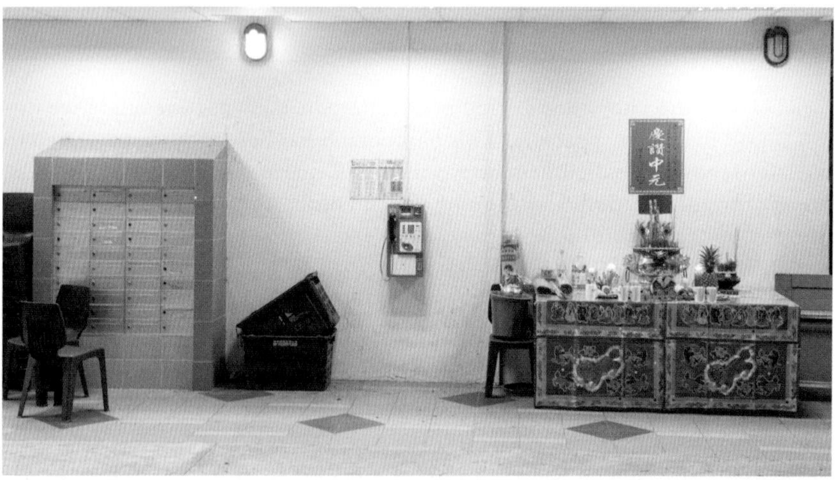

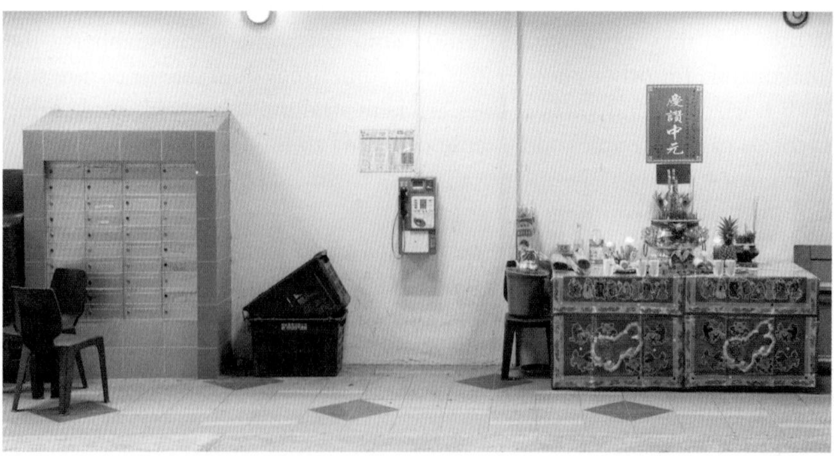

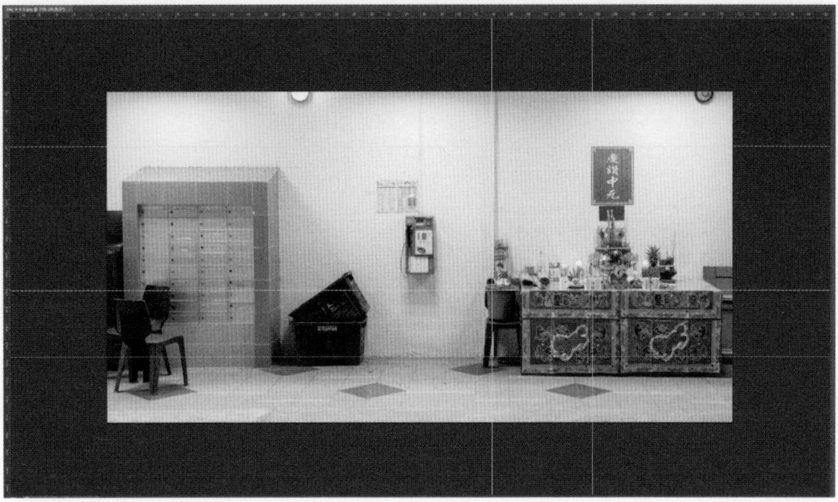

Figure 4.7a/b/c A temporary altar is set up along a corridor near the food centre in Teck Ghee Court. 4.7a shows the original photograph with an uneven floor (tilted to the right). 4.7b shows the corrected floor, rotated, skewed and cropped in Photoshop. 4.7c shows the corrected photograph with guides overlaid to ensure that the lines are straight and aligned.

Juxtaposition is a powerful compositional tool that allows a photographer to introduce *contrast* in various aspects of a photograph. In its simplest form, juxtaposition is often used to denote size and scale – for example, putting a human being somewhere in a landscape photograph to show the relative size of a geographical feature like mountains, a canyon or a lake. Juxtaposition can also be used to show contrast in shades or tones (light vs dark), colours (especially opposite colours), shapes (round vs square, sharp vs soft) and lines (lines running in different directions from each other within the photograph). In documentary photography and photojournalism juxtaposition between subjects and subject matter is often used to create surreal images of the scene. For example, Joel Meyerowitz's photographs of New York City tell stories of race, identity and class, often by juxtaposing residents and individuals against each other (Meyerowitz 1963), and using strong contrasts of light and shadow to illuminate and obscure parts of his images.

In my study of Teck Ghee Court, I sought especially to contrast the everyday with the exceptional. Although the placing of itinerant altars and burning of *kim zua* is a year-long practice, these rituals reach the peak of their prominence in everyday life during the Hungry Ghost Festival. As such, the contrasts between sacred and profane and mundane and spiritual are accentuated and made tangible. Like Figure 4.7, each

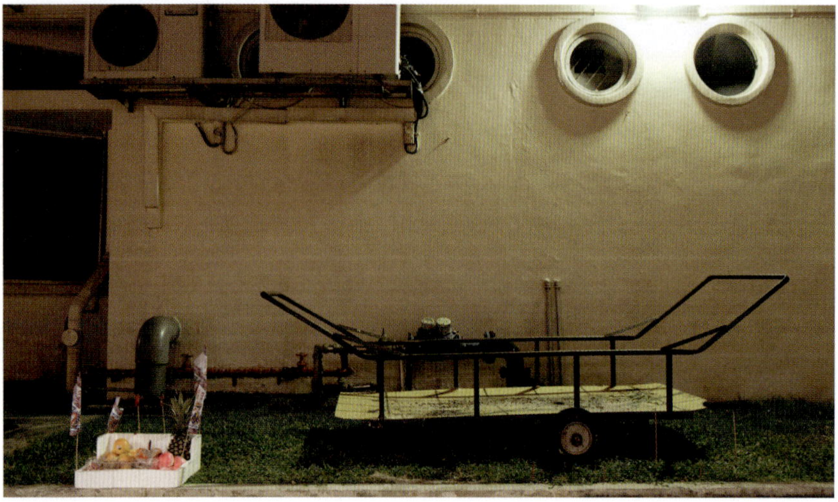

Figure 4.8 Cart and altar side-by-side. Notice again the way I have photographed these objects straight on, rather than from the side. I also knelt down so that I did not have to tilt the camera down from eye-level.

photograph was an attempt to visually juxtapose these concepts, but at the same time show through their juxtaposition how imagination and physical reality co-exist within the same physical space. In Figure 4.8, I found an old cart parked by the side of the central market against a grass verge, its job of hauling goods done for the day. Next to it, a hawker had placed a temporary altar using a cut out from some Styrofoam padding, using the density of the padding to hold candles, incense sticks and fruit. Placed so close to the cart, these two objects presented to me the everyday intertwining of commercial and spiritual life for hawkers in Teck Ghee Court, where fate and luck have as much to do as produce and business acumen. Placing them together but against each other in a photograph was my way of telling that story.

Conclusion: multiple perspectives

Typical camera settings: No particular focal length, aperture or shutter speed.

How do we further represent space in photographs? As mentioned at the start of this chapter, when documenting space, we would often begin with mundane photographic depictions. These would attempt to simply show the space "as is," and while the descriptive element is useful for mapping and inventory purposes (Collier and Collier 1986), mundane depictions rarely attempt to develop a coherent visual narrative of the space – i.e. to elicit the social character of the space itself, or the identities that have been layered over through the different acts and interactions of the individuals dwelling there.

Instead, it is important to consider a particular space from multiple angles through one's camera. This does not mean one saturates the area with photography, but rather, that one makes considered use of photographic techniques *from more than one perspective.* Multiple perspective photography allows you to tell different stories and situate an object, set of objects, person or people in the multiple contexts that are beyond the camera's viewing angle. I will illustrate this with a particular altar near Teck Ghee Court.

As I wandered through the high-rise flats that surrounded Teck Ghee Court, I encountered a liminal, albeit more permanent altar positioned at the bottom of a flight of stairs. Although temporary, the altar was intricate and complex, involving urns for incense sticks for passers-by to offer a prayer, a poster indicating the purpose of the altar (and suggested lottery numbers for any appeased spirit to bless), and various offerings for different kinds of spirits, including that of child spirits, who are believed to be too short to reach the altar table, and hence have their offerings left on the ground, customised to their tastes (packets of milk, sweets, toys and biscuits).

No single photograph of this altar would have been able to express the way it occupied the space. Furthermore, the bottom of the staircase was on the edge of the sheltered void deck of this particular block of flats, opening up to a *juxtaposing* and contrasting corridor of darkness (at night). Its place at the bottom of the stairs also gives vital clues to the inhabitants of these flats, with one other informant assuring me that an altar this elaborate often indicates the presence of a spirit medium and house temple, both of which operate in an open–hidden tension with state regulators of space (see also Chapter 8 on portraits). As such, it became necessary to create multiple portraits of the same space, but at times "sacrificing" elements of the primary subject (in this case the altar) to show aspects of spatial interactions. Putting these photographs into a collage, I was then able to explain how this itinerant altar helped individuals re-imagine a mundane stair-landing as a spiritual crossroads.

Multiple perspectives are just one example of how you can make use of a single focal point to tell different stories to your readers about space and place. Too often we are overly focussed on a particular angle from which we want to photograph a particular subject, forgetting that moving around, even slightly, can also challenge our own visual understanding of a scene. The key, then, to photographing space is to move and dwell within that space, to see it as a fluid and interpretive text that one can sense and experience.

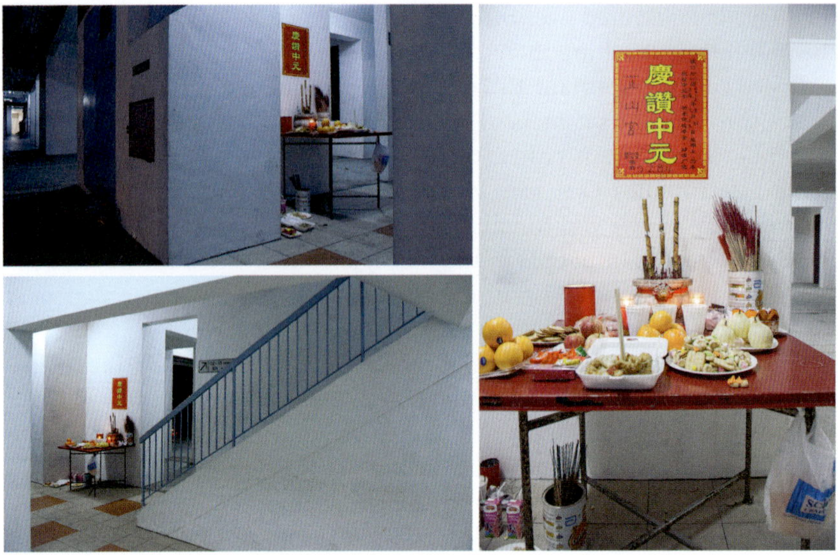

Figure 4.9a/b/c (clockwise from top left) This collage of photographs shows the altar from different perspectives. Figure 4.9a situates the altar in the brightly lit void deck of the flats, offering a contrasting exposure of covered and uncovered, inside and out. Figure 4.9b shows a close-up of the altar and its accompanying poster, contextualising its use and artefacts that make up its character. Figure 4.9c positions the altar as a secondary subject to the staircase, which in this case also makes use of the staircase as a leading line to draw the reader's eye towards the altar.

Chapter exercises

Photographing space and structure

Practise with composition and positioning here – when photographing space, where you place yourself and your camera (and the focal lengths that you use) can have a dramatic effect on how your photographs present your subject.

1 Pick a space that you are not entirely familiar with – first ask yourself why this space might be significant to the people who dwell inside. What structures or corners appear particularly interesting?

2 Get an "overview" photograph – a wide-angled shot that encompasses as much of the place you are photographing

as possible. Try photographing this overview from different angles and positions by circumnavigating the place and photographing at regular intervals. Try as much as possible to photograph the space "head-on," rather than at an angle.

3 Practise with the different compositional tools covered in this chapter.

   a. Vantage points – if there are high-rise public spaces available, try getting an overview shot from top down, but be careful! Also try to photograph structures from the ground-up, especially high-rise structures
   b. Straight lines – Turn on the gridlines on your camera (if possible) and try to align the floor / horizon of your photograph with a horizontal gridline. When you have done this, try to misalign the same scene, tilting your camera to the left or right. This second photograph will show how different some photographs can look when tilted.
   c. Juxtaposition – Look for interesting objects positioned next to each other, whether by design or accident, these tell a story of spatial arrangements and relationships. Don't be fascinated by a single object, but rather photograph elements together and in groups.

4 Do not be satisfied with one image of one space – this is a key mistake when starting off with using photography as a research tool. Be patient and wait to see if the scene changes, whether that is with the light or the movement of individuals.

chapter 5

Photographing everyday life 1 – action and interaction

Key technical concepts

- Gaining access through practice
- Action and interaction
- Framing (repoussoir)
- Positioning "elements" (rule-of-thirds)
- Focussing, focus lock and recomposing

Case study keywords: Singaporean Chinese weddings

Introduction

Social researchers are often positioned as observers to events in communities and groups they are studying. This observer role puts them in an excellent position to be photographers as well, but then raises further questions about the extent to which one can take photographs and in what manner. In Chapter 3 we discussed the level of "intrusion" that carrying certain cameras brings (and does not bring). In this chapter I am going to show how by using one's role as a photographer with some degree of technical repute, access to photographing everyday life becomes easier, more available and offers greater opportunities to create strong visual narratives. I will also show the different techniques one can use when photographing consumption, interaction and negotiation – common elements of the everyday life of our informants (Ingold 2000; Lefebvre 1991; Pink 2012a), regardless of culture or geographical location. In particular, I will be breaking down the various techniques used to develop a photojournalistic aesthetic.

When gaining access to a particular group or community, social researchers using visual methods can take both active and passive roles, either by participating deeply in the life of the community (Hingley 2011) or observing passively as outsiders (Junker 1960). Hingley (2011), for example, recounts how in order to photograph various faith communities in the United Kingdom, she befriended them through offering to give car rides or photography lessons. Her use of digital cameras and the ability to immediately show images allowed her to more quickly establish rapport with her informants. In my own research on Singaporean Chinese weddings, and some aspects of Chinese religion, I have found that active participation as a photographer or "professional photographer" places me in a unique position to conduct my visual research. I am given more access than if I had been a more minor participant, and my photographic outcomes are often a useful way to forge and maintain relationships with my informants. Before I explain how I transformed this practice into research, I will briefly outline the Singaporean Chinese wedding as the context in which this and other chapters are situated.

Chinese weddings in Singapore

As a postcolonial nation-state, Singapore has rapidly evolved both socially and economically over the last 50 years since gaining independence. Initially a British Crown Colony, Singapore was also briefly a Japanese colony during the Second World War, then a state in a newly formed Malayan Federation before finally becoming a nation-state in 1965. Its geographical position has made it a prime trading hub for both the region and the world, and consequently also a migration destination, particularly for individuals from China. Many scholars have traced the path of migrants from China (see Wang 1991), and it is not in the purview of this book to document these paths. Suffice it to say, Cohen (1997) notes that as a nation-state, Singapore remains one of the few in the world where the Chinese immigrant population now also comprises the majority host-society. At the last count, individuals who consider themselves to be *Chinese* account for about 80 per cent of the overall population in Singapore.

This large proportion of Chinese individuals has also given rise to questions about the Chinese diaspora (Cohen 1997) and Chinese identity in Singapore (Heng 2015), particularly in terms of interventions by the state, which sought to shape notions of Chineseness into a single homogeneous category in the 1980s through to the early 2000s (Kong and Yeoh 2003; PuruShotam 1998). My research in weddings attempts to explore notions of Chineseness through the practice of wedding rituals, and how Singapore's position in the confluence of global economic, cultural and media flows has shaped such notions.

Singaporean Chinese weddings are highly ethnicised, syncretic and hybridised events. Like many wedding rituals around the world (Mead 2007), they are also a site for consumption and performance. I have argued previously that weddings are an excellent site for understanding everyday life because of their consociative structure and use of concentrated bursts of activity, effectively acting as a parable of how individuals experience and perform their ethnic identities (Heng 2011). It was noted as early as the 1950s that Singaporean Chinese wedding rituals were already truncated, modified versions of wedding rituals that took place in China in the immediate past (Freedman 1957). Freedman's observations of the structure of wedding rituals in Singapore in the 1950s still bear strong resemblances to what we see now, albeit with some modifications. It begins in the morning, when the groom leaves his family home to travel to the bride's family home to fetch her. There, he must engage in "door games" – rituals of forfeit in order to appease the bridesmaids (such rituals have also been noted in other cultures: see James 1977 and Rorie 1934). Once he has retrieved his bride, they travel to his home for a tea ceremony, where cups of sweetened tea are served to family elders. The ceremony is then repeated back at the bride's home for her family. The morning rituals often conclude before noon, but some couples may then make their way to church or a temple for a religious ceremony in the afternoon. Finally, the wedding often culminates in a large banquet, frequently held at a hotel or restaurant, which can have anywhere from 100 to 1000 guests. This, of course, is a very sweeping overview of the Singaporean Chinese wedding, and as I show how photography techniques can be used to photograph interaction, ritual and people, I will deal with the nuances that occur throughout the day and night.

Getting access through practice

Prior to beginning my postgraduate studies, I had been freelancing as a wedding photographer for about nine years, doing simple commercial photographs for wedding day events. I had started by shooting on film in the 1990s, and only transitioned to digital photography in 2003 when the

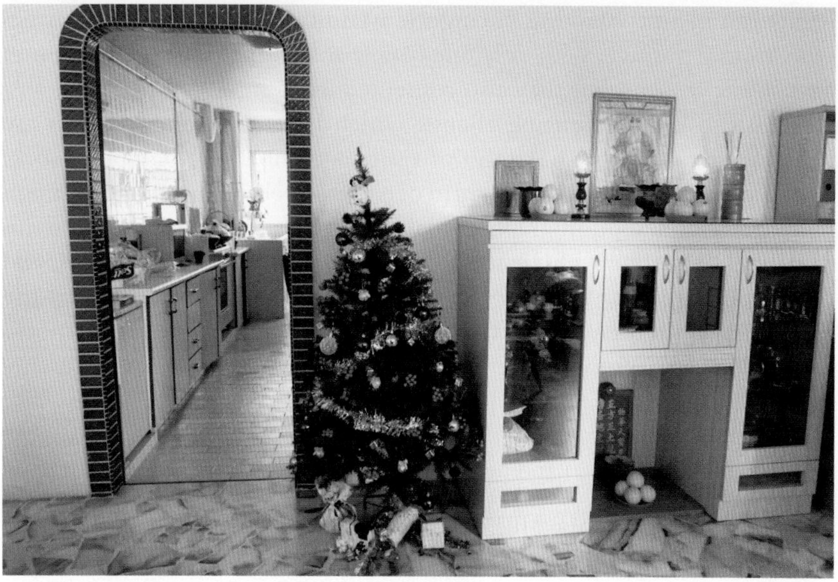

Figure 5.1 One of my favourite photographs, displaying a mix of everyday, religious and cultural life in my informants' home. Photographed around 2006.

prices of DSLRs had fallen to affordable levels. This move to digital photography proved to be the turning point not just in my appeal as a photographer, but also in the technical standard of my photography, because I finally had control over post-processing. Rather than entrusting my prints to a professional lab, I was able to determine almost exactly how I wanted my photographs to look, and to rely on the lab more for printing (which was and still is an important aspect of the photographic process).

However, what I learnt was that competency creates access through professionalism. If I could prove that I was at least competent with a camera, could capture the requisite scenes in a wedding, and deliver the wedding album in an acceptable amount of time, given the right price point there would be couples willing to hire me as a professional freelance photographer. Around the time I moved to digital photography, I had also picked up other relevant skills in the creative industry, most importantly the ability to design and produce my own website. I advertised my services in an online wedding directory, and, despite not having a proper photo studio, was able to secure clients by meeting them at cafés in town and showing them samples of my work. A further chance collaboration with a photo album boutique in town also provided more opportunities to publicise my work. When meeting with potential clients, I would also disclose to them my role as a researcher (which at that time was part of my PhD), and ask for their permission to conduct research into their consumption habits and identity-making during the wedding. The response was overwhelmingly positive, with only one couple abstaining (but still hiring me) for privacy reasons, but they also consented to be interviewed.

Thus the key to securing clients, which in turn meant access to my field, was to develop a portfolio of easily accessible photographic work. This is most often found in the form of either a website or a blog, although many professional photographers maintain both as a way of reaching out to new clients. The website acts as a "best of" collection of images, and the blog is a regular update of the most recent shoots conducted by the photographer. Either way, such channels allowed me to signal my competency to potential informants.

"Looking" professional

When taking the role of a professional wedding photographer, I also had to "look" the part. Starting out in the 1990s meant that professional wedding photographers were (and still are) expected to comport themselves in certain ways, especially when it comes to equipment. DSLRs with professional lenses (indicated by their larger size) are considered the norm, and whilst in previous decades a large flashgun (and flash diffuser) was also common, today's photographers are more mixed, with some opting to go without a flashgun. However, the size of the camera tended to be a signal of professionalism in Singaporean Chinese weddings. I thus carried at least one DLSR with a normal zoom lens, along with a flashgun attached for when I would be asked to take informal portraits in mixed lighting situations. (The flashgun also added to the overall size of the camera, making me look even more "professional.")

In my bag, I would also carry spares of everything, and a number of extra lenses in anticipation of different and/or unexpected room sizes. Singaporean flats vary widely in terms of size and layout, and in some rooms I would need to use a very wide zoom as I would be standing almost next to or in front of the subject. If there happened to be a ceremony in a religious building, I would always carry a telephoto lens to compensate for restrictions on movements and placement during formalised rituals.

Useful tip: As a professional, I would also carry more equipment than I normally would if I had been there solely as a researcher. Backup cameras, lenses, batteries and memory cards are all important, because all are liable to fail at the most inopportune time. When you are appointed or have agreed to deliver a set of images to an individual, group or institution, it is important to maintain a professional presence.

When I began as a professional photographer, I would endeavour to dress to look the part – not only would my camera bag be large and black, I would also wear a photographer's vest with numerous pockets for film, batteries and lenses. More recently I have chosen to carry less on my person, and leave my bag in an inconspicuous area when shooting. I would also choose my outfit to match more closely to a groomsman, allowing me to blend in more with the wedding party and shoot in more relaxed conditions – in the next section I will explain why "blending in" becomes important when photographing everyday life.

Action and interaction

During my research, I noticed how many wedding clients would freeze or deliberately pose when they detected a camera was aimed at them. Other participants were more camera-shy, and would immediately turn away or raise their hands when they knew a photographer was trying to take a photograph (this tends to be less of a problem at weddings, where most individuals are happy to pose, but in other situations they may be less obliging). In other situations of everyday life, taking another individual's photograph requires one to be more surreptitious, even if implicit consent is given, as this allows us to create portraits of interaction that are less affected by our intrusion as researchers.

In Chapter 4, I discussed the importance of photographing structure and/or subject. When photographing individuals or groups going about their everyday lives, we can think about this in terms of action and interaction. Edward T. Hall echoed this idea with his concept of proxemics (1982) – emphasising the need to consider "spatial proximity and physical relationships" (Beck and Grajeda 2008). By this I do not mean that we *need* to photograph people close to each other talking, emoting, running or walking, but that our photographs should evoke the sense of living and dwelling, of interacting, however minutely, with the individuals and spaces in which they are being photographed. I will deal with each of these in turn.

Action is defined here as both explicit, kinaesthetic movement like walking, running and jumping, as well as more nuanced micro-movements such as posture, glances, facial expressions and positioning. Action is important to photographing everyday life because it gives us clues as to an individual's comportment and to the circumstances and context of the environment. Action also adds that sense of "life" to an image – as evidenced by Doisneau's photograph of a couple kissing at the *Hotel de Ville* (1950) or Jacob Riis's work on *Lodgers in a Crowded Bayard Street Tenement* (1890). In each of these photographs, individuals are pictured engaging in everyday life, whether that is love (Doisneau) or

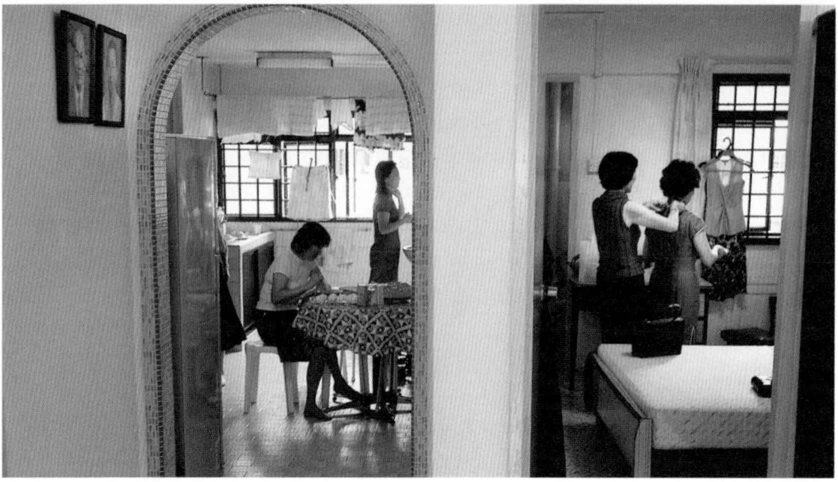

Figure 5.2 In this photograph, family members are getting ready for the morning's wedding rituals. Using door frames as framing devices, I juxtaposed four different individuals moving and interacting with each other and with the home. Two other "actors" are present in the portraits hanging on the left wall. The image not only shows mundane actions of preparation, but also exposes an overarching story of the relationships between the individuals pictured in that space.

simply existing (Riis), their body language, comportment and positions telling us stories of their emotions, existence and identities.

A subset of movement is interaction. Interaction is defined here as the ways in which individuals interact with one another and/or with their environment, consciously or unconsciously. For example, two individuals may interact with one another whilst talking, but in other photographs we might be able to juxtapose two other individuals who are not interacting deliberately with one another and co-opt them into a *photographed performance* of everyday life (Lefebvre 1996). In doing so we are then able to achieve not just a document of what individuals are doing, but a portrait of everyday life in a particular space. Figure 5.2 shows one such example.

Framing

Typical camera settings: No particular focal length, aperture or shutter speed. When standing further away from the subject a longer focal length can help to compress elements together to situate one subject within a frame.

Figure 5.2 also explores an often-used device in photography called framing. Framing is defined as positioning the subject within another subject that encompasses it. At the most basic level, the technique leads the viewer's eye towards the subject in a frame, bringing attention and focus upon the subject. In Figure 5.3, I had just arrived at Lily the bride's home at 6a.m. in the morning, and was preparing to photograph the first ritual of the morning, a session of make-up that takes anywhere from two to three hours. Professional make-up artists are often employed for this, and engage in transforming the bride into a performative body, suited for the rest of the day's ritual consumptions. Framed within an ethnic lens, the make-up ritual (which one might argue would also include the donning of the white wedding gown) often reflects the transportation of transnational cultural norms (Gilroy 1993) associated with "Western" modes of weddings. To this end, I wanted to show the fleeting but crucial relationship between Lily and the make-up artist – an intimate yet professionally distant connection. I also wanted to show the bride in the moments before her transformation and ensuing performance. I noticed that a large mirror was placed precariously on her table, next to a smaller vanity mirror. When she turned to face the make-up artist (standing), I framed their interactions with each other, as well as a more detailed facial expression in the vanity mirror. The positioning of the mirrors allowed for a double-framing of the subject, not only drawing attention to two instances of action/interaction of the same person, but also giving some insights into the layout of the room as reflected in the mirror.

Figure 5.3 also demonstrates the use of a *repoussoir*, an object along the left or right foreground of an image that directs the viewer's eye into the composition. The device is used not just in photography but also in other disciplines of the visual arts. In this case the repoussoir is the vanity mirror showing Lily's face and the hand of the make-up artist, which makes us do a double-take and leads us to a "wider" frame of the two interacting in subtle and tentative movements.

But at the same time the type of frame can also further contextualise and position the subject in the circumstances of his, her or its environment. In Figure 5.2, I sought to show the way individuals were also compartmentalised in their everyday lives in state-subsidised housing, and to give viewers a clue into the structure and nature of such housing. The door frame on the left, covered in mosaic, is an example of older state-subsidised housing, revealed also in the shape of a rounded archway.

Framing also allows one to create a sense of depth and space in an image. Because a frame is often some kind of foreground, it immediately places the object at a distance *behind* and *inside* it. In Figure 5.4, I have photographed two rituals simultaneously. One is the bride's make-up (in the bedroom), and the other is the bride's mother praying at the family altar. By framing the bride in the doorway of her bedroom, I am able to

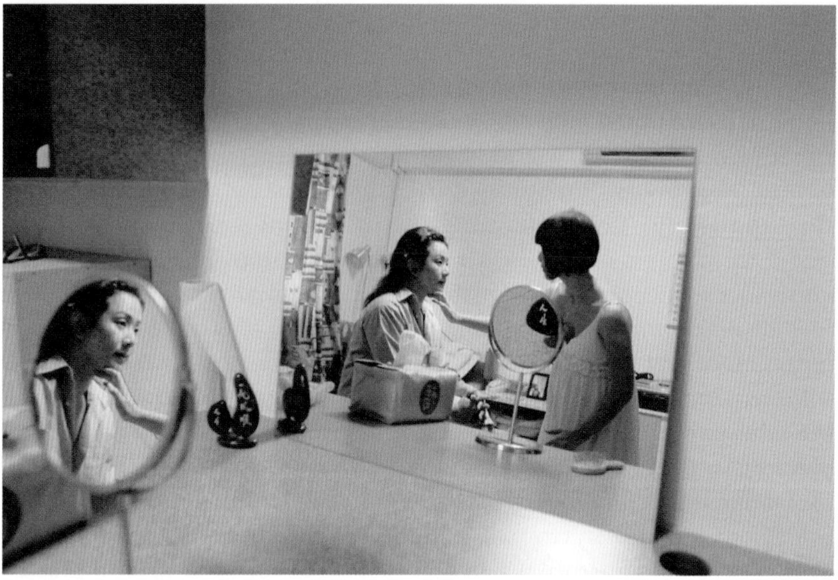

Figure 5.3 Chinese brides in Singapore often prepare for wedding rituals by undergoing a ritual of transformation, commonly employing a professional make-up artist. Preparation and anticipation are key elements of establishing the wedding as a highly concentrated burst of everyday activity.

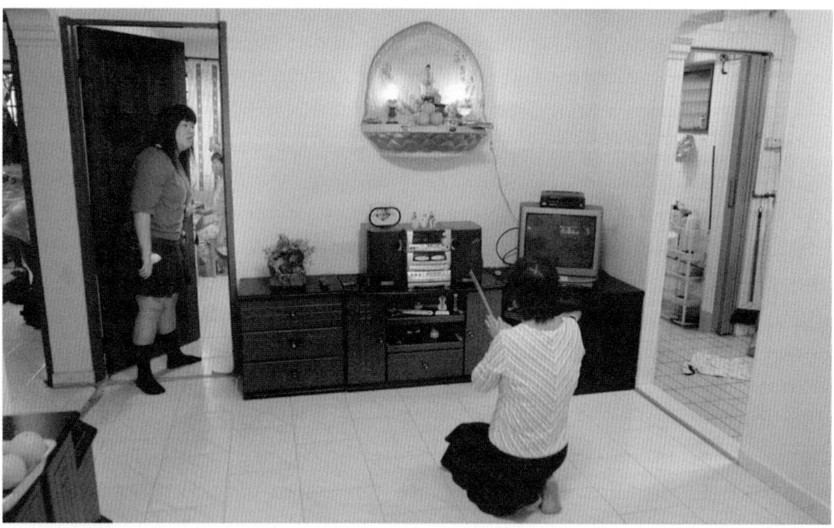

Figure 5.4 Although it is considered a "special" day, many families still go about regular chores in the morning before the wedding begins. Prayers are offered, breakfast is cooked, coffee is drunk. Such photographs also allow us to develop a sense of rhythm that takes place on other days within the household.

show the depth of the flat and rooms. The kitchen and bathroom on the right of the photograph are also framed by a doorway, giving us an idea of the relative width and depth of other rooms.

That said, we do not need structures to create frames and create framing effects. Figure 5.5 shows the aftermath of the first ritual of the day, where Calvin the groom has brought Veron, his bride, back to his family home. Before they return to Veron's family home, Calvin's father, Mr Ang, requests that they pray at the family altar. You can see how Veron and Calvin, who stand in the foreground of the photograph, frame Mr Ang in the background, drawing our eyes to him as he prepares incense sticks for the couple to pray with. The two empty seats to the left of the couple also frame another object – a plastic stool that is temporarily brought out for extra guests – and in this way juxtapose the different elements of house furnishings for the occasion.

Useful tip: When composing a photograph, you are effectively framing the subject in the confines of your camera. Think about whether this framing is useful, or if you are omitting vital information about the subject. Many photographers often frame a photograph too tightly – thinking that this is good composition – but forget the contextual circumstances that would enrich a visual researcher's understanding of the photograph.

Positioning elements – the rule-of-thirds

Typical camera settings: No particular focal length, aperture or shutter speed.

When thinking about photographing everyday life, we are also looking for the interaction between individuals and that between individuals and the environment. In the previous section, I discussed how framing can help us focus on particular scenes and people in a photograph, but also how every photograph is effectively an act of framing. Part of this process is deciding who and what to include inside a single photograph, particularly one that stands alone and is not in a sequence of successive images of the same scene. Beyond inclusion, one also needs to think about how the different elements in any photograph come together to develop a single-image story.

In Figure 5.6a, we return to Lily, the bride whose make-up ritual I featured in Figure 5.3. Dan (in white) has completed the "door games" and retrieved Lily, and the two are walking down a central stairwell from Lily's flat. Lily lives in a five-room Housing Development Board (HDB) flat (see Chapter 4 for a description of HDB flats). Like many older flats, hers does not have an elevator on every floor, hence

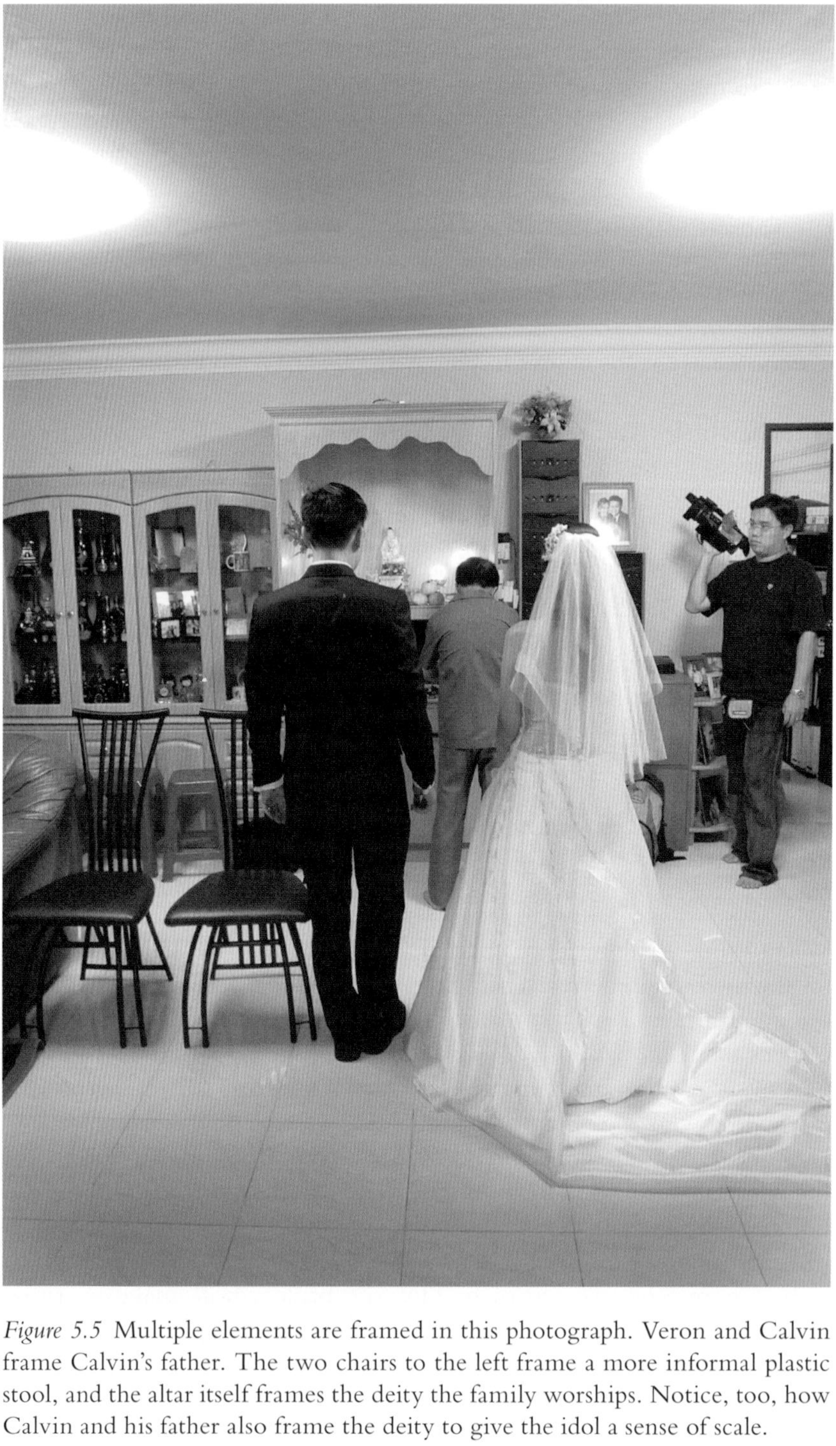

Figure 5.5 Multiple elements are framed in this photograph. Veron and Calvin frame Calvin's father. The two chairs to the left frame a more informal plastic stool, and the altar itself frames the deity the family worships. Notice, too, how Calvin and his father also frame the deity to give the idol a sense of scale.

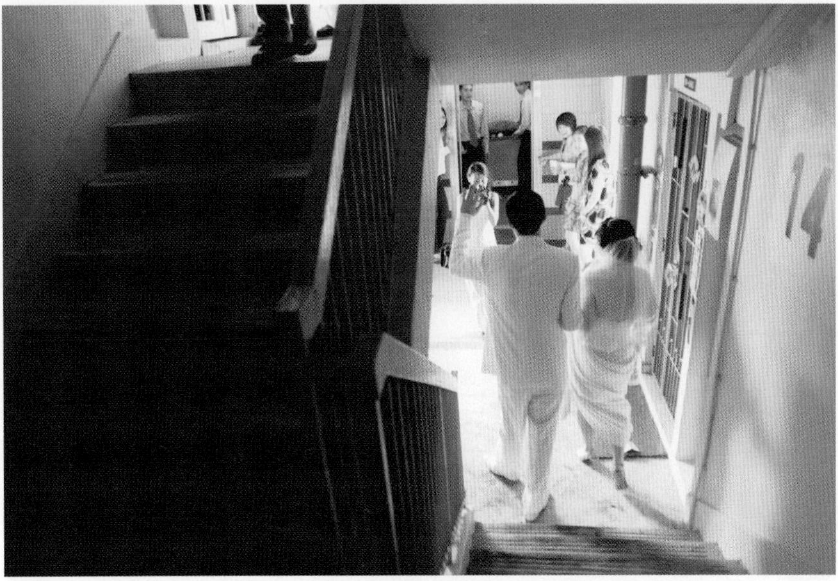

Figure 5.6a Dan has fetched Lily from her parents' home and is proceeding to his family home. He waves to my assistant who has positioned herself in front of the couple.

the opportunity for me to photograph the couple's movement through typical transitory spaces in their everyday lives – the staircase and lift landing.

These transitory spaces in HDB flats are purposefully barren and minimal. Raw concrete and external pipes and cables ensure lower building costs, which keep the prices of social housing low in Singapore. These ascetic features contrast powerfully with the consumptive character of Singaporean Chinese weddings, and it was my desire to show that contrast between everyday and "special-day" in these images. On top of that, I wanted to give the reader an impression of the journeys of these individuals on other days. To do this, I positioned the couple to the right of the photograph, capturing the full length of the stairwell as well as a glimpse of the feet of one of their groomsmen. I also kept a low enough stance so that the angle of my lens captured two more groomsmen holding the elevator, and three bridesmaids standing in an informal "welcome line," all meant as a way to accentuate the social and cultural status of bride and groom on their wedding day.

Figure 5.6 also demonstrates the use of the rule-of-thirds, where elements of a photograph are positioned using nine equal sections created through two horizontal and two vertical lines. This results in four intersections and four observable overlapping lines. By positioning elements

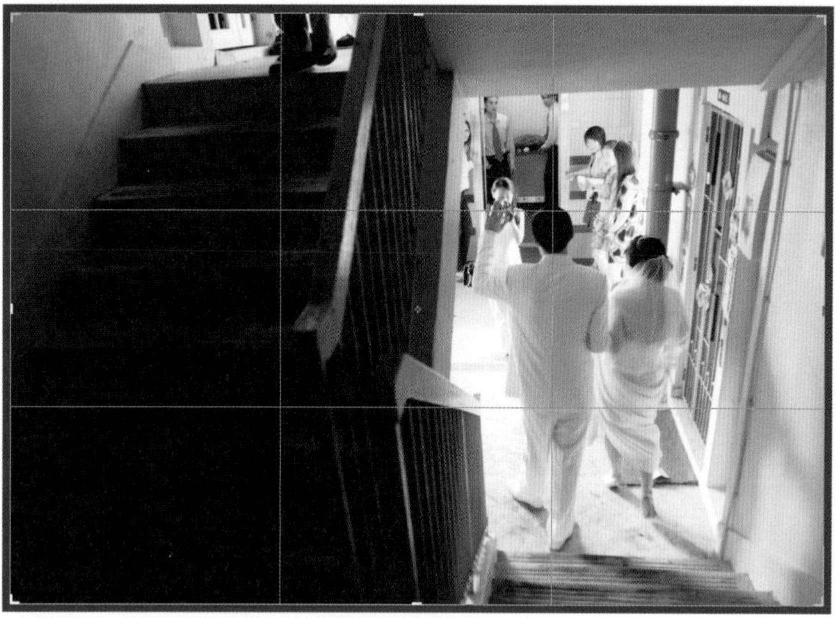

Figure 5.6b The same photograph, now with gridlines showing the rule-of-thirds. Dan's head is positioned on the intersection of two lines, moving him off-centre. This also positions Lily in the right-third of the image. The groomsman's feet are also positioned on or near the left vertical line.

or points of interest in the photograph on an intersection or along a line, the rule argues, elements in the photograph will appear more balanced and aesthetically pleasing.

At the same time, the subject or subjects in a photograph do not always have to be sitting on an intersection or along a gridline. In my experience, dividing elements into the "thirds" of a picture (either horizontally or vertically) while keeping the subject near an intersection or line (and not directly on) will also achieve a balanced effect.

In Figure 5.7a, I had followed Joe and Samantha to their wedding at a five-star hotel in Singapore. Religious space is highly regulated in Singapore (Kong 1993), and many newly established and independent churches are unable to find or afford land to build dedicated structures. As such, many churches rent commercial spaces such as convention centres and hotel ballrooms for their weekly services and rituals. The result is stages adapted to altars and halls adapted to sanctuaries. Here, Joe and Samantha kneel at the altar on stage to pray, whilst friends and supporters reach out in a symbolic "laying of hands" upon the couple. Whilst all this happens, Samantha's flower girl, Ming, fitted with furry angel wings, stands oblivious to their fervent prayers.

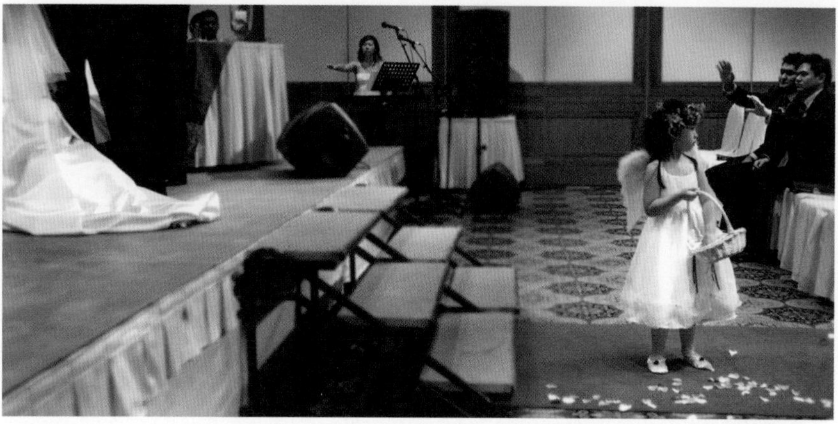

Figure 5.7a Evangelical Christian wedding ceremony at hotel in Singapore.

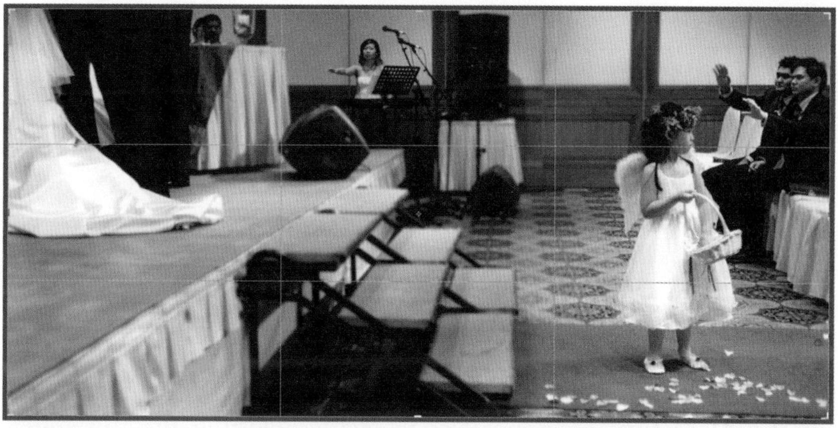

Figure 5.7b A modified use of "thirds" – placing different subjects off-centre for visual impact. In this case, Joe and Samantha occupy the left-third, their worship leader Mabel occupies the centre-third in the background and Ming and two other groomsmen occupy the right-third.

Useful tip: The rule-of-thirds is not a strict rule, but more of a guideline to encourage photographers to position their subject "off-centre." Even then, many photographers starting out tend to be overly aware of the rule-of-thirds, forcing every subject to one of the four intersections. This creates a sense of "compositional anxiety" where one is more concerned about composition than the actual act of photographing.

Finally, not all photographs need to adhere to the rule-of-thirds. Various photographers often point out that in order to create a photograph with symmetry, perhaps that of a building, tree or reflection, it is not always possible to then position elements along a line or at an intersection of lines. Furthermore, placing subjects in the centre of an image can create different kinds of visual effects, especially if it is a portrait of an individual in his or her surroundings.

Focussing, focus lock and recomposing

Typical camera settings: No particular focal length, aperture or shutter speed. Issue is more prevalent with longer focal lengths and smaller apertures where shallow depths-of-field make misfocussing more noticeable.

In order to understand how to execute the compositional techniques in this chapter, it is important that we also analyse and master the acts of focussing, locking focus and recomposing. *Focussing* is the process by which a camera's lens moves towards or away from a subject in order to sharpen the image of the subject (Harris 2016). Such a movement can be internal or external – by internal I mean the lens's internal mechanism moving in such a way that the image you see in your camera's viewfinder is sharp. By external I mean that the whole camera moves closer or further away from a subject until its image is sharp in the camera's viewfinder. The latter is most common when one tries to focus on a subject close-up, but overreaches the minimum focussing distance (the absolute minimum length the lens needs to be from the subject) and thus has to move the camera *away* from the subject. However, most of the time our camera remains static and we adjust the lens's mechanism.

There are two broad methods of focussing – manual and automatic (or autofocus). Manual focus involves manually adjusting the lens, often using the lens's focus ring. Autofocus involves using the camera's electronics to activate motors in either the camera or lens itself to achieve the same effect. Whilst most lenses for DSLRs allow for both manual and autofocus, smaller compact cameras (especially consumer-grade ones) and smartphones rely almost exclusively on autofocus. (There are exceptions of course – professional and enthusiast compact cameras often include a manual focus option.) In DSLRs, autofocus is often the most convenient way to focus on a subject, although some will argue that with practice, manual focus is faster and more accurate. For the purpose of this section I will be discussing how to best make use of autofocus when composing a photograph.

To engage autofocus in a DSLR, it is important to master the "*half-press*." This is where one presses gently on a camera's shutter release but not all the way down. This engages the camera's motor, which drives the lens to rotate and focus on the subject in the camera's *focus area*, which is an amalgamation of several *focus points*. By default, a camera's focus area is in the centre of the viewfinder, often bounded by right-angled symbols or half-circles. When a subject is placed within this focus area, it becomes the object upon which the camera will focus. Oftentimes the focus area will also light up when it has focussed on a subject, and some cameras provide audio confirmation of focus via a beep.

Useful tip: Depending on the camera, focus areas can be very large (computing from multiple points within the camera's view), central, or very specific. More advanced cameras allow photographers to change the focus area to a distinct part of the camera's view, allowing the photographer to always focus on a subject that is off-centre. This is particularly useful when photographing static scenes where the primary subject is always off-centre – for example, a series of students receiving their graduation certificates on stage.

If one were to hold down the shutter release in half-press, this would typically lock the camera's focus on the last subject that was focussed on. While still holding in half-press, it would then be possible to shift the camera and lens and move the subject within the frame whilst still maintaining focus. This is known as *recomposing*. Recomposing is necessary when you want a particular subject in your photograph to be in focus, but that subject is not in the centre of the camera's frame. Returning to Figures 5.7a and b, I had to lock my focus on Ming by placing her in the centre of the camera's frame, locking the focus, and then recomposing such that she would then be in the right-third of the photograph. If I had simply focussed on the centre portion of the image, I would be focussing on the loudspeakers in the background, and as I use a wide aperture, this would have caused Ming to be blurred and the loudspeakers to be sharp.

Useful tip: Half-presses are now only one way of engaging autofocus in some cameras. Cameras with touchscreens (and smartphones) now also routinely allow users to set a mode where pressing anywhere on the touchscreen will command the camera to focus on that particular spot and release the shutter. Such a method removes some need for recomposing. Likewise, advances in technology allow for the use of other buttons on a camera to activate and lock focus. See Mansurov (2012) for more details.

Conclusion: capturing decisive moments – awareness and anticipation

The photographer Henri Cartier-Bresson is famous for the phrase and corresponding book *The Decisive Moment* which, according to Kim (2010), "was that split second of genius and inspiration that a photographer had to capture a certain moment." A photographer, particularly one working in street photography, documentary photography or photojournalism – genres where action and interaction feature heavily – relies on being able and prepared to capture decisive moments in her photography. And while luck does play a part – Cartier-Bresson himself admitted in an interview that one of his most iconic photographs of a man jumping a puddle had an element of chance to it – the ability to capture decisive moments can be honed through practice and planning. In this section I will consider a few techniques that can help one photograph moments in everyday life.

The first is to develop a wider view and sense of a scene, which involves being environmentally, spatially and cognitively *aware* of what is going on *all around* you, particularly in areas that are outside of your field of vision. If you are photographing an event at which everyone is focussing their attention in one direction, it is often fruitful to turn around and look in the opposite direction to note if something there is interesting and worth

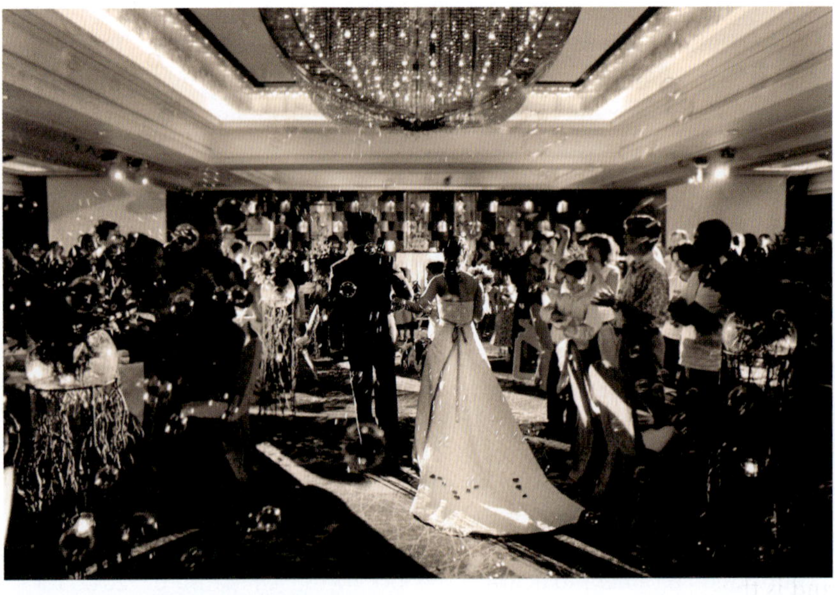

Figure 5.8 A bridal couple walks down an aisle in a five-star hotel in Singapore, complete with a bubble machine.

photographing. Likewise, if everyone is pointing their cameras / smartphones from one angle, I realise that angle will be covered extensively, and move away to find another angle to photograph the same subject from.

In trying to photograph weddings as a site of consumption and performance, I often attempted to portray the full spectacle of the wedding as a performative event. Nowhere is this more evident than in the evening banquet walk-in – a syncretic ritual which mimics a bride's church walk-in, but instead with her husband and in a secular environment. However, with this come all the trappings of a staged *event* – hotels and restaurant venues often try to outdo each other in making the act as spectacular as possible. In the 1990s this involved pouring dry-ice smoke onto the aisle (this still happens today). More recently venues have become more innovative, with the use of multi-coloured LEDs, pyrotechnics, bubbles, creative spotlights and confetti.

When I started out photographing weddings, I found that most if not all photographers would position themselves at the *front* of the banquet hall, photographing the bridal couple as they made their triumphant entry into the venue to the rapturous applause of their guests. But I also found this angle difficult to take – the spotlight was often harsh and created lighting difficulties (see Chapter 9). I also realised that this position was overused and clichéd, and thus sought a new angle. I realised that the spotlight cast a strong silhouette of the couple, while at the same time illuminating everyone else through a backlight. Using a wide-angle lens, I am often able to capture the whole scene – bridal couple, visual effects, guests as spectators and spatial arrangements all in one moment. This was my decisive moment in a wedding, which I found was being mimicked by other photographers a few years later.

The second is to *anticipate* people's behaviour during their actions and interactions. Part of this comes through practice, observation and experience. For example, in my fieldwork in weddings I photographed a good number of them as a professional before I approached it from a research perspective. As such, my repeated observations and participation in weddings allowed me to anticipate certain actions that were more likely than not to happen – in other words, I was anticipating behaviour based on previous experiences. This could be the positioning of individuals during particular rituals, participants' expressions, their reactions to certain events and words, and so on and so forth. One significant ritual in Singaporean Chinese weddings is the tea ceremony, where the bridal couple serve cups of tea to their family elders. The acceptance of that tea becomes a symbol of the elder's acceptance of the spouse into their family, and is thus a socially important aspect of the wedding. Many individuals consider this the "moment" in a Singaporean Chinese wedding where the couple are considered to be "properly" married, and thus also a

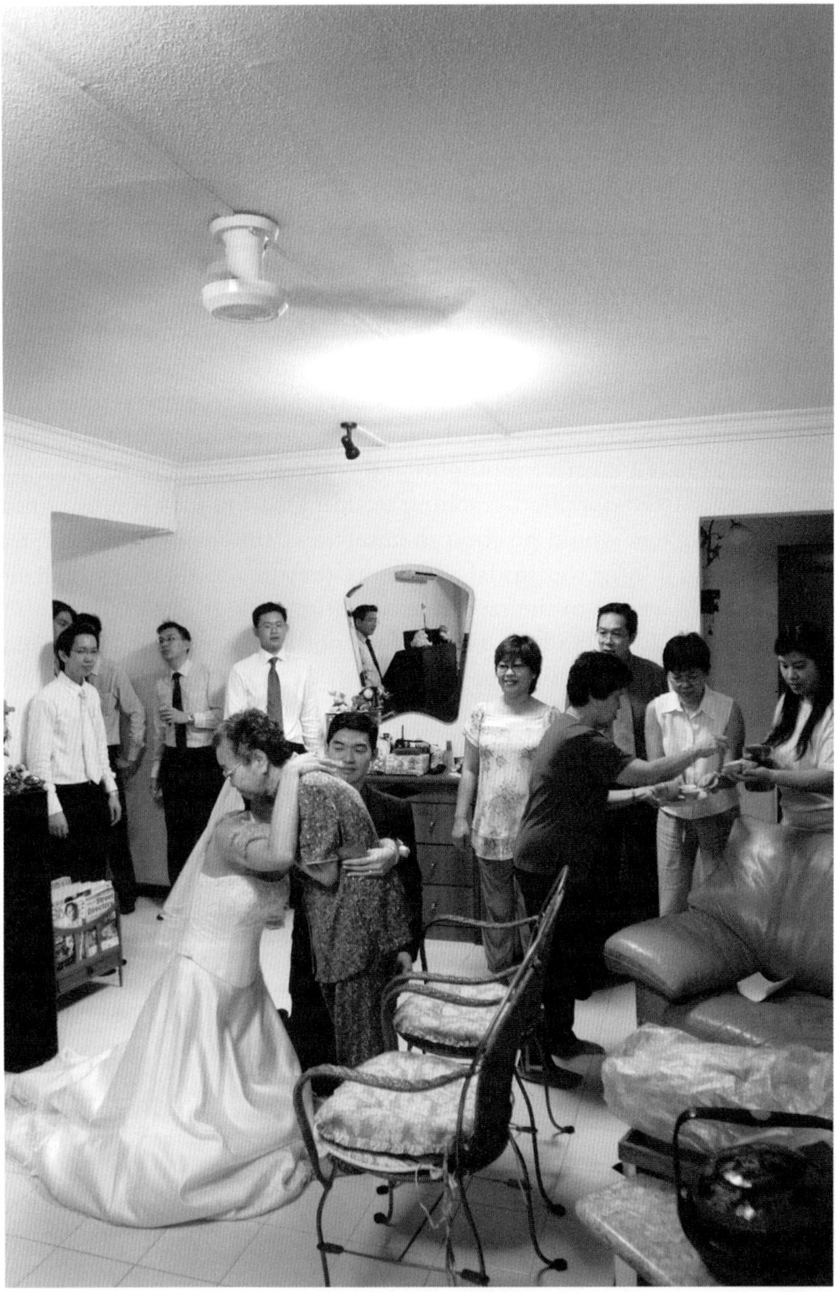

Figure 5.9 Anticipating emotion.

moment in which they cement their status as adults, ready to leave the family home to set up a new family unit.

The tea ceremony (and the wedding as a whole) is thus also a transition point for many young Singaporean Chinese individuals, who are also aware of the emotional significance of the event. Knowing this, I make sure that I prepare myself for moments in which individuals react emotionally to each other, making outward gestures of affection they would not normally have done. In Figure 5.9 I photograph Sarah, who hugs her grandmother in a sign of gratitude, love and, to a certain extent, finality in her rite-of-passage. Many of my informants explain to me that they choose not to display affection or even praise on an everyday basis, attributing this behaviour to "Chinese culture," but for a moment in a day they choose to relinquish such inhibitions.

Anticipation and awareness work for any number of genres in photography, and not just those that involve the documentation of everyday life. For example, if we are aware of the way light falls upon a building or space, we will be able to photograph that space at a certain time of day to create portraits of a certain ambience. Likewise, if we anticipate the movement of individuals along particular paths and trajectories in the same space, perhaps into stray beams of light or cast shadows, we can also time our photographs to capture these moments. Anticipation, especially in repeated actions, is a very effective tool to ensure a consistency of quality in our photographs. In the next chapter, I will be considering in more detail how we photograph and engage with such particular acts of repetition – rituals.

Chapter exercises

Everyday life – interaction

Unlike space and structure, shooting everyday life has more practical and ethical issues, especially if you have not yet received explicit permission to shoot. However, it is often acceptable to conduct some form of street photography in many parts of the world, usually as a tourist. In this case, you will want to start practising with cameras that have as little of a field presence as possible.

1 Find a particular public space where photography is common; this could often be an area that is popular with tourists and where taking images has become an acceptable practice.

2 Look for moments in which individuals are interacting with each other and with their space. Avoid the temptation to photograph the obvious or, at least, look beyond the obvious once you have photographed it. Many photographers will gravitate immediately to vendors, performers and the dispossessed – creating portraits that while they are important to the texture of a space, tend to show only one aspect.

3 Practise with the different compositional tools covered in this chapter.

   a. Framing – Position objects or people within a framing device – doorways, archways, and windows are a good start, even if the object / person and frame are not immediately or intuitively related. When you are comfortable with static objects, you can start experimenting with more non-obvious frames, or with using other elements to the left or right of the main subject to lead readers' eyes into the image.
   b. Rule-of-thirds – Turn on the gridlines option in your camera if you can, then try to position interesting elements or your primary subject at the intersections of the vertical and horizontal lines. If you are trying this for the first time, set your camera to Program mode (fully automatic) and use a wider lens to reduce depth-of-field issues (see Chapter 7 on depth-of-field). Also try to photograph scenes along a level plane to begin with (not too much distance between the foreground and background). Once you have got used to the rule-of-thirds, you can use longer lenses and different subjects.
   c. Focus lock and recomposition – Sometimes, it might be useful to learn this technique before trying the rule-of-thirds, but autofocus systems, combined with face-recognition focussing are becoming so much more advanced that the traditional sequence of mastery is up for debate. Nonetheless, learning to lock focus and recompose is still important.

      i. Start by selecting an object or person that you want to focus on.

ii. Aim your camera directly at this subject and then focus on the subject by pressing your shutter release halfway.
iii. Keeping your finger's pressure steady on the shutter release, move the camera to the left or the right such that you are moving the focus area off from the subject.
iv. Press the shutter release fully to take the picture with the focus still locked on your initial subject

chapter 6

Photographing everyday life 2 – ritual

Key technical concepts

- Three ways of photographing ritual
  - Landscape of ritual action
  - Portrait of ritual interaction
    - Waist level photography
  - Ritual details
- Photographing sequences as both literal and expressive record

Case study keywords: Bukit Brown Cemetery

Introduction

Ritual, religious or mundane, is a key aspect of everyday life. As many social researchers have noted, ritual is an important way for us to understand the values, ideals and norms of an individual, social group or culture (Evans 1998; Graburn 2001; McLaren 1999; Tong 2004; Wong 2001). Anthropologists have long incorporated photographs of rituals into their analysis – for example, Chan and Yung's (2005) study of Chinese street opera (often a ritualistic affair) in Singapore relied on images to express the outside/outdoor nature of entertainment and contrast this with the evolving role of theatre in Chinese ethnicity. Similarly, Hockings's (2010) study of funeral rites, Bezner's (2002) analysis of wedding images as evidence of ritual as a core aspect of American culture and Chappell, Chappell and Margolis's (2011) consideration of old school photographs showing ritualised schooling practices are evidence of the efficacy of photography to document, illustrate and illuminate ritual practices.

However, as Gold (1997) has noted, the dichotomy between the interpretation and creation of visual images amongst academics, especially sociologists, still stubbornly remains. This implies that photography of ritual can, and often does, fall into a system of mundane documentation, *followed* by interpretation on hindsight. The social researcher photographing the ritual thus often sees the image as nothing more than a record. But, as Lury (1998:2) has also pointed out, photography not only represents, but shows us a new "way of seeing," so photography should help us to "see" rituals in different ways when we look through the camera. Rather than just photographing the actions and procedures of ritual, we must photograph it in a way that evokes the sense, emotion, identity and culture that is so often performed in and expressed through ritual.

Bukit Brown Cemetery and its rituals

For a cemetery in Singapore, Bukit Brown is large and expansive. Established in the 1900s as a clan-specific cemetery for Hokkien immigrants, Bukit Brown was eventually acquired by the British colonial government to act as a municipal cemetery. It grew in popularity over the years, but closed in 1971 to new burials. Since then, nature has quickly taken over the landscape – particularly because of the cemetery's geographical location near to a central catchment area, barren deathscapes have become a lush, verdant tropical rainforest. The closure of the cemetery in the 1970s has also meant that infrastructure is lacking, especially artificial lighting and re-paved roads (more on this in Chapter 9 on night photography). As such, Bukit Brown Cemetery stands as a complex space of urbanisation, de-urbanisation and re-urbanisation.

Despite its closure and apparent state neglect, the cemetery is still home to various annual rituals that take place throughout the year. Of special note are *Qing Ming* in March/April, an annual grave-cleaning ritual that is similar to All-Souls day, and the Hungry Ghost Festival in August/September (see Chapter 4 for more information on this festival). In addition, a recent Singapore government decision to exhume about 4000 graves from the cemetery to make way for a four-lane throughway has meant that many individuals are also engaging in exhumations of their ancestors for cremation and re-interment in columbariums. In this chapter, I will focus on rituals pertaining to *Qing Ming.*

In order to photograph rituals well, it is necessary to consider the different scales at which a ritual takes place, which can be categorised into three levels. Firstly, a landscape of ritual action, photographs taken at very wide focal lengths (17–24mm) from a distance, with the ritual contextualised in a wide space and given little visual precedence. Secondly, a portrait of individuals operating in their ritual space, photographs taken near to the subjects but at wide focal lengths (24–30mm) to show the actions and interactions of subjects. Thirdly, a zoomed-in detail of ritual actions and/or object, photographs taken using longer focal lengths (70mm and above) that crop out distracting elements to focus on particular actions done in rituals, or expressions of the subject. I will deal with each of these in turn.

Starting out: developing a landscape of ritual action

Common camera settings: Very wide to wide focal lengths (14–35mm), small aperture (f/8 and above in daylight, f/4 in lower light conditions). Tripod in very low-light conditions.

Qing Ming Jie (清明节), literally translated as "Pure Brightness Festival," is a tomb-sweeping ritual that occurs on the fifteenth day after the Spring Equinox, typically in the first week of April. The festival has its origins in ancient China, where individuals held ceremonies to honour their ancestors. The intention of the ritual is similar in diasporic Chinese Singapore – *Qing Ming* is an occasion for families to reunite around the graves of relatives (usually grandparents, parents or significant ancestors) to perform acts of filial piety and to appease the spirits of the dead by offering incense sticks, food and paper effigies of money, gold and clothes. In Singapore and parts of South-East Asia, there is also an additional practice of placing coloured sheets of paper known as *ya zhi* (压纸) on the mound of the tomb, as an indication to other branches of the family that descendants have visited the grave. Finally, individuals identifying with Teochew traditions will eat cockles at the grave and then strew the shells over the grave mound, symbolising a wealthy family with gold strewn on the ground.

My own experiences with *Qing Ming* began long before my fieldwork in Bukit Brown. As a child I would be awoken early in the morning, at about 4a.m., when my parents would bundle me and my sister into a car and drive to *Khong Meng San* (光明山 Bright Hill) temple, where my grandfather's ashes were stored in a columbarium. I was too young to remember the significance of what we were doing, but these memories served as a connection to my own identity as a diasporic Chinese individual when I stepped into Bukit Brown to document what was to be one of the last *Qing Ming* festivals for individuals whose ancestors' graves were affected by the planned road to be built by the state.

I arrived very early in Bukit Brown on the first day of *Qing Ming*, at about 5a.m., and positioned myself in my car near the gates, to watch individuals and groups slowly make their way to their ancestors' graves. My first task was to document the ritual landscape, the general *feel* of the space with rituals going on. Instead of immediately photographing, I sat in my car, watching the rain pelt the windscreen, observed figures walking in a line, holding umbrellas and large oversized bags of folded *kim zua*, ready to be burnt. I drank in the air of ritual, the anticipation of performance.

With that, I stepped out into the cemetery and followed the main single-lane road around the periphery of the centre, also one of the areas most affected by the road (and hence with the highest number of exhumations). I carried one camera but with two lenses, one wide for landscapes, and a telephoto to zoom in from afar so as not to intrude on semi-public rituals (I and other fieldworkers that day would ask permission for any close-up photographs). I took two kinds of photographs – the first worked less well than the second. In the first, I attempted to photograph the ritual of burning as it happened, but from a distance using my telephoto lens. This had little impact other than the images appearing voyeuristic and opportunistic. It also seemed to betray my shyness in not wanting to approach complete strangers in public (this was one of my first assignments in Bukit Brown). The photographs were neither of a landscape nor of a ritual, but of something in between that did little to add to any textual observations I was making.

Another attempt, this time using a wide-angle lens, proved to be more effective. Here, I integrated the character of the landscape with the ritual act of burning *kim zua*, allowing the landscape of Bukit Brown Cemetery to swallow up the ritual, leaving only a tell-tale sign of ritual. I also made use of an early rising sun (the sun at a low angle creates dramatically different lighting conditions – many photographers call the first hour of sunrise and the last hour before sunset "golden hours"). In Figure 6.1, I photographed into the light, creating a silhouette of the large tree in the foreground as well as the individuals framed by the smoke emanating from their stack of burning *kim zua*. Notice, too, how the smoke is framed between two trees in the background. I also converted the photograph to black and white to put emphasis on form, action and structure, and used Adobe Camera Raw to increase the contrast and clarity settings, as well as to deepen the "blacks" (see Chapter 11 on post-processing).

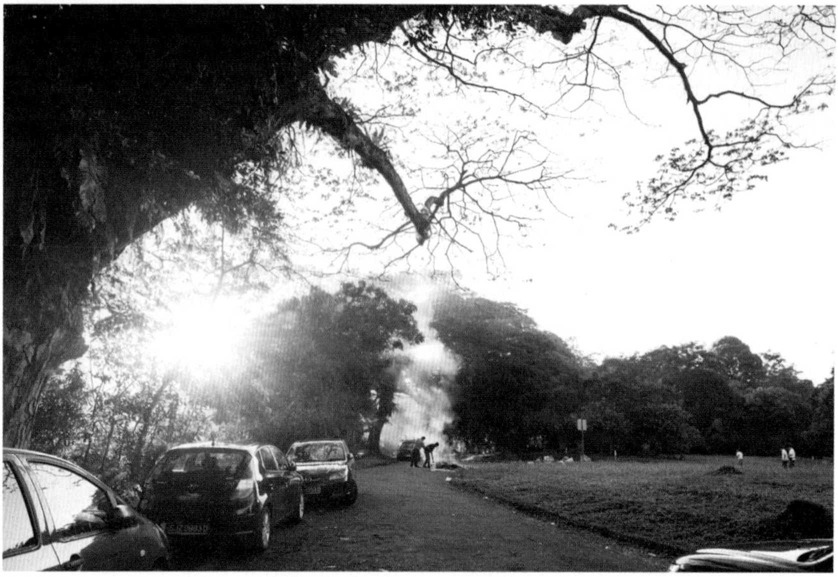

Figure 6.1 A landscape of ritual action – individuals burning *kim zua* at the cemetery's roundabout. The photograph only partially adheres to the rule-of-thirds (see Chapter 5), in that subject matter is separated into three segments, both horizontally and vertically, but no single point of interest sits on the intersection of the imaginary grid.

Useful tip: Don't just photograph the ritual itself – go early and photograph the setting up (if there is one). That will allow you time to watch for interesting locations and anticipate where particularly important events will take place. Keeping a respectful distance during setup will also acclimatise participants to your presence with a camera.

Photographing rituals from a wider angle and a distance seems counter-intuitive. After all, are we not trying to photograph the intricate and detailed movements and actions of the celebrants? This is partially true, but in situations where the environment is as important as the individual for the ritual, photography helps us to create a portrait of that space, developing a context that is important to our later, more detailed descriptions and analysis of the ritual. In the case of Bukit Brown, the natural landscape of rainforest is critical in our understanding of the significance of such rituals – it betrays the macro-level neglect accorded to the space, having been closed to new burials by the state in the 1970s. This closure meant that individuals were only able to carry out micro-levels of maintenance, clearing only the graves of the individuals they were related to. Developing

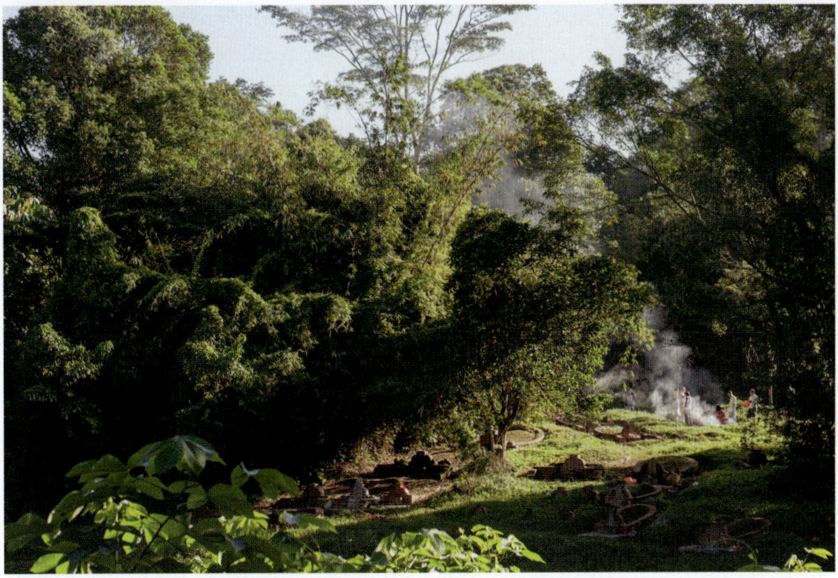

Figure 6.2 On a ridge, I spotted a clearing where a family were burning *kim zua*. Using a standard zoom lens, I zoomed in to 70mm (almost telephoto) and framed the family between the trees, using some plants and trees to give a sense of scale to both the individuals and the tombstones in the foreground.

infrastructure by the clearing of large trees, building of roads or installing of street lighting proved to be impossible, and, in hindsight, this was a precursor to the state's narrative of redevelopment for economic progress. Rituals like *Qing Ming* could thus be seen as a micro-level subversion of state narratives of space and how space should be used, as was also the case in Teck Ghee Court in Chapter 4. It was thus important not just to situate my subjects in their environment, but to document and characterise the environment as a key factor in understanding the social significance of *Qing Ming* and other rituals that took place in Bukit Brown.

Creating a portrait of rituals – wider angles near subjects, lower angles for more impact

Common camera settings: Wide to standard focal lengths (17–60mm), large to medium apertures for better shutter speeds (f/2.8–f/5.6). High ISO to compensate in lower light conditions.

Once I had finished the landscapes of Bukit Brown, I rendezvoused with a team of researchers who had arranged to meet with a family of informants who had given their consent for us to observe their *Qing Ming* rituals. Serene (F, 40s, Chinese) is the great-great-granddaughter of Tan

Quee Lan, a prominent Chinese businessman in Singapore. The year that we met Serene was especially significant, because it was her first *Qing Ming* festival since rediscovering the cluster of graves housing Tan Quee Lan and other family members in Bukit Brown (see Tan 2012 for a full account of her story). She had spent several years searching for these graves, but at the same time felt that there was a supernatural force in the guise of dreams leading her to a family reunion in Bukit Brown.

Serene had brought her family to perform *Qing Ming* – including her two children, Alexander and Elizabeth, and her brother and sister. Accompanying them was also a distant relative who had relocated to neighbouring Malaysia, but was also a successful businessman in his own right. We met at the mouth of the hill in which the graves were located (Bukit Brown is roughly divided into four or five separate blocks or hills) and proceeded to walk in through a well-trodden path in the undergrowth, hewn out by local caretakers. The caretakers had also cleared the undergrowth around the graves, leaving a small clearing in which the family could perform rituals and researchers could film, photograph and make observations.

The clearing was very useful in that it allowed a large group of individuals to move about and interact freely, whereas in most cases in Bukit Brown one's movements would be more restricted owing to the density of neighbouring graves and undergrowth. I began as I normally would by photographing the space in which the ritual was taking place – mapping out the clearing as well as the positioning of the gravestones. What I also did was to ensure that the rituals were portrayed with sufficient detail for two purposes – the first was to ensure proper photographic documentation (both for the project and as a field note reference), and the second was to situate individuals within the ritual – its artefacts, space, protocol and procedures.

It should be noted that these photographs are also the most common ones we see in academic publications that employ visual methods to document ritual action. Hence, these are also the most challenging to make different and more interesting. The first step is to acclimatise oneself to the ritual – what it is, what is happening, who are the key subjects, artefacts and actions to be photographed and so on. This means that the first series of photographs will often be highly descriptive, effectively a sequence of images showing who did what, where it was done and how it was done. But it is only through this process of acclimatisation that we can transcend the mundane.

The "right" moment

However, mundane photography does not have to be uninteresting. There are two ways in which we can photograph rituals but still retain elements of *studium* (see Chapter 1). The first is to wait for particular moments during the ritual in which action and interaction are more obvious and/or dramatic. This does not mean that we only photograph "energetic" or theatrical moments, but within any particular sequence within a ritual, there will be some moments that lend themselves better to photography than others. During *Qing Ming*, it is common to offer food and drink at the graves of one's ancestors – which is seen as a way of paying respects and nourishing and pleasing their spirits. However, there needs to be a system in which one knows when the spirit has partaken of the offerings and is satisfied. To this extent, celebrants often engage in *pua puay*, which is to take two red-coloured, kidney-shaped blocks of wood (known as *jiaobei* [筊杯]) and toss them on the ground. If they land face-up and face-down respectively, it is interpreted that one's ancestor is satisfied. If not, the process must be repeated until the aforementioned result is obtained.

To photograph *pua puay*, I took a series of images from the time Serene knelt at her great-great-grandfather's grave to the time the blocks of wood landed at her knees. In a typical academic publication, I might only be able to use one image from this series – so I would have to choose, both at the shooting stage and at the curation stage, which moment would best depict the ritual, i.e. which was the "right" moment. In Figure 6.3 I chose the point at which the blocks of wood left her hands in mid-air. Technically this meant that I needed a constant shutter speed that was fast enough to capture the motion, necessitating a larger aperture (f/4 and below) and a comparatively fast shutter speed (in the forest, with the density of shadows, I had set my ISO to 3200 to ensure a faster shutter speed to prevent camera shake).

Useful tip: Revisiting rituals is essential to good photography – repeated attempts mean that you become familiar enough with a ritual to anticipate what happens next, and where to best position yourself when shooting.

Lower angles for more impact

The second way involves finding more innovative angles to photograph the same subject. Too often when attempting to document an event unfolding in front of us, we are tempted to photograph at eye-level, meaning we raise the camera to our eyes and photograph from whichever position we are in. This often results in "snapshot"-style photographs, images that appear to be casually and carelessly composed. I propose that this is due to the large majority of casually composed images being

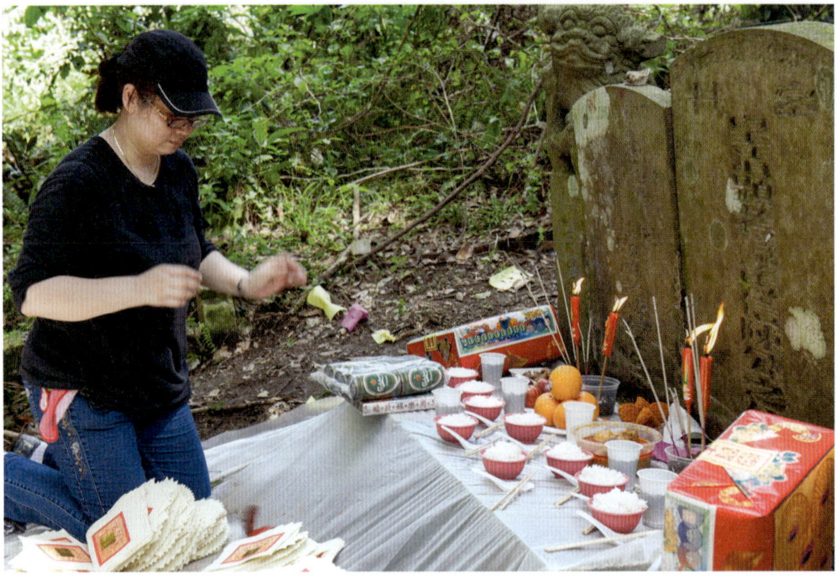

Figure 6.3 With a stone guardian lion looking on from top right, Serene drops the *jiaobei* onto the ground in front of offerings of food and paper effigies of beer cans. A slightly slower shutter speed (owing to the overcast forest foliage) means that Serene's hands and the blocks of wood are blurred – this works to enhance the storytelling capacity of the image, indicating movement and action rather than staticity. Notice also how the subjects are divided into three vertical segments (see rule-of-thirds, Chapter 5).

created at eye-level, so that an average viewer is more likely to associate such images with a common pool of material. Of course, it is not possible to always avoid photographing at eye-level, but one way to make what seems mundane appear more interesting is to change the angle from which you are shooting.

Consider the act of burning *kim zua* – this is a ritual action meant for celebrants to send money to their ancestors in the netherworld. The burning transforms the *kim zua* from effigies of money or gold into actual gold that can be spent on bribes and other expenses in the netherworld. Burning *kim zua* takes place all year round, and is particularly prominent during *Qing Ming* and the Hungry Ghost Festival (see Chapter 4). Since it is a commonly performed ritual, photographing it from eye-level would make the action even more mundane. I was thus challenged to find a way to photograph such burning up-close and make it a bit more fresh and interesting. I chose to photograph from waist-level, squatting near the burning point and zooming out to capture more of the action within a single frame. I was rewarded with a series of Alexander and his

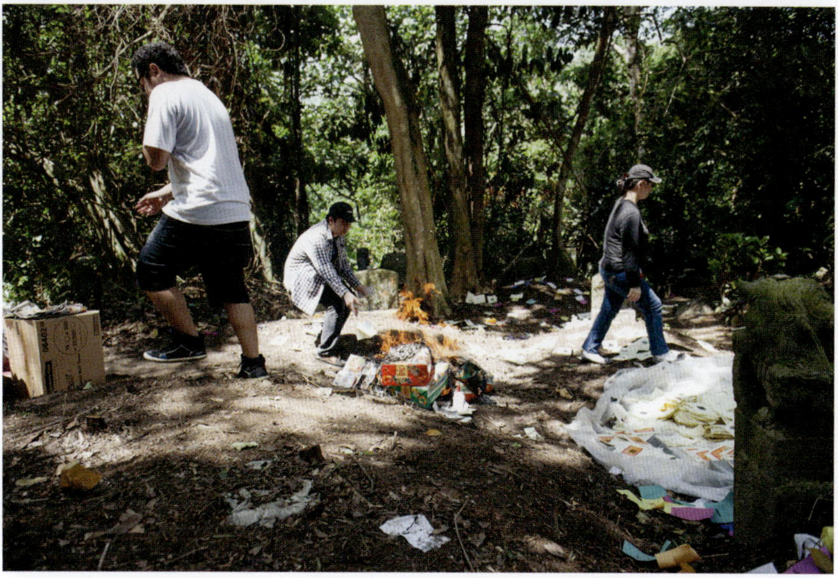

Figure 6.4 This was at the end of a long sequence of photographs, where I was observing how Alexander and his uncle were gingerly throwing *kim zua* onto the burning pile of offerings. I waited for the moment at which they would throw the offerings onto the fire, then back away quickly, and was fortunate enough to catch Serene on the right as well.

uncle burning *kim zua,* but in a way that showed a certain sense of action, motion and interaction (see Chapter 5).

"Waist-level" photography has two important advantages. One, because most individuals have an eye-level above an average waist height, it is an angle that is less often seen in vernacular photography. This immediately offers a different perspective to what is "normally" seen, making the photograph appear more interesting and informative. Two, with enough experience, it is possible to "shoot from the hip," meaning one approximates distance, angle and focussing and takes a photograph without referring to the viewfinder. (Some cameras have dispensed with this randomness by introducing LCD viewfinder screens that flip upwards, allowing you to photograph from almost any angle.) Doing this can often appear less intrusive and if your subjects are distracted or less observant, they may notice the act of photography less, allowing them to behave more "naturally." This is particularly useful when photographing in environments where your presence is tolerated but not encouraged, or when you need to covertly photograph something without your subjects knowing (assuming this remains ethical for you to do so).

Zooming in: photographing rituals in detail

Common camera settings: Standard to telephoto lens (50–90mm+), large to medium apertures for better shutter speeds (f/2.8–f/5.6). High ISO to compensate in lower light conditions.

At the start of the ceremony, I had also spent time talking to and photographing Serene and her family doing preparatory work. In Figures 6.5a and 6.5b, I demonstrate how creating a close-crop in contrasting light can give a greater impact to the ritual act. Here, Serene and her two children are flexing and folding the *kim zua* to prepare for its burning. *Kim zua* needs to be manipulated in certain ways before it is ready to be offered, either rotated into a stacked fan-like arrangement, or folded into an ingot shape (to reflect ancient Chinese gold ingots).

Figure 6.5a shows how a ritual might typically be taken at a focal length of 38mm. Shot at eye-level pointing downwards, the image is cluttered with many distracting elements that are not necessarily useful to the primary purpose of displaying ritual – Serene's sister Medina stands on the left, and a researcher's video camera lens has intruded on the right. Whilst these elements are useful in a wider analysis, they are best left out for an image such as this.

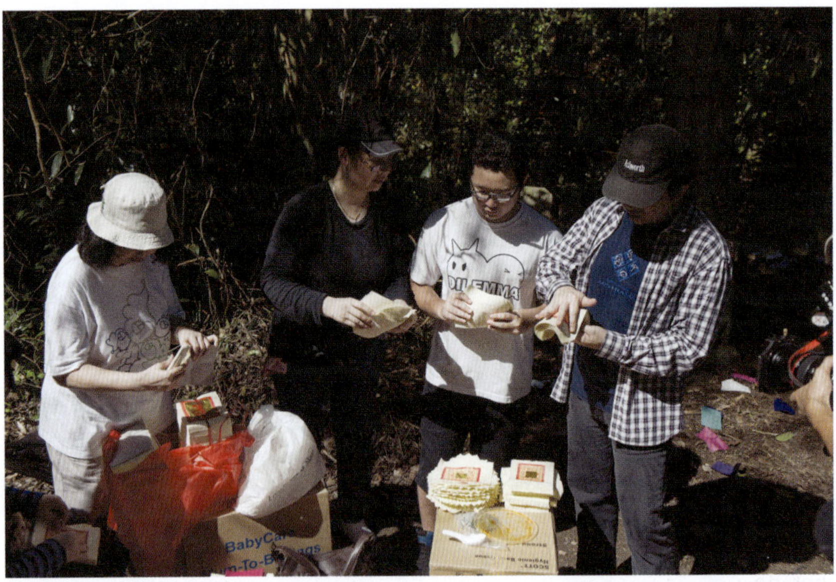

Figure 6.5a A photograph that is useful as part of a descriptive sequence of "what happens," but does less in creating an evocative understanding of the ritual.

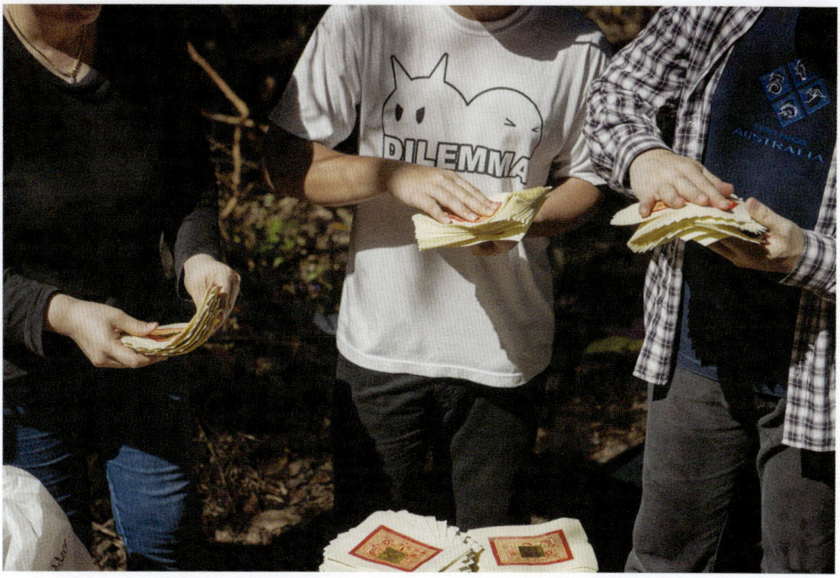

Figure 6.5b Zoomed in at 70mm (or three footsteps closer) – a close crop captures detail such as the design on the *kim zua* and the synchronised motion of Elizabeth and Alexander. Zooming in closer removes distractions but at the same time also removes contextualising images. Such close-up details are best paired with wide-angled photographs.

Conclusion: going beyond "what happens" photography

As you read through this chapter, you will notice a chronological disconnect in the way I have told this story, and this is intentional – the three ways of photographing rituals need not be three *phases*, in that they do not necessarily follow one after the other. In fact, when doing a larger study it is useful to create a separate way of categorising photographs according to the scale at which you have photographed them (in addition to any other ways you are observing these actions).

However, in order to create a more evocative visual study of rituals, it is also necessary to consider what kind of photographs can depict more than just "what happens," or, as Edwards (1997) has termed it, the "descriptive" form of images. Descriptive photographs are important, because they are part of a wider sequence of documentation that brings its own ethnographic value. Yet we must also work towards photographs that do more than that, that exceed their own descriptiveness of ritual and expose its emotional and spiritual aspects. This kind of photography goes beyond showing a literal record of the ritual, but makes use of the

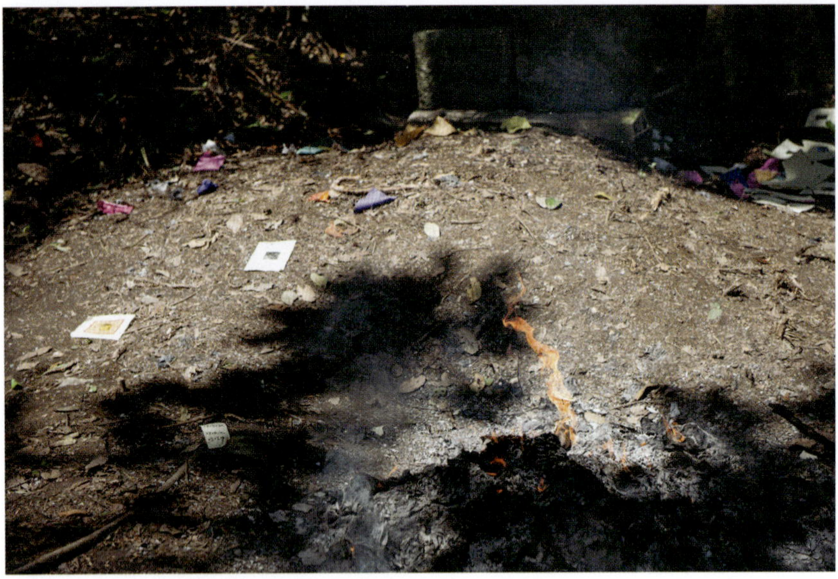

Figure 6.6 Fire, forest, forgetfulness.

subjects and environment to create abstract images that suggest and tease out the intangible facets of everyday life that textual description cannot portray. Figure 6.5 makes one such attempt.

Figure 6.6 shows the smouldering remains of *kim zua* and other paper effigies of clothes and offerings burnt for Serene's ancestors. The overhanging foliage breaks around the white-hot ash, as if the single lone flame is trying to worm its way out. In the background a single worn-out tombstone sits surrounded by scattered bits of coloured paper. There is no action in sight, no individual engaging, reacting or interacting. If anything this photograph documents the space and/or objects poorly. But at the same time, it can also be read as a different kind of text (Chopra 1989; Knowles and Sweetman 2004). We can understand this photograph as an evocative artefact of Bukit Brown's present and future – an overgrown cemetery with little to no infrastructure (like wayfinding), leading to descendants losing track of their ancestors' resting places. The shadow of the tree looms over Serene's offerings and creeps into the centre of the photograph towards the tombstone. Photographs like these can work either as an introductory image in an essay (visual or otherwise), or as a final capstone on a series of more mundane images. Such images tend to share similar characteristics – they tend to be more abstract in their composition, show less literal and descriptive subjects, and require a closer reading to be understood (which at the same time, can also lead to a whole variety of different readings, which may or may not be your intention).

In this chapter we looked at the different ways in which we can photograph rituals, taking a *Qing Ming* ritual as a case study to better understand angles, space and cropping. However, my focus here was the photography of *actions* and *interactions* in rituals, and little has been said about the objects or other physical items. In the next chapter, I will be looking at the ways in which we can photograph the objects, artefacts and possessions of our informants in meaningful and ethnographic ways.

Chapter exercises

Everyday life 2 – ritual

Despite rituals being everywhere and all around us (everyday or otherwise), it is sometimes difficult to gain access to other individuals' rituals, particularly if they are of a personal and/or religious nature. However, opportunities to practise photographing rituals can come in the form of annual public parades, processions or celebrations. Alternatively, ask a close friend or family member for permission to document their daily life for a few days – home rituals are a particularly good opportunity to practise photographing ritual behaviour.

1 Start by looking at the space / landscape in which the ritual is taking place. If you are photographing outdoors, don't immediately focus on the ritual, but focus rather on the wider context in which the ritual is taking place. If you are photographing indoors, don't just photograph that particular space / corner / room in which the ritual occurs. Use a wide-angle lens to juxtapose and compare the ritual space to other related spaces.

   a. If the ritual is happening whilst you are photographing, practise the rule-of-thirds by positioning the overall act of the ritual to the left or right of the centre of the camera's frame.
   b. Experiment with different focal lengths; try to locate the ritual within its environment. If outdoors, what adjacent buildings, streets, individuals or institutions help to show a different perspective of the ritual taking place?

2 Assuming you have a chance to photograph rituals up-close, make sure you use a wide-angled lens, preferably a zoom, to photograph the ritual from various angles and focal lengths. Often, individuals will choose to photograph a particular ritual from only one vantage point and use the same focal length throughout the duration of the ritual. Whilst consistent, it ignores the opportunities to find better angles and more interesting compositions. If possible, try to move around your subject as the ritual is performed – don't just stay in one spot.

3 Go low where possible – many photographs of rituals are taken not at eye-level, but with the camera pointed down in an almost dominant form of observation. Instead, bend your knees and photograph on the same vertical axis as your subject. If they are kneeling, kneel alongside them. Such angles exhibit a sense of collaboration between you and your subject.

4 Experimenting with focal lengths also allows you to create zoomed-in details of smaller rituals. Although digital cameras have high resolutions which allow you to zoom in during post-processing, photographing ritual objects or ritual actions close-up ensures that future reference to such images is painless. So when photographing rituals, try to create a mix of wide angles and closer zoomed-in shots – this may not happen the first time you photograph a ritual, but repeated visits, especially to the same ritual, will allow you to anticipate actions as well as try new angles.

chapter 7

Photographing social and cultural inventories

Key technical concepts

- Minimum focussing distance
- Depth-of-field
- Distortion
- Developing a more abstract photographic understanding of objects

Case study keywords: Bukit Brown Cemetery, Chinese religion, Chinese weddings

Introduction

Objects are important to people – as Miller (2013) has aptly shown, objects bring comfort and meaning to individuals in their everyday interactions. In this chapter, I will be considering how we can photograph both single objects and collections of objects in a meaningful and useful way – or, to borrow from Collier and Collier (1986) – a cultural inventory. Collier and Collier's version of a cultural inventory was more literal, however, as their focus was on using photography as a tool of memory in this case, to remove the need for exhaustive textual cataloguing. In this case, we are not simply using photography in this way (although the by-product of our work does yield a useful set of images detailing these things), but also to expose the significance, emotions and meanings that individuals accord to these objects. Some of this has already been dealt with in Chapter 4 on space and how to photograph objects in space, but this chapter extends the argument to look more closely at the objects themselves.

Unlike other chapters, I will be using examples from all three case studies to give the widest possible view of how we can use a camera to photograph objects. I will begin by considering how we can photograph walls and the things that individuals adorn them with.

Photographing objects – minimum focussing distance

Typical camera settings: Wide-angle lens for multiple objects (24–35mm), medium to portrait telephoto lens for close-up, single objects (60–105mm), as narrow an aperture as possible to maximise depth-of-field.

Photographing objects in a collected and curated set is becoming increasingly popular, as evidenced by Peter Menzel's *What I Eat: Around the World in 80 Diets* (Menzel 2010) and his co-authored book with Charles Mann (Menzel and Mann 1994) – the former being a collection of portraits of families and all the food they eat in a week, and the latter a visual study of the material possessions of families around the world. Photographing objects by themselves also gives us a chance to study these artefacts in greater detail, which is sometimes lost if the artefact is part of a wider-angled shot.

> Useful tip: Don't just shoot an object from a single perspective or scale. Combine portraits of objects in wide-angled and detailed shots to develop a more nuanced understanding of both the character and the role of the object in its environment

There are two ways in which we can think about photographing objects by themselves. The first is a detailed, micro-study of the object in itself. This means photographing its form, its details and any quirks that make it interesting and meaningful. In other words, we are looking at what photographers call "macro photography" – a form of photography that reproduces a subject, often small to very small items, on a much larger scale in a photograph – magnifying details and the subject itself. Although a much more technical discussion can be had about reproduction ratios (the scale at which an object is reproduced on a camera's film or sensor plane), our concern here is how to photograph objects effectively in the field. There are three main issues here – the kind of lens and its minimum focussing distance; aperture and depth-of-field; and the kind of lighting available when photographing the object or objects.

To illustrate these issues, I will consider the photography of exhumed and recovered artefacts from Bukit Brown Cemetery. As part of my fieldwork in Bukit Brown, I was tasked with photographing not just exhumation rituals, but also the objects that were recovered from exhumed graves. These included, but were not limited to, scraps of clothing, coins, funerary artefacts like miniature cooking pots, spectacles and jewellery. With the permission of the descendants of the exhumed individual, I also photographed any remains that were found. Owing to the high rate of decomposition (due in part to a tropical environment and the cemetery's proximity to a rainfall catchment area) and the age of the graves, these remains were often limited, but did include skulls, bones, bone fragments, teeth and gold teeth. In other words, I was working with small to very small artefacts in the field, without much specialist equipment. In the field, my brief was not to scientifically and exhaustively document each object, but to capture the social, spiritual and cultural significance of their presence in these graves, whilst at the same time retaining a level of detail that would afford us a decent level of analysis.

The first thing to do would be to isolate the object or objects from distracting elements, and this usually means filling the frame with the object. To do this, one has to move close enough to the object with a camera so that the object fills most of the space within the image. This is where we have to consider the minimum focussing distance of a lens, defined as the minimum distance between the subject and the camera's sensor that will allow the lens to focus on the subject. This distance is measured from the focal plane mark – a small circle with a line through it, commonly found on the prism of DSLRs. Technically, you can tell what the minimum focussing distance is by looking on the body of the lens, which indicates a range of distance between infinity (∞) and a number. This latter number is the minimum focussing distance. Practically, if your camera is too close to the subject, the lens will not be able to focus on the subject, and you will have to either move away from the subject, or move the subject further away from you. Macro lenses that offer a 1:1 reproduction ratio, that is, they are able to capture an image's full-size on the sensor when focussed as close as possible, have very small minimum focussing distances, whilst other less specialist and less expensive lenses can typically only create an image that is 1/5 the size of the actual object on the camera sensor.

Useful tip: As many graves contained artefacts, I would carry a 105mm macro lens to photograph very small objects. Oftentimes, using a 24–70mm lens set at 70mm was enough, but having a macro lens achieved two things. One, I could photograph almost any small artefact, and two, the lens doubled-up as a telephoto lens when I needed to shoot from a distance

Depth-of-field – a short but important diversion

When I was able to fill the frame with an artefact to my satisfaction, I then had to consider the depth-of-field and hence the point of the object on which I was focussing. Depth-of-field is defined as "the degree of depth within the field of view that . . . has acceptable focus" (Lockhart 2015), where depth is defined as the distance *into* a photograph, which includes the foreground, midsection and background of an image. (Lockhart also explains the physics behind the reasons for depth-of-field variations in aperture and focal length). Shallow depth-of-field is often characterised in photographs as a blurred background or foreground, and is commonly seen in portraits and close-up photography. Deep depth-of-field is often characterised in photographs as the entire depth of the photograph being sharp, and it is common in landscape and architectural photographs.

Depth-of-field is largely controlled by three factors – aperture, focal length and the distance between the subject and camera (focal plane). These are summarised in Table 7.1.

Useful tip: To see how depth-of-field can change dynamically as you adjust camera settings on the same subject, see the Bokeh simulator and depth-of-field simulator at http://dofsimulator.net/en/ (Retrieved 3 Jan 2016).

Table 7.1 Depth-of-field factors

Aperture	The wider the aperture (smaller number), the shallower the depth-of-field
Focal length	The longer the focal length (larger number), the shallower the depth-of-field
Distance between subject and camera	The nearer the subject is to the camera, the shallower the depth-of-field

Hence, shooting closer to the subject at 200mm, f/2.8 will produce a much shallower depth-of-field than shooting further away from the subject at 24mm, f/8. In Figure 7.1, we see Ah Teck (M, 70s, Chinese) beginning the process of exhumation of the grave of Khoo Seok Wan, a literary scholar and poet who was born in China in 1874 and died in Singapore in 1941. Despite the aperture being wide open at f/2.8, I was also shooting on a short focal length of 24mm, and standing away from Ah Teck. This resulted in a medium depth-of-field, where the majority of the participants were still sharp, and it was only those in the background who had begun to appear blurred.

As the exhumation progressed, fragments of bone and artefacts started to emerge. Bone fragments were carefully extricated from the grave by hand and placed into a red basin to be ritually washed with rice wine before being placed in a white plastic bag for transport for cremation. In Figure 7.2 I have captured Ah Teck deep inside the freshly dug grave, combing exhaustively for remains before emerging to place them inside the red basin for further sorting.

In Figure 7.2 we see Ah Teck's hands polishing the dirt off a coin-like object. Zooming in at 60mm because I was on the other side of the pit, my shallow depth-of-field meant that only Ah Teck's hands were sharp (I had focussed on his hands and the artefact as they were the most

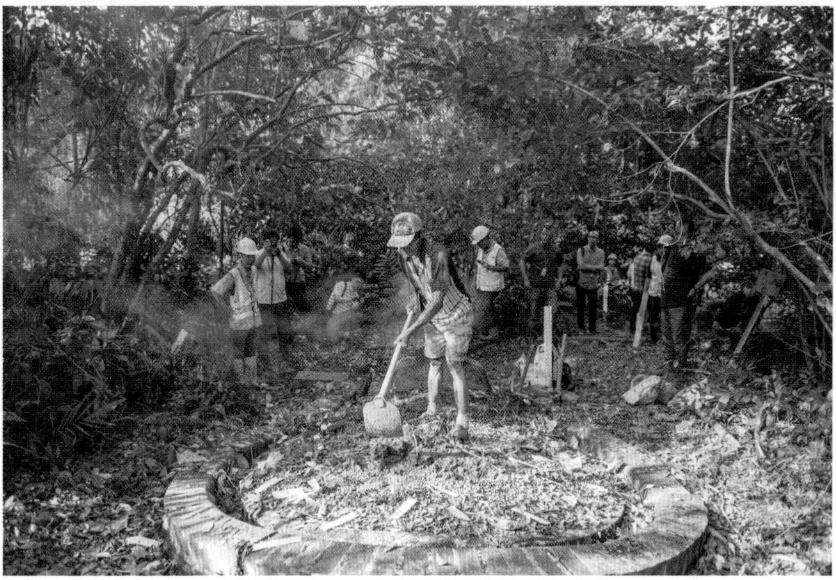

Figure 7.1 Ah Teck brings his changkul (a combination of shovel and hoe) down onto the tomb of Khoo Seok Wan (24mm, f/2.8) – sharp foreground, midground and slightly blurred background.

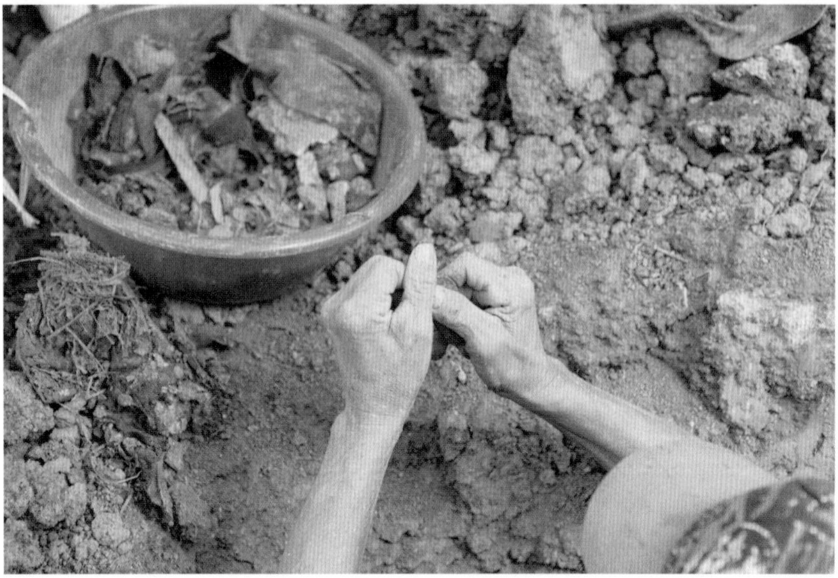

Figure 7.2 Ah Teck discovers an artefact from Khoo's grave (60mm, f/2.8) – sharp hands, blurred foreground and background.

important subjects). Note how both Ah Teck's cap in the foreground and the red basin containing bone and clothing fragments in the background are blurred, indicating a shallow depth-of-field.

As Ah Teck continued to polish the artefact, it emerged as the Total Abstinence Medal, cast for the Total Abstinence Society in India in the late 1800s. He handed the medal to David, one of Khoo's descendants, who gingerly examined the inscriptions. It was a poignant moment for one to hold a "lost" artefact of one's ancestor for the first time. So, instead of placing the artefact on a white clipboard for "proper" documentation, I asked David to hold it out for me to photograph. What was important in this photograph was not the grave itself, but the medallion and David's hands. Hence, I zoomed in close to eliminate distractions using an even more shallow depth-of-field.

Thus we can see how depth-of-field plays an important part in isolating the object, both from its background and from its foreground (where applicable). When shooting objects up-close in the field (without a tripod), we tend to use settings that minimise the depth-of-field – a longer focal length (70mm and above), a wide aperture to give a fast enough shutter speed to prevent camera shake, and we will probably be very close to the artefact. It is thus important to be careful about two more factors. The first is the way the object is positioned before it is photographed. In Figure 7.3, the individual holding the medallion was

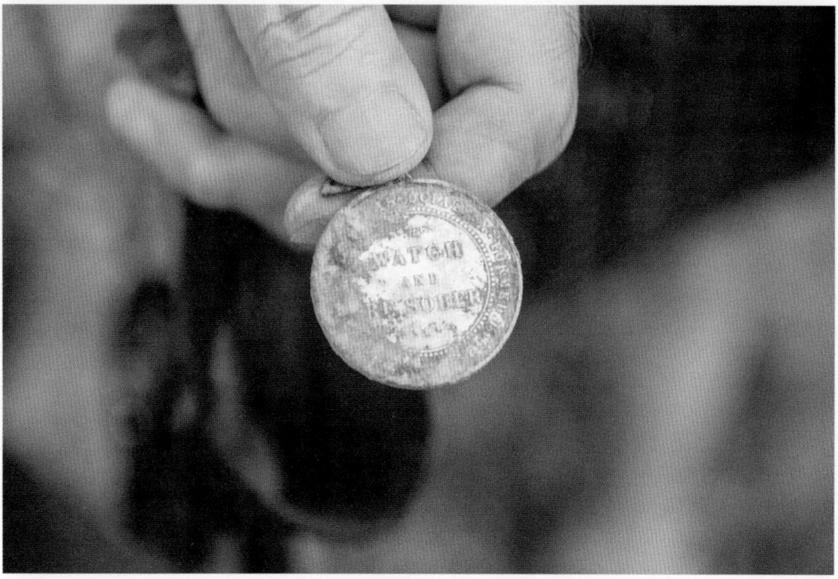

Figure 7.3 The medallion held by one of Khoo's descendants. Shot at 62mm, f/2.8, but with the lens at its minimum focussing distance to the medallion, this has turned the background into an indiscernible blur. Even the last two fingers of this hand are blurred.

able to keep it steady for me to photograph, allowing me to contextualise the medallion in the hands of the deceased's descendants. However, if the individual had been unsteady, and the medallion had been moving, it might have moved in and out of the minimum focussing distance, perhaps also causing the medallion itself to become blurred. The second is the type of light falling on the object. When photographing artefacts in Bukit Brown, I would try to get an even light that was not too harsh falling on the artefact to ensure a uniform level of illumination. Direct sunlight would often cause problematic shadows (especially for three-dimensional objects like earrings or spectacles). I would also avoid shadows or the shade of trees as this would reduce my shutter speed, forcing me to open up my aperture and reducing the depth-of-field further.

Objects with depth are also susceptible to depth-of-field issues. If you are working with a very shallow depth-of-field, ensuring that you are focussing on the object is not enough, as protrusions and extrusions of the object may become blurred, as they did in Figure 7.4. If your camera has a high enough resolution (and you have no other lens with a better macro capability), then it might be better to photograph from a further distance, with a wider focal length and narrower aperture to ensure that the whole object is sharp, and then crop the image in post-processing to produce a large enough object.

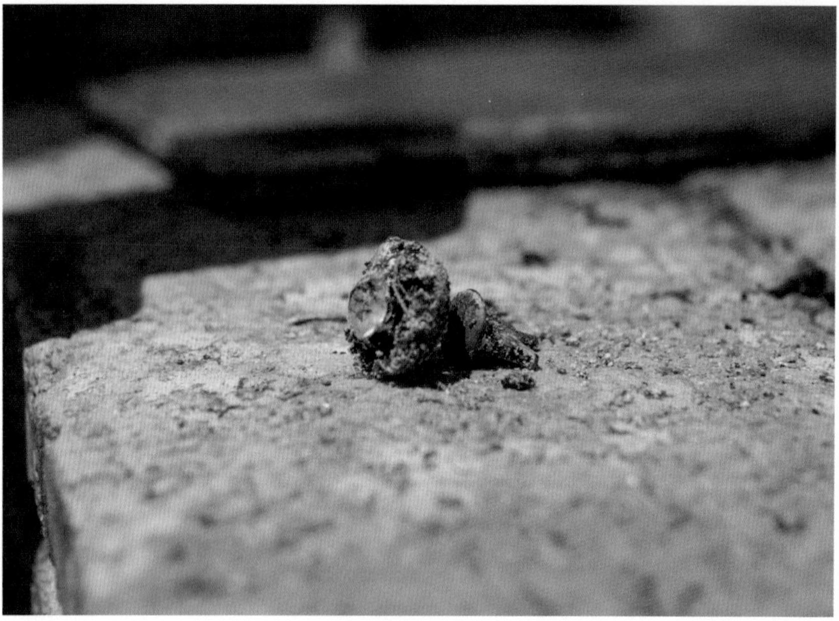

Figure 7.4 An earring from another exhumed grave. Despite shooting at 38mm at f/8, I was using a lens with a low reproduction ratio, meaning that I had to go in very close to the earring. The result is a depth-of-field that is so shallow, only part of the earring itself is sharp – the crown which protrudes outwards and towards the camera is blurred. (The image itself has been cropped digitally to make the earring appear larger.)

Useful tip: Depth-of-field is an important factor in many different kinds of photography – and is usually one of the first things taught to photographers. If you are shooting on fully automatic mode with face-recognition auto-focus, depth-of-field becomes less important, but as you progress and start to take on more decisions (like setting the aperture, focus and exposure), depth-of-field will become more of a concern.

Photographing multiple small objects in the field

When Khoo's grave was completely exhumed, we had retrieved numerous artefacts, including scraps of clothing, bone fragments, medals, coins, as well as miniature versions of pots, claypots and stoves. Yong Hung, the site co-ordinator, had brought along a white clipboard and various measuring devices (for size and colour) to photograph these artefacts as a collection. In a static, closed environment, we would use a lightbox with controlled studio lights to properly illuminate the object. In a jungle with

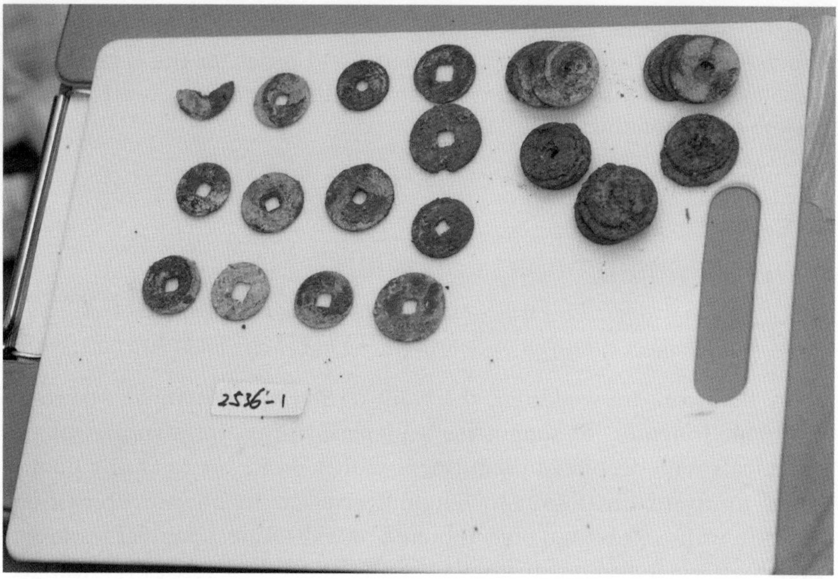

Figure 7.5 Coins photographed at the grave site. Try to fill the frame as much as you can to get as large a reproduction of your subject matter as possible.

limited time (Khoo's descendants needed to leave for the cemetery registration office), we had to make do with what we had.

Faced with multiple objects, one would need to choose the best angle in which to photograph them together. It is easy to simply aim the camera downwards and correct the image later, but with depth-of-field issues, shooting from an angle can cause some objects to be more blurred than others. Instead, where possible place the objects on the ground (or as low to the ground as possible), and select an area with even lighting, preferably not with a strong directional light that will cast a shadow on the objects. If this is not possible, turn on the flash feature on your camera (or add a flashgun) to fill-in the shadows (more on this later). As such, Yong Hung placed the clipboard on a small foldable stool, and I stood over the clipboard and positioned the camera as perpendicular to the clipboard as I could to photograph the artefacts, and in the case of Figure 7.5, a collection of retrieved coins.

Useful tip: Firing your flash in broad daylight – the final part of photographing small objects is the use of fill-in flash in conditions where the available light is not optimal. This could be a particularly shaded area, or a strong directional light casting shadows upon the object. Turn on your on-camera flash or flashgun, and if necessary ensure that your camera is set to force-fire the flash (if you are in daylight, the camera's meter may decide that the flash is not necessary). You may need to lower your ISO and narrow your aperture in order for the camera to achieve a shutter speed that will sync with the flash. See Chapter 9 for more details on the use of flash.

Photographing objects on walls

Typical camera settings: Very wide- to wide-angle lens (14–28mm), f/4–8, Lower ISO for minimal noise, turn on in-camera grid for level horizontals (see Chapter 4).

In my fieldwork on weddings, the walls of homes and temples served an important function for supporting and performing the identities of the individuals who decorated them (Heng 2012). From art to family photographs to award certificates to religious artefacts to interior decorations ("feature walls" – textural objects bolted to walls – are a popular feature in contemporary Singaporean homes), walls and other vertically arranged objects (like bookshelves and display cabinets) give clues into the everyday lives and identity-making processes of my informants. During my research into Chinese weddings in Singapore, I would almost always begin each wedding day in the home of the bride (see Chapter 5 for more details). I would also be given access to the family bedrooms, where the bride would be having her make-up done. Throughout the day I would follow the bride and groom back to the groom's home, where they would also often spend time in more intimate spaces like the bedroom (where there would be air-conditioning), resting and performing certain rituals like eating food meant to bless them, such as *tang yuen* – small flour balls in sweet syrup – or *mee sua* – noodles with eggs in a sweet syrup. Both are meant to bless the couple with a happy (sweet) marriage and fertility (in the case of eggs).

It would be in these spaces (bedroom, living room, dining room) that I would see the personalities of my informants emerge on their walls – what was important to them, the things, people or values that they treasured. It was not just art, but also study desks with old photographs and memories pinned up.

In Figure 7.6 I had the time (and permission) to explore the common areas of Eliza's (F, 30s, Chinese) home, in which her father Ngiam had great influence in terms of interior decoration. I set the focal length to a very wide angle of 17mm, which enabled me to capture the entire expanse of his wall of pride, despite standing only 2 metres or so from the wall itself. In rooms or spaces where movement and positioning is limited, having a very wide-angled lens is very useful for photographing walls, or including multiple elements within a single frame. Of course, it is possible to use a narrower focal length, create multiple images and combine them

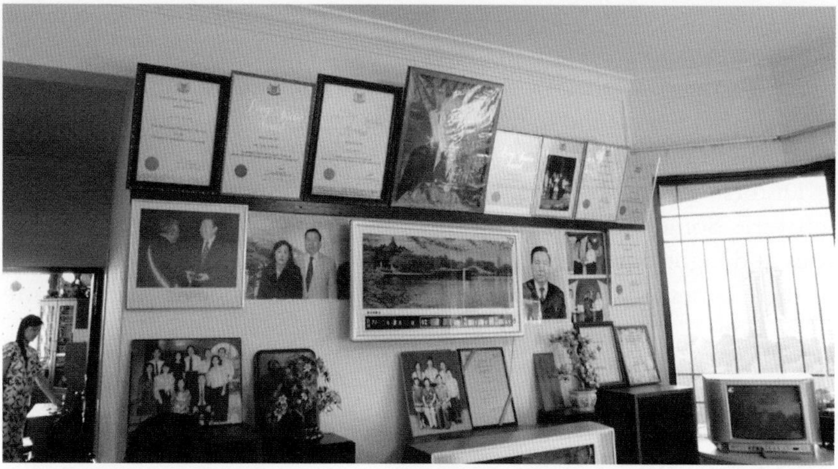

Figure 7.6 Ngiam's (M, 60s, Chinese) home in 2005 – a lifelong civil servant, Ngiam displays his certificates not in an office or study, but in the living room above the communal television, such that anyone in the family watching television would also observe his achievements. On the top tier are various long-service awards and (plastic wrapped) artwork, and in the middle tier is a photograph of him receiving his award from the then President of Singapore. In the centre is a curious piece of technology, a digital frame showing temperature and humidity. Notice one of the wedding celebrants placed on the left to indicate scale.

together in a photo-processing software (some cameras even include this as a feature), but this tends to be more time-consuming and requires additional skills to do well. Another alternative is to use the "panorama" function on many consumer cameras and smartphones. This is where you swing the camera across in a 180-degree arc, while the camera captures a series of images and pieces them together in real-time. Usually used for landscape photography, panoramas are useful in documenting everything from space to multiple points of interest across a wide horizontal plane. I will discuss the use of panoramas more in Chapter 10 on smartphone photography.

One problem with the use of very wide-angled lenses (and even more so with panoramas) is distortion. Distortion occurs when the curvature of a lens, necessary to achieve a wide angle of view, causes the subject positioned in the edges of a photograph to bend and/or expand. This is affected largely by three factors: the focal length, the distance of the subject to the lens, and the lens itself. Firstly the focal length of a lens tend to correlate with the amount of distortion at the edge – the shorter the focal length (i.e. the wider the lens) the more distortion there is. Often distortion becomes more visible from 21mm and below. Secondly, if a subject is very close to the lens, it tends to become more distorted. Hence, if you are using a lens with a high level of distortion (and you want to avoid subjects in the photograph becoming distorted) you should position the camera further away from all subjects. Finally, professional and high-quality lenses tend to minimise distortion, so two lenses of the same focal length may have very different levels of distortion.

Distortion can be corrected using various kinds of post-processing software. Some software companies, like Adobe who produce Camera Raw and Lightroom, work with camera manufacturers to include profiles of their lenses in the software to provide a certain level of automatic correction.

Walls and informants – reflections and adjoining rooms

Typical camera settings: Wide-angle lens (24–35mm), wide to medium aperture (depending on depth-of-field desired – f/2.8–f/5.6).

Instead of just photographing walls, it is also possible to integrate and/or juxtapose the individuals who have decorated them. This could be as simple as asking your informants to pose with the wall, but there are other more creative ways to approach this composition. Reflections and adjoining rooms are two useful mechanisms that one can use. Reflections on walls mostly occur through the interaction between the subject and mounted mirrors or mirrored surfaces, the latter often being the glass of photo-frames or a television screen that has not been turned on.

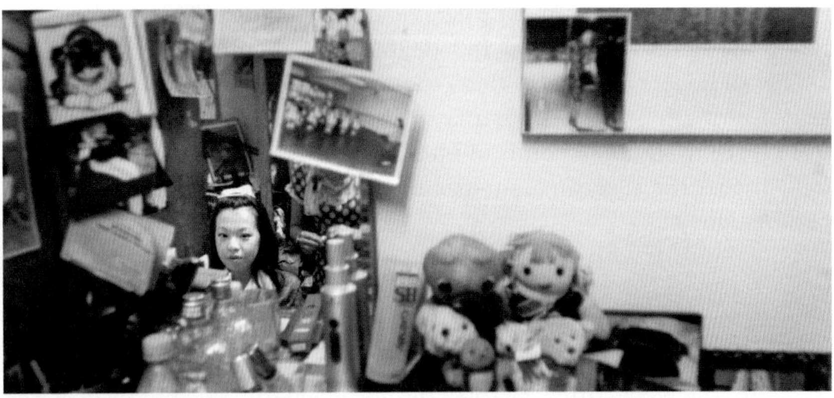

Figure 7.7 Yeok Tsui (F, 20s, Chinese) in 2006. Yeok Tsui has lived in this flat in Central Singapore with her parents for all her life, and her desk/make-up table is a menagerie of memories and life-narratives. I used the mirror to frame her face amongst her belongings, creating two portraits – one of her items, and another of herself.

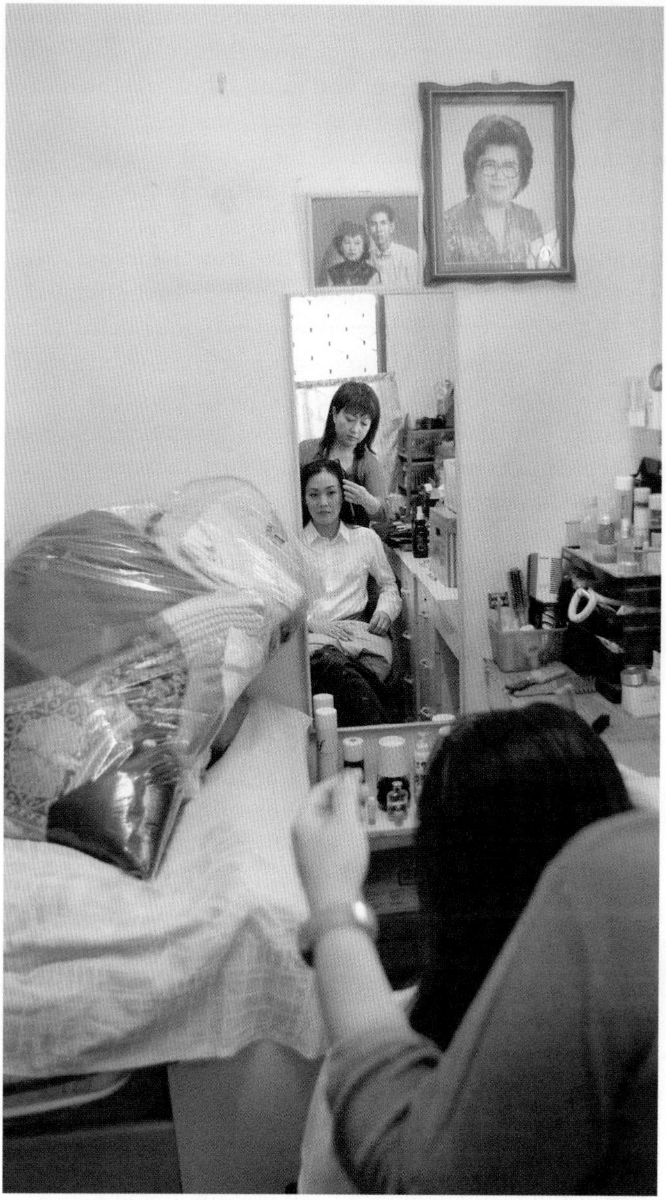

Figure 7.8 Yi Ling (F, 20s, Chinese) in 2004. Sitting in her parents' bedroom (which is usually the master bedroom of a house or flat), Yi Ling is framed in the mirror having her make-up done. Placed above the mirror is an old portrait of her parents, and to the right of that is a portrait of her grandmother. In a single photograph I am able to show three generations of Chinese Singaporeans without deliberately trying to show three generations of Chinese Singaporeans. Notice also a recently removed photograph to the left of Yi Ling's parents' portrait, with the shadow of dirt a tell-tale sign of memories displaced.

Reflections personalise and personify the material culture of the photographed wall. They create an additional story in which the artefacts on the wall can be given a deeper and more ethnographic meaning.

In Chapter 5, I discussed the use of door frames as a framing device. At the same time, the adjoining room that is fronted by a door frame is also a useful way of positioning one's informant(s) in relation to a wall and its artefacts. In Figure 7.9 I was photographing Winnie's wedding. Her family home was a three-room HDB flat (two bedrooms and a living room), and relatively small given the number of individuals residing inside, yet was elaborately decorated with religious items (a very large statue of a Buddha was perched somewhat precariously on a shelf near the main door) and numerous photographs arranged around a Disney- and cartoon-theme. The photographs themselves are of Winnie's sister, Lee Chin, and Lee Chin's son – reinforcing my initial observations of a close-knit, lower-middle-income family where grandparents provide childcare support in the daytime or over the weekend (a common phenomenon in Singapore where most young households are dual-income). The wall shows signs of constant updating – photographs displaying nuanced progress in the life-stages of a first grandson – so much so that some photographs are simply wedged between, rather than placed in frames.

I could have simply photographed the wall of photos and frames and left it there, but instead I also tried to include some human interest by positioning this wall as the foreground of my shot, and Winnie in the background with her bridesmaids. In doing so I tried to show a degree of activity within the home. But Figure 7.9 was not as successful as I had hoped. Firstly, I had used too large an aperture (f/2.8) and created too shallow a depth-of-field, meaning that although Winnie was sharp, the wall of photographs was not (that said, it might also be advantageous if I had wanted to anonymise Winnie's nephew but still retain the pervasiveness of his photographic presence). A slightly narrower aperture of f/4 or f/5.6 would have been more suitable. The second factor was timing, although the bride and groom tend to be my primary concern when doing fieldwork, using Winnie as a primary subject here was less helpful. It would have been more meaningful if I had waited for Winnie's nephew to be in that room before composing and taking the shot.

Foregrounds and walls

Typical camera settings: Very wide- to wide-angle lens (14–28mm), slightly narrower aperture to take into account artefacts in the foreground (f/4–f/8), grid-lines for composition.

Oftentimes walls are preceded by other objects – in Figure 7.6, Ngiam's wall of pride had a console and television as part of the overall design, and

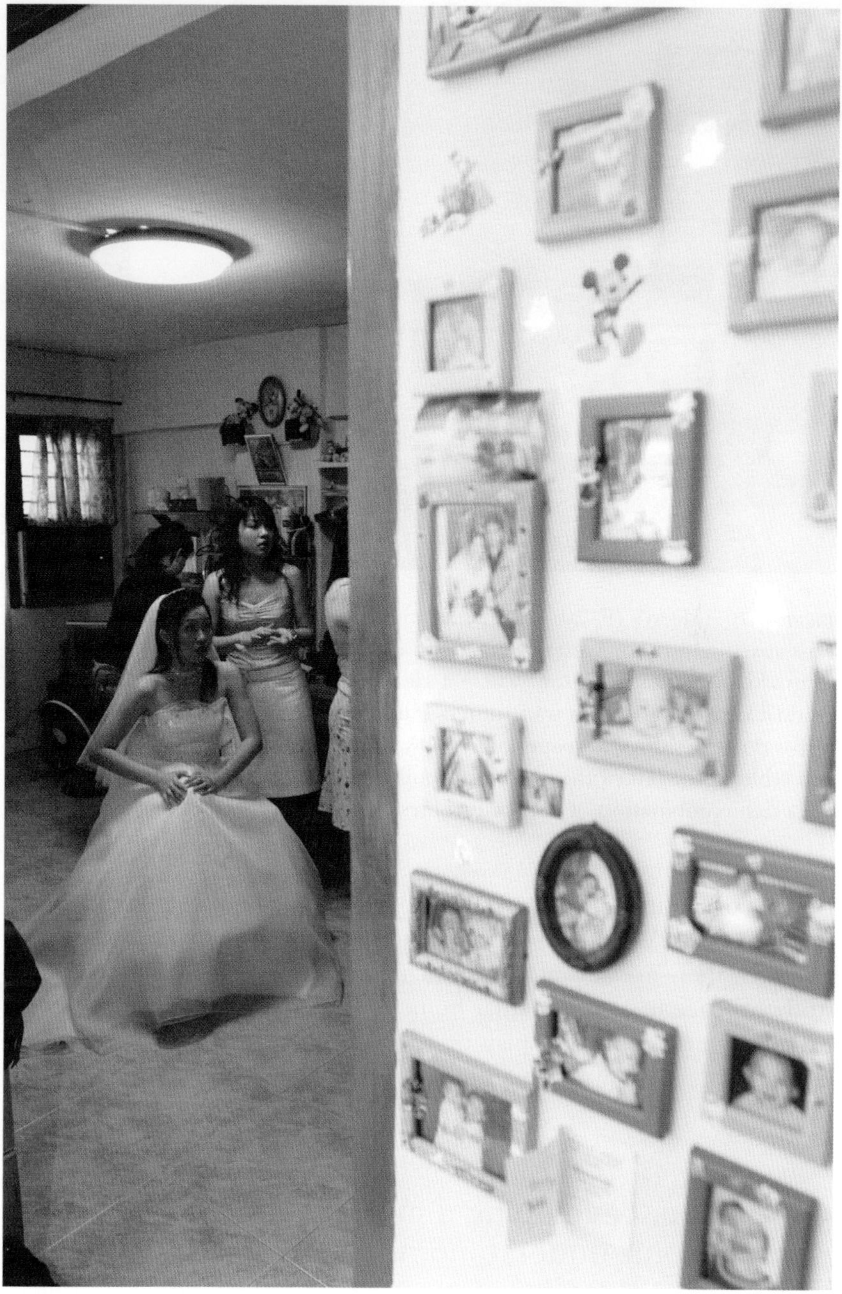

Figure 7.9 Winnie waiting with her bridesmaids for the next phase of the wedding day.

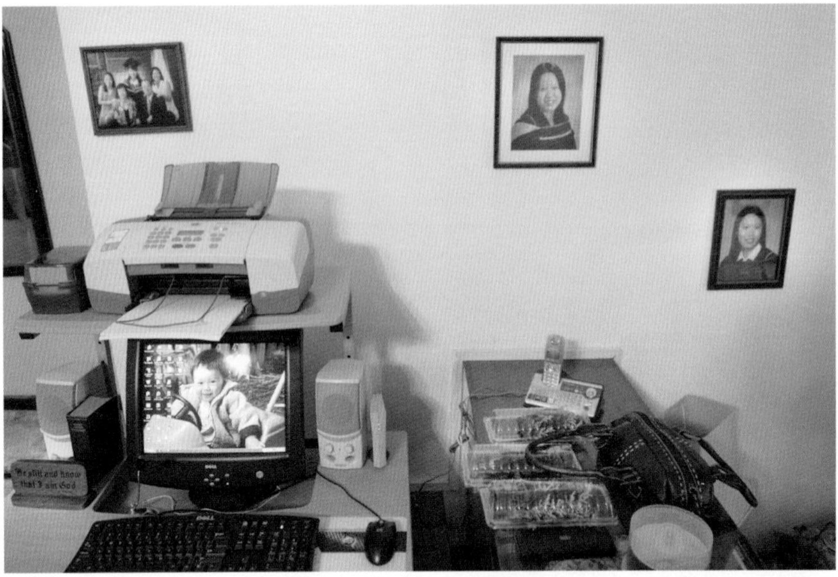

Figure 7.10 Eileen's (F, 20s, Chinese) family home in 2008, an upper-middle-class apartment in the west of Singapore. I was first intrigued by the positioning of graduate portraits on the wall – a clear sign of the value of education and graduation as a significant transition of status in the family. What complemented this was the desktop wallpaper of Eileen's nephew, as well as a Christian artefact and bible to the left of the computer monitor. Within this photograph we then see a rich combination of faith and values.

I would often find tables, desks and bookshelves complementing artefacts hung on walls. Whilst we might want to zoom in and focus only on wall artefacts, there are advantages to including the wall as part of an overall study of space in any particular home. This is especially so if the wall is part of an area for work, play or worship. In Figure 7.10, we see how keeping an eye on ornamentation on a desk can add even more meaning to what is on a wall.

Conclusion: developing a more abstract photographic understanding of objects

At the beginning of this chapter I considered work by Edward Weston and other photographers who looked beyond the mundane depictions of objects. Weston in particular interrogated the form and structure of objects by lighting and shaping them to re-imagine the way we think about their purposes and identities. When we are done photographing an object as a visual record for our observations, what else could we do to evoke a deeper and different understanding of the material artefacts that texture our everyday lives? Some photographers have attempted to do this, by situating their work within an academic environment of visual studies (see for example, Heng 2014; Keiller 2009; Leet 2013) Such abstract reasoning of objects through photography brings up many other theoretical implications and considerations, which are likely best discussed in another book. But in this conclusion I offer a few technical suggestions to photographing objects in different and less descriptive ways.

Firstly, think about *how* you as a researcher would re-imagine the object. What else could it say about the subjects, informants or spaces that you are investigating? Is there a wider but more hidden story that cannot be told by simply photographing the objects as seen? In my research on Chinese religion, I am often intrigued by the need to burn and destroy effigies as offerings. Whilst there has been much research that has gone into the study of burnt sacrifices, the act of destroying and remaking in Chinese religion in Singapore is an opportunity to examine the moment where material and immaterial worlds collide, where an effigy is made real in the spiritual world through its destruction and transience. One informant gleefully asked me once after a large amount of *kim zua* was burnt, whether my camera had captured the spirits collecting the money in the fire. This transience has informed my photographic practice to include more abstract photographs of fiery destruction, particularly at the point of physical combustion. In Figure 7.11 I show one such image.

Secondly, if and where possible, consider the form of the object *in isolation* from the field. In some situations there is value in taking an item and bringing it into a controlled "studio" environment. By this I do not mean a fully equipped photo studio, but a place in which you have the time and luxury to photograph the object at your leisure, using different sources and strengths of light, different backgrounds, angles and focal lengths. Finally, consider the physicality of an object for its own sake – its textures, surfaces, density, form and so on. In my work in Teck Ghee Court (see Heng 2014, 2015 and Chapter 4), I was particularly concerned with the material aftermath of worship and offerings during the Hungry Ghost Festival – the leftover ashes that gave the neighbourhood a different, albeit temporary look and feel. In Figure 7.12, I chose to crop an image of a huge stack of *kim zua* as it burnt and disintegrated. This was, of course, after photographing the whole ritual of stacking, praying and setting alight these offerings, but once that was done I was left to ask if there was something else I could do visually to my subject. In this case, it was trying to offer a radically different perspective from my previous, more mundane images.

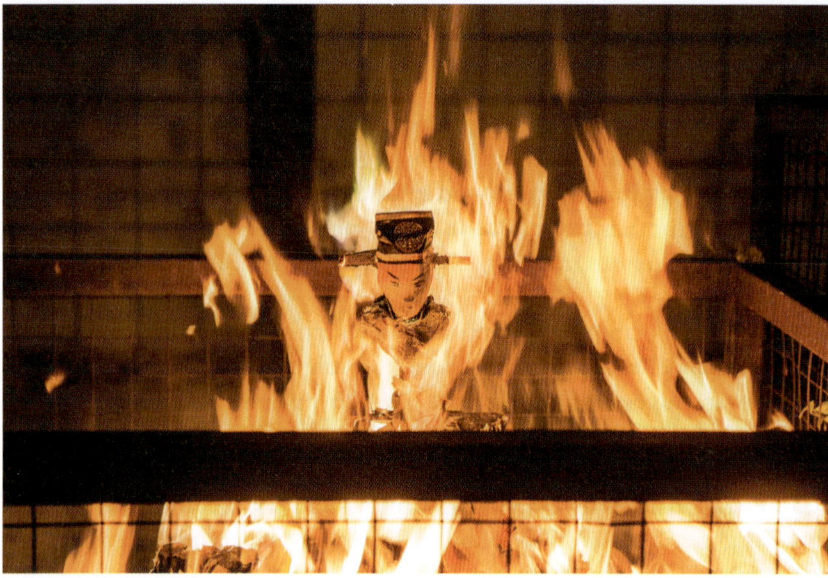

Figure 7.11 At a combined temple in the north of Singapore, devotees burn paper effigies of lost souls whom they implore to carry their sins for them as they *guo ping an qiao* (过平安桥) or "cross the peace bridge," an annual ritual meant to cleanse an individual of their sins for the coming year. Although I did also photograph the effigies in their material form, I continued to photograph the burning mass and flames as they disintegrated.

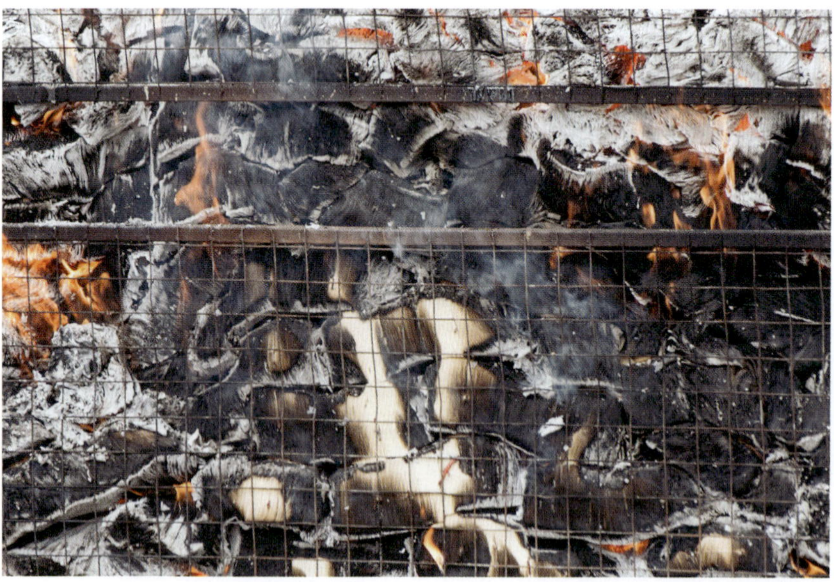

Figure 7.12 Kim zua burning.

Chapter exercises

Social and cultural inventories

When photographing objects, it is good to practise with objects of a variety of sizes, from small to large, so as to get an idea of how different positions, angles and focal lengths can portray each object. To get even more experience, try and make sure that you have access to a lens / camera with a macro function (some smartphones are capable of this, but for practice, try it with a DSLR and macro lens).

1 Experiment first with depth-of-field. In brightly lit conditions, set your camera to aperture-priority mode with automatic ISO. Set a focal length of 50mm–70mm, then pick two objects, and set one in the foreground and another in the background with a distance of at least 30cm. This could be as simple as placing two cups apart from each other on a table.

   a. First, set your aperture to as low a number as possible (this is usually f/3.5 or f/4.5). Then focus on the object in the foreground and take a photograph. This should create a blurry background, with the object in the background appearing blurred. This is a shallow depth-of-field.
   b. Next, set your aperture to about f/8 to f/11, then do the same and photograph the object in the foreground. You will notice that the object in the background is now sharper. This is a deeper depth-of-field.

2 Next, try to see what your minimum focussing distance is. Set your camera on manual focus, and try to go as close to a small object as possible – this could be an espresso cup, a tube of toothpaste or remote control. Try focussing on the object such that the object appears sharp in your viewfinder. If this cannot happen no matter how much you focus, try moving a bit further away from the object and trying again. Keep repeating this until you can make the object sharp. This would be the minimum focussing distance of your lens.

3 Search for opportunities to develop cultural inventories of all sorts of spaces. In Chapter 7 I have discussed walls

in particular, but various other typologies present opportunities for practice. For example, think about the exterior of homes, and the way individuals arrange and decorate these exteriors, using the front door as a unifying visual factor. If you are photographing at home, look around for the way you arrange items and objects against walls, and these need not simply be what is on the wall, but the furniture and other items stacked against these walls.

4 Try to create an abstract interpretation of an object or groups of objects. Instead of interpreting the object simply as an object, think about how its shape, lines, colour and other attributes represent the ways individuals give meaning to it. Ask yourself how you can photograph these attributes in ways other than simply depicting the object "as is."

chapter 8

Photographing people

Key technical concepts

- The basic "field portrait"
- Wider angles and environmental portraits
- Candid portraits: people in action
- Conclusion: "faceless" portraits

Case study keywords: Chinese religion, spirit mediums

Introduction

Portrait photography is usually considered to be the taking of photographs primarily of individuals who are posing for the photographer (although this is not always the case, as we shall see later). Drawn from the idea of painted portraits, portrait photography was not initially possible in the early days of photography, where photographic exposures required individuals to sit perfectly still for several minutes (Ford 2005). As technology has improved and progressed, photographic portraits, especially those taken in studios, have continued to be very popular with individuals. Scholars have grappled with the implications of posed photographs. Kesting (2014), for example, considers how migration in South Africa is framed and how migrants are made visible through mundane passport photographs as well as more artistic projects, whilst Rose (2012) looks at more informal portraits in the guise of family snapshots and what she calls the visual economy of distribution of images through the mass media. Other scholars make use of portraits taken by themselves in their research, as Harper, Knowles and Leonard (2005) did with British migrants in Hong Kong, or Pinney (1997), who reflects on the contradictions between his own practice of creating posed photographs in India and the different gazes associated with the desires of how his subjects wanted to be represented.

Photographers themselves have used portraiture to establish the human condition in a myriad number of ways, and many of these have been in the field. As Di Bello (2012) notes, an early example of an environmental portrait was that of Isambard Kingdom Brunel, by Robert Howlett (1857), who pictured Brunel against the backdrop of the construction of the *Great Eastern* steamship. Photojournalists combine portraiture work in the field with other kinds of documentary photography as well. George Rodger's famous photographs of the Nubas (1949) as well as James Natchwey's haunting and prize-winning headshot of a Hutu man in Rwanda (1994) use portraiture to bring out not only the personalities of their subjects, but also the social circumstances surrounding their condition and existence. In Asia, photographers like Zakaria Zainal (2012) and Sim Chi Yin (2014) continue to interrogate the social lives of their subjects through portraits. Zainal's photographs of Gurkhas in Singapore expose a little known sojourning community who continue to lead impermanent lives in a country where they cannot gain citizenship. Sim's photographs are more environmental – documenting the cramped and closed everyday lives of rural migrants in Beijing, who rent tiny segmented rooms in the basements of the city's buildings.

People are at the heart of many social science studies, whether it is their behaviour, values, interactions or themselves. In previous chapters many photographs of space, artefacts and actions also included the presence of people, as both primary and secondary subjects. In this chapter I will discuss in particular how to photograph people as the primary subject through the topic of portraiture. To do this, I will be using case studies from my work on Chinese spirit mediums, or *tang-ki,* in Singapore.

Chinese religion and *tang-ki*

The term "Chinese religion" refers to a syncretic mix of Taoism, Buddhism and folk religion (Dean 1995; Lee 1986). It is sometimes called *shen*ism (Elliott 1955), where *shen* literally means "spirit," and thus the worship of spiritual beings, particularly deities from the Taoist and Buddhist canon. *Tang-ki* are the spiritual leaders of a particular segment of Chinese religion followers (DeBernardi 2012), and are characterised by their ability to enter into trances in which they are believed to channel deities from both heaven and the underworld. During this trance, they are no longer themselves, but the deity who possesses them, and thus take on the personality, voice, behaviour and, with the help of their followers, dress and weapons of that deity (Chan 2006; Heng 2016).

During my fieldwork in studying place-making amongst practitioners of Chinese religion, I encountered several *tang-ki,* who operated in both "official" (Kong 1993) temples and more unofficial spaces like their homes (especially HDB flats, see Chapter 4) and industrial estates. I also met and photographed them whilst documenting Bukit Brown Cemetery, in which they were a regular feature during the Hungry Ghost Festival as they led their followers in rituals to appease the dead. *Tang-ki* typically belong either to a temple or a *sintua* (神坛), the latter literally translated as "spirit altar" – denoting a group of practitioners who worship and perform rituals together, but do not have an "official," consecrated site of worship. These *sintua* tend to occupy residential homes and industrial units, and are the main focus of my visual research.

Five basic crops in portrait photography and natural crop lines

When choosing to photograph an individual, a photographer may choose to include all or part of the individual's body. As such, there exist five commonly used crops of an individual – a full crop, which is the entire body; a three-quarter crop, which is somewhere around mid-thigh; a half-body crop, which is from the waist up; a chest-up (or bust-up) crop, which is from the chest; and a headshot, which includes only the subject's head. Gomez (2010) proposes that there are four crops – full, three-quarter, bust-up and head, but I argue that a half-body shot should also be considered as a basic, commonly used crop, as evidenced on the cover of Les Back's (2007) *The Art of Listening*, as photographed by Paul Halliday, where the subject shows off musical tattoos on her arms.

There is no hard and fast rule as to which crop is the most appropriate. Many photographers start with three-quarter, half-body and chest-up crops (as did I when I first started photographing individuals) – and I will cover this in the next section when I discuss the basic "field portrait." Otherwise, there are a number of issues one might consider when deciding on which crop to choose. One, how much of the subject's body is important for the story that you wish to tell about the individual? Perhaps there is something particular about their clothes or posture so that every part needs to be included, hence necessitating a full-body crop. Or perhaps the expressions of your subject, their frown lines or eyes, are more important, necessitating a headshot. Two, are there particular parts of the body that need to be shown in greater detail? In digital photography, especially with high-resolution cameras, it is possible to digitally crop the image at the post-processing stage, and thus narrow in on a particular part of the photograph. But this does not always yield the best image, as other factors like depth-of-field (see Chapter 7) can mean that a particular section will not prove to be sharp. This means that it is better to crop in-camera (if possible) to ensure that you have captured the desired and important details. Finally, how important is the environment in which the portrait is taken? Does it help us to understand the subject better, or is it crucial to the subject's identity? If it is the latter, a full-body crop to include much of the subject's surroundings would do much to add layers of meaning onto the image (look further on in this chapter for the section on environmental portraits).

Natural crop lines

When photographing tightly cropped portraits, either full length or half-body, there remains a question as to where to crop the body of the subject. The human body has natural crop lines, particularly at its joints – meaning the fingers, wrists, ankles, toes and knees – and cropping at these points can sometimes produce an awkward image. Cropping at these points causes a break in the visual flow of the body, making the subject appear more "stumpy" (Milicia 2015) and less flattering. This occurs most frequently when photographing a group of individuals and the photographer crops the image at the subjects' ankles, causing them to appear as if they are floating. Meyer (2012) provides a useful infographic giving guidelines as to where it is advisable to crop and where it is not. His infographic also points out that it is possible to crop the top of an individual's head off – as we are often used to seeing people wearing headgear. However, cropping along natural crop lines is more obvious in photographs where the individual is the primary subject, and where the body is evenly lit and takes precedence in the image. In environmental portraits where the individual's importance is on par with his or her environment, such cropping may seem less obvious (see Figure 8.2), especially if these lines are shrouded in shadow.

A basic field "portrait"

Typical settings: Medium to long telephoto lens (50mm–135mm), wide aperture to isolate subject (f/4 and below).

One of the first things that beginner photographers learn is a basic portrait photograph – a close-cropped composition of an individual using a long telephoto lens and a wide aperture to blur the background and isolate the subject. These crops are usually at the shoulder or waist (i.e. head-shots or half-body crops) and are very useful for a study of the individual as *the individual*. In other words, if you are seeking a detailed study of the individual, their expressions, features, dress/comportment and otherwise, these portraits are a useful way to capture such characteristics. Walker Evans' *Alabama Tenant Farmer Wife* (1936) is an excellent example of the use of simple portraits to capture human emotion and experience. In the photograph, Allie Mae Burroughs is positioned against the hard wooden plank-walls of her home, accentuating the frown-lines, grey hairs and thin-lips of her facial features. Such detail is best brought out in a close-cropped portrait, rather than a wider-angled, environmental portrait.

In one such instance, I photographed Ah Heng, a spirit medium of more than 20 years, who had entered into a trance for his *sintua's* annual *yew keng* (游境), a procession involving the *tang-ki* inspecting the boundaries of his or her territory. (In contemporary Singapore the procession is more about the establishing and maintaining of social networks between allied temples and *sintuas*.) Ah Heng's *sintua*, *Xuan Jiang Dian* (玄江殿), finds its origins in the early 1950s – and is currently situated in central Singapore, near to the central business district. The *sintua* has moved many times since its inception, from an HDB flat to the back of an office to more "official" grounds next to another temple.

Like many *tang-ki*, Ah Heng has more than one deity he maintains a contract with – an agreement for the deity to possess him and do work through his body. In Figure 8.1, Ah Heng channels *Shan Cai Tong Zi* (善财童子), also commonly spelt amongst devotees I've met as *Shancai Tongzi*, the Child of Wealth – a popular deity in Singapore who appears in various guises in Buddhist, Taoist and folk stories. Amongst Chinese religion practitioners in Singapore, *Shancai* is a deity capable of healing, blessing, giving advice and serving the community.

In Figure 8.1, I used the 70mm telephoto portion of my standard zoom lens to zoom in on Ah Heng's upper body (this is after I had photographed his full body and comportment extensively as he entered a trance). Setting the aperture at f/2.8, I reduced the depth-of-field to a minimum and blurred out both his helpers in the background and foreground. An added advantage of this is that the two followers' heads in the foreground also act as a framing device to bring our attention closer to Ah Heng.

To best create these portraits, it is usually advisable to use a longer telephoto lens of 80mm and above – portrait photographers tend to favour longer lenses as they tend to compress facial features and suffer from less distortion, thus giving a more flattering look to their subject. All things being equal, longer lenses also allow for more shallow depth-of-field, allowing the photographer to isolate subjects more from busy and distracting backgrounds.

The downside to these kinds of portraits lies in their ubiquity. Because they are one of the first kinds of images photographers learn to take, they

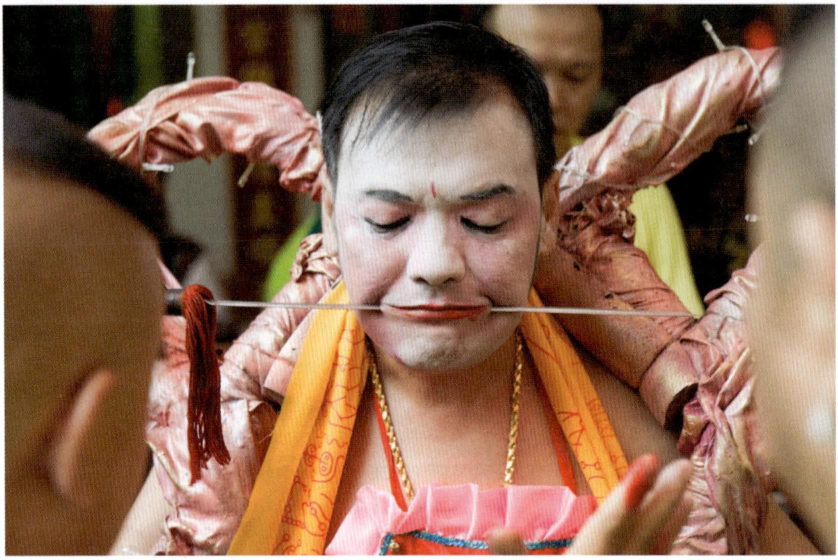

Figure 8.1 Ah Heng wearing the vestments of *Shancai Tongzi*, with a specially customised harness mimicking the flowing scarves that are typically depicted in his idols. Pierced through his mouth is a representation of a soldier of the heavenly armies.

also tend to be too easily dismissed as unimpactful or unimportant, especially those that mimic the vernacular, everyday "snapshot" photograph. Complicating this further is the rise in popularity of selfies, which are effectively photographic self-portraits but using a particular angle of lens that fills the frame of the image, increasing the expectation of mundaneness amongst viewers. However, field portraits remain popular in the visual study of individuals. One excellent example is the project *Humans of New York* by Brandon Stanton (2013), a series of simple field portraits of individuals in New York, coupled with a short (but now increasingly longer in recent posts on the author's Facebook page) account by each person.

Useful tip: When photographing these portraits, experiment with angles, direction of gaze and expressions, especially if the individual is posing for you. Also experiment with shooting in landscape or portrait format, and see if the rule-of-thirds works for your subject (see Chapter 5). Finally, many photographers recommend focussing on the eyes when shooting closely cropped portraits.

Wider angles and environmental portraits

Typical settings: Wide to very wide lens (35mm and below), medium aperture to extend depth-of-field (f/5.6 and above).

Instead of a close-cropped portrait, many photographers try to contextualise their subjects within an environment, usually one that develops a narrative around the subject. For instance, Harper, Knowles and Leonard's (2005) study of British migrants in Hong Kong included a wide, low-angled shot of a war veteran standing outside a memorial for fallen soldiers, an annual ritual of his. These are known as environmental portraits – photographs of individuals or groups situated within their environments. Environmental portraits are useful in the field because it is there that we encounter our informants. This style helps us to situate our informants within the places and spaces in which we observe and photograph them.

To create an environmental portrait, first use a wide- to very wide-angle lens. This allows you to bring more of the space around the subject into the frame of the image. In my first visit to a house temple, I was introduced to Han, a friendly gentleman in his 50s, who had been serving as a *tang-ki* for the last 20 to 30 years. Han's home is a three-room (two bedroom) HDB flat in the east of Singapore, a modest space of about 1000 square feet. The altar, ritual chair and secondary altar table take up more than half of his living room space, leaving enough for a small sofa set and a television for him and his family. For a *tang-ki*, the altar is a core component in his or her spiritual practice – the focal point upon which trancing rituals begin (a *tang-ki* commonly looks upon the idol of the deity that he or she is attempting to channel).

Han was at home, both literally and metaphorically speaking, when I visited to interview him. Prior to the photograph, he sat shirtless in the living room reminiscing about his past as a *tang-ki* and the ways in which his service to his gods helped the people around him and his neighbours – he was particularly famous for helping to improve the chances that legal cases would go the way of his clients, and counts non-Chinese religious practitioners, including individuals from monotheistic faiths, coming to consult him for help. I convinced Han to pose for a single photograph in front of his altar, altar table and chair. Han, bemused by my interest in him as a person (he had initially thought I had only wanted to know about the art of being a *tang-ki*), gamely put on a shirt not matching his ritual trousers to pose for a portrait.

In this case, I had the choice of photographing only the top half of Han's body, perhaps positioning him closer to the largest idol on his altar. However, I also noticed the way the light in his altar cast spectacular shadows onto the wall. I also wanted to show the spatial arrangements

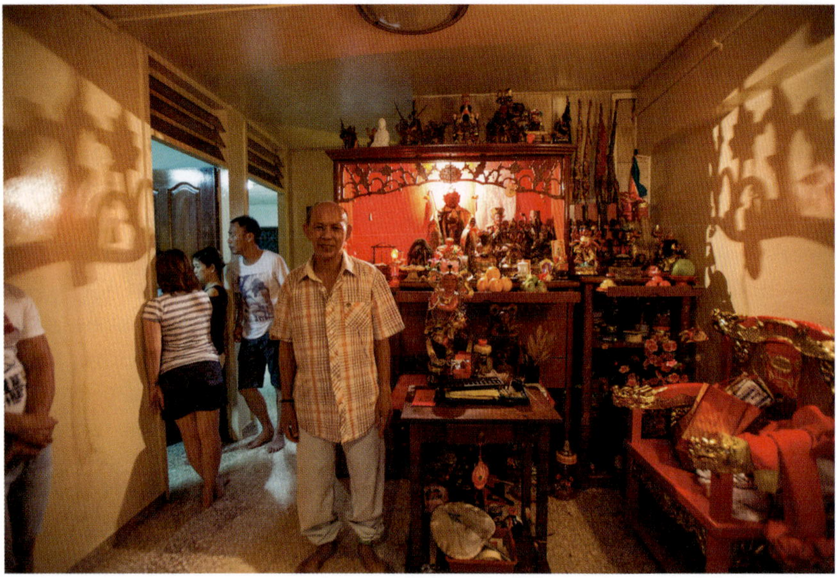

Figure 8.2 Han, a *tang-ki* living in the east of Singapore, within his house temple. Shot wide at 17mm, so I had visible distortion at the edges of the photograph, including the ceiling. It was important to keep Han at the centre of the image to reduce distortion of his body. Notice also how I accidentally cropped his toes – given that the ceiling light above was probably less important, I should have angled my camera further down to include Han's entire body, as well as the base of his secondary altar table.

of this house temple – the prominence of the altar, the way everyday, mundane and profane life continued all around these spiritual centres. On the left of the photograph are the flat's two bedrooms, with Han's followers having a conversation around other matters. I chose to include this as well to show the mixing of sacred and profane space.

Useful tip: Shooting from different angles can affect the way we perceive a subject in a photograph. A photograph taken at lower angles, such that the subject is looking down onto the reader, often gives an impression of power and authority, whilst a photograph taken from higher angles creates a more flattering portrait, giving a sense of approachability to the subject.

Candid portraits

Typical settings: Longer zoom lens to reduce field presence (70mm and above), higher shutter speed to freeze movement (at least 1/40s: faster moving subjects will still cause a blur, though this is not entirely undesirable).

Unlike posed portraits, candid portraits are photographs taken without the individual or individuals knowing or posing. Candid portraits can often be taken whilst the individual is moving or in action, as the lack of knowledge of their photograph being taken means that they are not pausing to pose. Candid portraits have long been associated with genres such as photojournalism and street photography, where a "natural," unposed portrait of an individual often yields a more meaningful series of images. Notable works include those of Martin Parr, whose work weaves between that of documentary and portrait photography. Parr's photographs of New Brighton (2009) create a fascinating portrait of working-class leisure consumption in the United Kingdom that is both enchanting and disturbing at the same time. One might also consider Dorothea Lange's famous image of Florence Owens Thompson, better known as the Migrant Mother in *Migrant Mother, Nipomo, California* (1936), which combines elements of candidness and static posing – Thompson's gaze is averted from the camera, her children framing her on either side hiding their faces from Lange – to develop a powerful portrait of the Great Depression.

To create a candid portrait, it is likely that you have to photograph surreptitiously. This is different from secret photography, where the subject is completely oblivious to your presence as a photographer. Candid photography may or may not be secret, but in an academic setting with ethical considerations of primary concern, it is likely that the subject knows of your photographic presence (see Chapter 2). Thus, part of the "soft-skills" of developing candid portraits involves getting the subject to be comfortable enough with your presence, such that they effectively ignore you as you photograph. In some situations where your main role is to *be* the photographer, subjects will often pause to pose once they know a camera is trained on them. In such circumstances it is important to position yourself in ways that make you less visually prominent, allowing for more unposed moments.

In one of my first encounters with *tang-ki* and their followers, I followed *Fu Tian Dian* (*福天殿*), a *sintua* located in an industrial unit in the west of Singapore. This particular *sintua* (now disbanded into two separate *sintua*) consisted of five *tang-ki*, three of whom were in their 20s, with the other two being older, in their 40s and 50s. On this occasion, *Fu Tian Dian* had chosen to hold their annual celebrations at a town square in Bukit Batok, a suburb on the west side of Singapore. Tentages were rented and set up, and temporary altars and ritual spaces were sacralised for three days. These celebrations are often done to commemorate the birthday of the chief Deity of the *sintua*, which, in this case, was *Xuan Tian Shang Di* (玄天上帝), the Supreme Lord of the Dark Heavens (Tan 2001). As part of these celebrations, three of the five *tang-ki*, two of whom I befriended later on, travelled with their devotees to Lim Chu Kang Cemetery for rituals to appease the dead, bless objects for auction (to raise funds for the *sintua*), and empower objects, particularly Chinese coffins, for future rituals.

The rituals took place at about 11p.m. with little ambient light save for the joss sticks and candles used by devotees. When I stepped out of my gatekeeper's car, the devotees quietly reminded me not to use a flashgun, as this would disturb the *tang-ki* in their trance. In Figure 8.3, three *tang-ki* sit at their tables, all in a trance and said to be possessed by the spirits of *Tua Ya Pek* or *Di Ya Pek* – the enforcers of the underworld, also collectively referred to as *Tua Di Ya Pek* (大二爺伯). Such deities are often called upon to perform exorcisms, give advice, improve one's fate (or luck) or hand out lucky lottery numbers. Here, they are busy blessing small artefacts that will later be auctioned off at a dinner – with such items believed to bring the owners good fortune. It is through these auctions that the *sintua* is able to partially fund itself and its rituals.

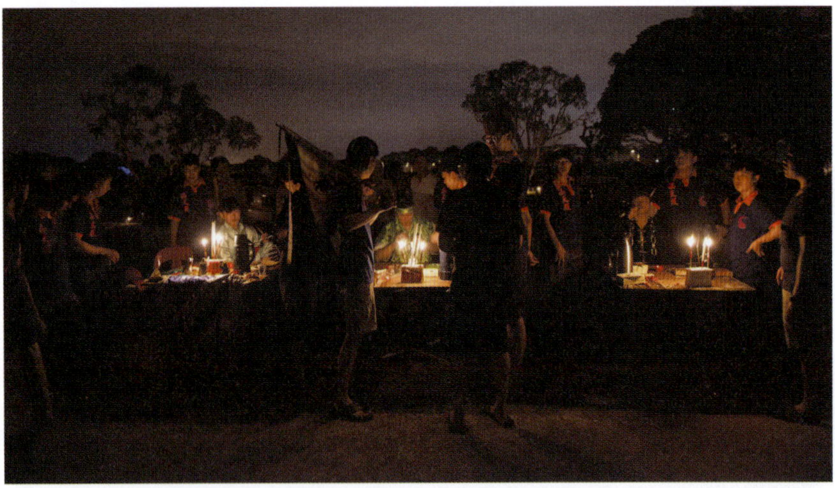

Figure 8.3 Using a wide-angled lens (24mm) but standing at a distance, I sought to photograph the three *tang-ki* being attended to by their devotees. When in a trance, *tang-ki* are accorded the social position of a god, and are thus treated to food and drink that their deities favour, as well as accorded great respect and deference. By spot-metering on the candlelight (see Chapter 9), I was able to photograph this candid group portrait without the use of a flash or tripod.

Useful tip: To best capture candid portraits, many photographers favour a medium- to long-telephoto lens, so as to reduce their photographic presence. However, depending on your relationship to your subjects, as well as your style of photography, it is equally possible to capture candids by using a wide-angled lens. Subjects who have become accustomed to your presence are more likely to ignore you as you do your work.

Usually it is important to maintain a minimum shutter speed to freeze your subject. Because subjects are not pausing to pose, they will likely be moving or engaging in some kind of action. Three considerations are helpful here. The first is to keep a higher ISO setting on your camera so as to ensure that shutter speeds remain fast enough. On many DSLRs it is also possible to specify a "minimum shutter speed" in your settings, where the camera will adjust the ISO settings based on your current aperture and shutter speed. The second is to anticipate moments of pauses. In Figure 8.4, I saw one of *Fu Tian Dian's* devotees, Ling, lighting joss sticks from candles on a table laden with food offerings for the dead. To do that, he would have to stand still whilst holding the joss sticks over the flame long enough for all of them to catch fire. Despite the dark, and having a slow shutter speed of 1/30 sec, which is too slow to freeze normal human motion, I waited for him to pause before taking the picture.

The third consideration is that some blur is inevitable, but also useful and aesthetically pleasing. In Figure 8.4, the joss sticks in Ling's hand are slightly blurred, caused by Ling lifting them away from the candle's flame. Such blurs give a sense of motion and movement, adding life to the

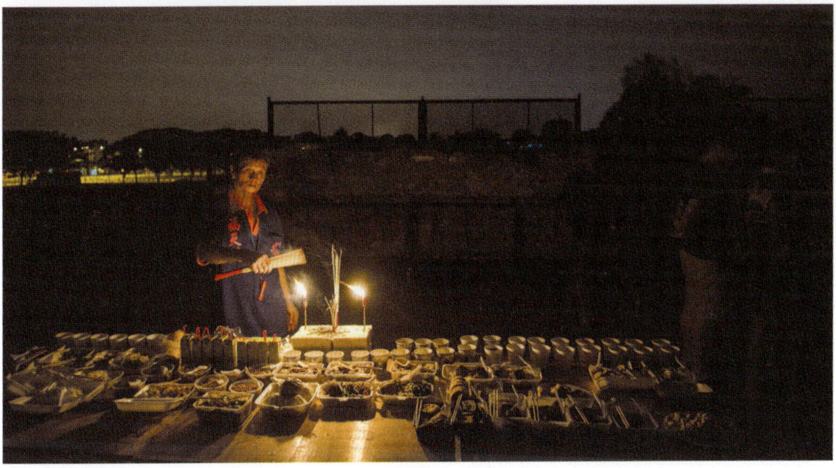

Figure 8.4 Ling lighting joss sticks, half-body crop environmental candid.

image without the need for animation or moving images. Blurs are also useful in revealing the expressive, kinaesthetic nature of the human body.

Conclusion: "faceless" portraits

When taken to the extreme, blurs are also very useful in hiding the identities of one's informants, especially when anonymity is desired. In Figure 8.5, Nick, a medium operating out of his family's HDB flat goes into a trance to channel his main deity, the Monkey God *Sun Wukong* (孙悟空). Whilst the process of trancing varies from *tang-ki* to *tang-ki*, most involve some degree of rocking and jerking motions. In Nick's case, and also owing to the comportment of his deity, such motions are extraordinarily violent, with Nick's arms flailing and his body swinging back and forth. Two of his devotees hold his bench steady whilst the rest look on in the background.

However, it is not always possible or convenient to use blurs to mask an informant. At times we must find other ways to afford our informants anonymity. This is where the idea of creating a "faceless" portrait is useful. A faceless portrait aims to depict or portray an individual whilst concealing or at least partially obscuring the individual's face. Whilst this

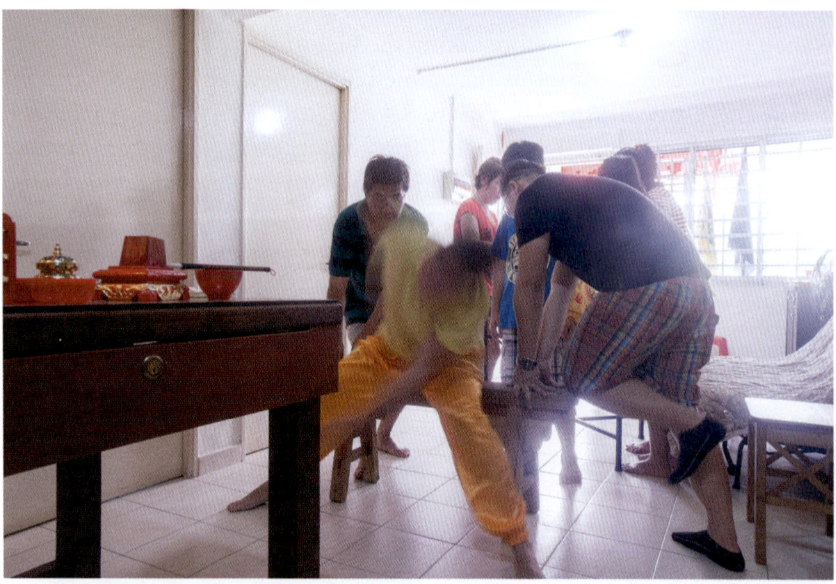

Figure 8.5 Although Nick gave me full permission to use his identity in my research, this photograph is a good example of how to anonymise an individual through the use of slow shutter speeds and faster body movements. Shooting at f/11 causes the shutter speed to drop to 1/8 sec, meaning that only individuals standing still would be frozen, whilst most other movements would be blurred.

is sometimes done for ethical reasons, there are two other potential advantages to this style of portraits. One, faceless portraits force the viewer to consider other aspects of the individual – their dress, comportment and other parts of the body which the photographer may want to bring to the viewer's attention – these could be the hands or feet, or perhaps simply the presence and action of the body in its environment. Two, faceless portraits, depending on the composition of the photograph, re-centre the gaze of the viewer from subject to subject and environment. Since there is no gaze from the subject, the viewer can be made to reposition his or her consideration of the subject *within* that image.

Such portraits, which rely on the angle of the camera as well as the positioning of the subject, have been used to great effect by other photographers. Graham Smith's *Thirty Eight Bastard Years on the Furnace Front. Mess Room for No.4 and No.5 Furnaces. Clay Lane, South Bank, Middleborough* (1983) shows his subject with his head bowed low, squeezed to one side of the mess room. Such a photograph achieves two things – not only does it evoke the sense of exhaustion and helplessness on the part of the community that Smith was documenting, a working-class, heavy industry in its twilight years, it also affords his subject both anonymity and presence simultaneously. At the same time, such a photograph contrasted with other images made by Smith in the same project, juxtaposing itself against a whole range of standard, environmental and candid portraits.

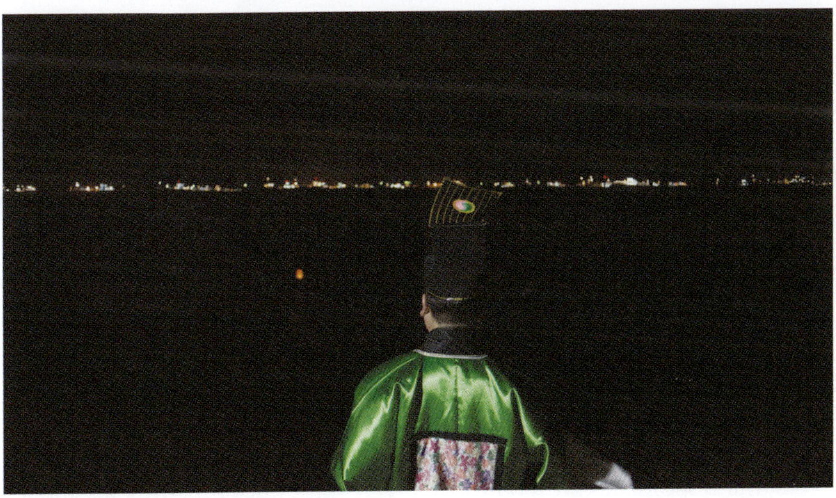

Figure 8.6 A Taoist priest stands at the beach in the east of Singapore, preparing for the *Chao Du* (超度) – a ritual of salvation meant for lost souls during the Hungry Ghost Festival. With a single video camera light illuminating the scene, the viewer's attention is drawn not just to his ritual vestments, but also to the single lantern to his left, floating in the sea to call out to wandering spirits.

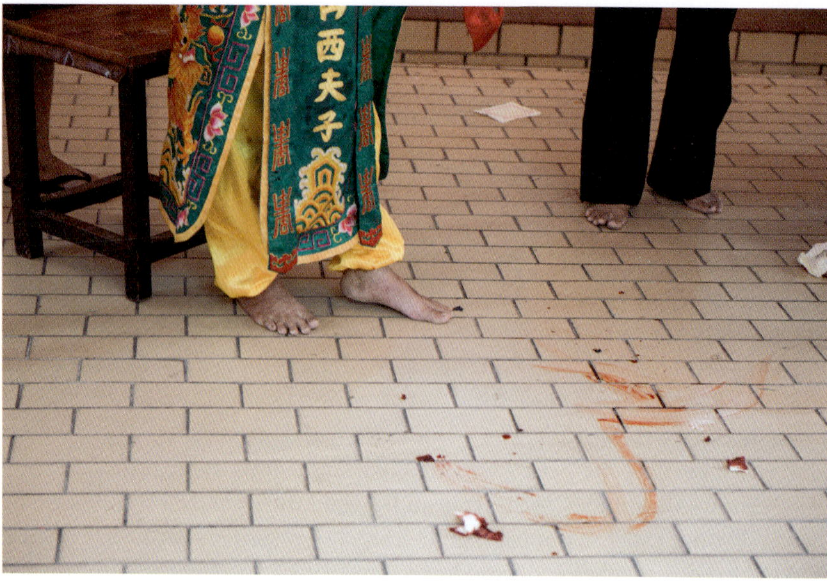

Figure 8.7 A *tang-ki* in North-West Singapore prepares for the arrival of other temple groups as part of their *Yew Keng*. The red ritual dye is used for all sorts of purposes, including the writing of consumable paper talismans that devotees burn into water and drink. *Tang-ki* typically go barefoot when in a trance, along with their closest devotees.

In my own photographs, we see a more conventional faceless portrait in Figure 8.6 – photographing an individual from the back – and a more unconventional version in Figure 8.7, where the focus is solely on the vestments and bare feet of a *tang-ki*. By doing a reverse half-body crop, showing only the legs, attention is then diverted to the floor and streaks of red ritual dye left by crumpled up *kim zua* (see Chapter 4) used to wipe the sweat of the *tang-ki*. Such unconventional faceless portraits can potentially add an interesting angle to a photo essay – opening up new understandings of the spatial dynamics surrounding the subject.

Whichever approach you take with portraits, always remember that the key to photographing people is your relationship with them, whether spoken or unspoken, implicit or explicit, formal or informal. If you establish yourself in a position of trust with your subject, you are more likely to be able to evoke the response, expression or pose you want out of them. This applies even in scenarios where you are simply an observer in the field, and where you are unable to develop deep relationships with your subject. In this case a careful mix of diplomacy and positioning can establish your presence without being intrusive (for candids) but can also allow you to make yourself known when you want your subject to pose for the camera.

Chapter exercises

Photographing people

When practising portrait photography, it is probably easiest to ask someone familiar to model for you. This could be a family member, friend, colleague or classmate. If you are using this book in a class, work in groups to practise shooting portraits of each other. Make sure that you have a variety of lenses to practice with, as facial features can appear quite differently depending on focal length.

1 Start by creating portraits as you would normally photograph someone when you are on holiday, so that you know what a ubiquitous portrait taken by you looks like. Take half-body and full-body photographs.

2 Follow this up by practising the five basic crops in portrait photography. Photograph using different focal lengths (from 24mm to 150mm, in steps of 15–20mm):

   a. The entire body
   b. From the mid-thigh up
   c. From the waist up
   d. From the chest up
   e. Only the head

3 In each of these crops, try to photograph your subject from different angles along both the horizontal and vertical axes. If possible try to shoot from a higher vantage point to create the portrait and then shoot from a lower vantage point. Try to position your subject differently, asking them to vary their pose once they become comfortable with you photographing them.

4 Position your subject within a larger space and photograph them as they are situated in that environment. Use a wide-angle lens to capture more than just your subject. Think about how they relate to this environment – are they at home? Uncomfortable? Experiment also with how *much* of the environment you want to incorporate into this portrait. Finally, try positioning your subject in different ways within this environment. Practise using the rule-of-thirds to place your subject off-centre in the frame.

- Consider also the other compositional tools taught in Chapters 4 and 5 on photographing space and interaction; in particular try applying techniques like juxtaposition, level horizons and framing.

5 Finally, practise photographing your subject without showing their face – this could be done either by cropping or using creative angles (e.g. with their back facing the camera, or in shadow, or using objects to obscure their identity). Pay attention to their use of body language to convey what facial expressions would normally be able to tell. Watch how positioning and posture play a role in creating narratives around your subject.

chapter 9

Photographing in challenging lighting situations

Key technical concepts

- Understanding camera meters and metering modes
- Photographing against the light
    - Metering modes
    - Exposure lock
- Overriding camera meters in adverse lighting conditions
    - Exposure compensation
- Working in low/no-light conditions
- Conclusion: working with flashguns

Case study keywords: Chinese weddings, Bukit Brown Cemetery

Introduction

Up to this chapter, most of the photographic case studies I have been covering have involved photography in relatively simple lighting conditions. That is, ambient light is often readily available in the form of sunlight (photographing during the daytime) or through artificial means in the form of street or interior lighting. Using a camera set on "typical" settings, photography in these circumstances would tend to focus more on issues of composition and framing. However, once we consider photography in conditions where the light (natural or otherwise) is not optimal, there exist other issues that need to be taken into consideration. In this chapter I will be looking at how we might photograph our informants and their spaces in challenging, non-optimal lighting conditions. Originally conceived as a chapter on night photography, I have chosen to expand this to include other environments in which similar principles apply. It is important to note, however, that the principles covered in this chapter can be applied to many other conditions, especially when it comes to mixed lighting situations, or when you want to achieve a particular effect on an individual (see Chapter 12 on ethics).

Entire books have been dedicated to teaching night/low-light photography, though few in comparison to books on the more general types of photography in daylight. One excellent example is Keimig (2010), whose instructional book on night photography also includes an extensive historical chapter on night photographers, from the earliest examples like Joseph-Nicéphore Niépce's *View from the Window at Le Gras* (1826) to more comprehensive early collections by Paul Martin (*The Alhambra, London, by Night* 1895) and Alfred Stieglitz (*Icy Night, New York* 1898) to documentary photographers like Lewis Hine, who made use of a flash to illuminate child workers in factories (*A Midnight Scene in More-Jonas Works* 1912). In social science research, there is little visual work done in poor lighting conditions using ambient light – with most opting to make use of artificial light (Hine 1912; Schwartz 2009) to assist in their investigations. Such relationships with light indicate a more dominant stance of controlling factors, which has its advantages, but I propose that there are other alternatives.

A relationship with light

In my PhD thesis (Heng 2012), I discussed how a visual sociologist had to decide what her relationship with light would be when conducting fieldwork. Would it tend to be more dominant, in that the researcher seeks to control the amount and quality of light at all times and in all situations, or would it be more cooperative, in that some attempts at introducing light in certain circumstances are acceptable, or would it be fully adaptive, in that the researcher accepts and makes do with whatever light there is in whichever circumstances are presented to her? In the field, it often comes down to personal preference and style, as well as the kinds of photographs that one is trying to take. Is it an image that needs to document the minute and intricate details of an artefact in the field, or is it more about capturing the emotions and ambience of the scene? In the former, one might demand that artificial and controlled light is very important, but in the latter the choices are far more fluid.

As mentioned above, photographers who work in challenging lighting conditions adapt to and/or control these situations in a variety of ways. Weegee, the pseudonym of Arthur Fellig, is best known for his unrelenting photography of the streets of New York City. He is best characterised by his use of a flash, necessary in the mid-1900s when film and camera technology in low-light environments had not evolved to what it is today. A quick glance through Weegee's photographs shows how his use of a direct flash (firing a flashgun directly at his subjects) creates stark, detailed photographs that evoke a sense of confrontation and directness, including that of *Tenement Fire* (1939) and *Brooklyn School Children See Gambler Murdered in Street* (1941). In contrast to this, Henri Cartier-Bresson's approach to street photography is much more subtle. That subtlety shows in both his style and the way he engages with light, letting available light dictate the shadows and highlights in some photographs – for example his work on China in the late 1940s (see *Final days of the Kuomintang* (1948)), which interrogates the everyday life of Beijing's inhabitants on the street. Unlike Weegee, these photographs lack a sense of confrontation, which I propose is at least partly to do with the kind of light at play.

Understanding camera meters

Neither approach is necessarily wrong, but in doing fieldwork the ability and opportunity to use a flash can be limited. You might be photographing a sensitive ritual in which bursts of light might irritate your informants, or perhaps you might want to remain unobtrusive. Both the physical nature (the size of a typical professional flashgun) and emitted light of a flashgun have the potential to increase your field presence dramatically. As such, it is more likely, especially in social research, that you would be photographing without the use of a flashgun (though I will cover this later in the chapter). Here, I will consider the techniques that are useful in working with only ambient light.

Photographing in adverse, mixed and challenging lighting conditions requires us to have a reasonable understanding of how cameras determine settings in the exposure triangle. In Chapter 3 I discussed how an exposure is dependent on three main factors: aperture, shutter speed and ISO setting. Depending on the level of manual override, a camera can set one, two or all three of these, although most photographers will usually shoot on semi-automatic and allow for one or two settings to be determined by the camera. But how does a camera "know" the level at which a particular setting should be? The answer lies in a camera's meter. Simply put, a meter is the "brains" of your camera. It measures the light that is reflected off an object or objects and determines what the aperture, shutter speed and/or ISO setting should be to achieve a technically correctly exposed photograph.

Cameras can meter in a variety of modes, known as *metering modes*, which take all, part or very little of any particular scene into account. That is, when you point your camera at something or someone, a camera can measure reflected light off all, part or just a little bit of what you are trying to photograph – i.e. whatever is in the camera's frame. These metering modes go by many different names according to camera manufacturers, but can be generally placed into three categories: multi-metering, partial or centre-weighted metering and spot-metering. The first, multi-metering, means that the camera takes readings from almost every part of what is framed in small components, then calculates the averaged reading, together with other factors like where in the scene you are focussing. The second, centre-weighted metering, tends to place the most important readings in the centre of the camera's frame, with some weighting given to a small area around the centre. This means that not all aspects of the scene are taken into consideration. The third, spot-metering, only considers the smallest cell or zone in the centre of the camera's frame and bases the reading entirely on that zone. This can either give the most accurate reading or the most widely off-the-mark reading. For a more detailed explanation of metering modes, see Mansurov (2010).

In the next few images, I use a case study of a recent wedding I photographed just at the start of 2016 to demonstrate the uses of matrix and spot-metering. These events occur just after the morning bridal make-up is done (see Chapter 5), and signal the start of the wedding rituals proper.

In Figure 9.1, I await the contemporary version of a Chinese wedding procession. Initially conceived as almost parade-like, with sedans, gifts and family as a show of wealth (Wanyan 2008), the arrival of a groom in a Singaporean Chinese wedding is somewhat muted, with a single bridal car pulling up at the foot of the bride's family home's apartment block. A young male relative from the bride's (Valarie's) side of the family, holding two oranges, waits to open the door of the car for the groom (Benjamin). Here, I used a multi-metering mode, known as matrix metering in my Nikon, to capture the scene. The brightness of the background, along with the shadows cast by the overhead shelter meant that the camera's meter correctly exposed the background (notice the truck parked in the centre-left of the photograph), but underexposed Joseph, the bride's nephew. Whilst this creates an interesting silhouette, and is useful for anonymising subjects (see Chapter 12), it demonstrates the broad ways in which multi-metering works. If I had *not* wanted to make Joseph a silhouette, I would have used a spot-meter and taken a reading off him.

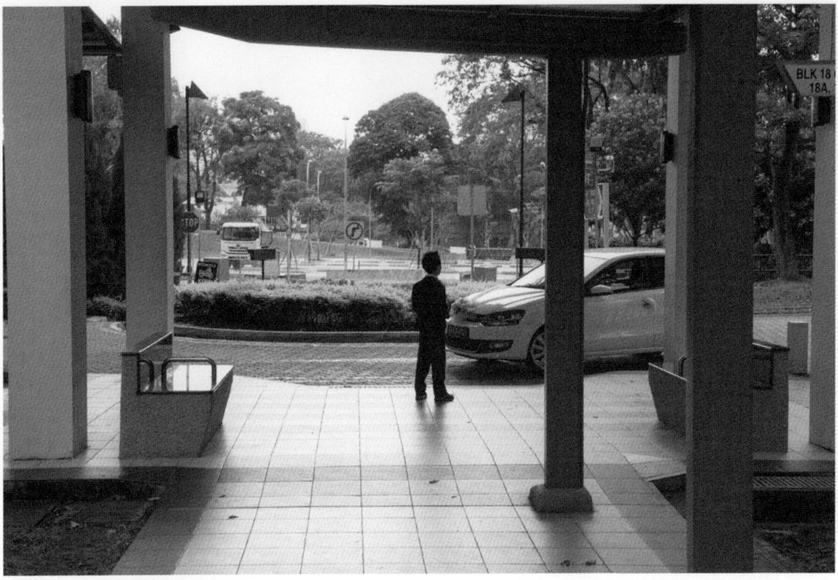

Figure 9.1 Waiting for the bridal car.

Spot-meters allow for the correct exposure of particular subjects in a frame. This means that if there is something or someone who is very important to the image, and other elements are *less* important, a spot-meter can help to ensure that the details of this subject are correctly exposed, but at the sacrifice of some or all other elements. Figure 9.2 shows one such example of how a background is "sacrificed" for the foreground subject.

In Figure 9.2, Joseph sits on the staircase waiting for the "door games" to commence. Door games are a common ritual across cultures, where grooms and their entourage attempt to gain entry into the bride's home, often seen as a symbolic act of violence and conquest. The menfolk will do everything they can to enter, and the women everything to prevent them. In the case of Singaporean Chinese weddings this usually involves the front grille being locked so that men and women can barter and play games. Some argue too that this ritual dates back about 3000 years to when the Duke of Zhou in China set out six particular rituals that constituted a marriage (Wanyan 2008).

In order to capture Joseph's expressions, I swapped to a spot-meter mode and took a reading off his face. Sitting in the interior staircase of this block of HDB flats, without the overhead lights switched on, meant strong sunlight from outside was casting shadows on Joseph and Sam, the photographer next to him. Thus, in order to get a correct exposure on Joseph (and not a silhouette as in Figure 9.1), I had to sacrifice detail in

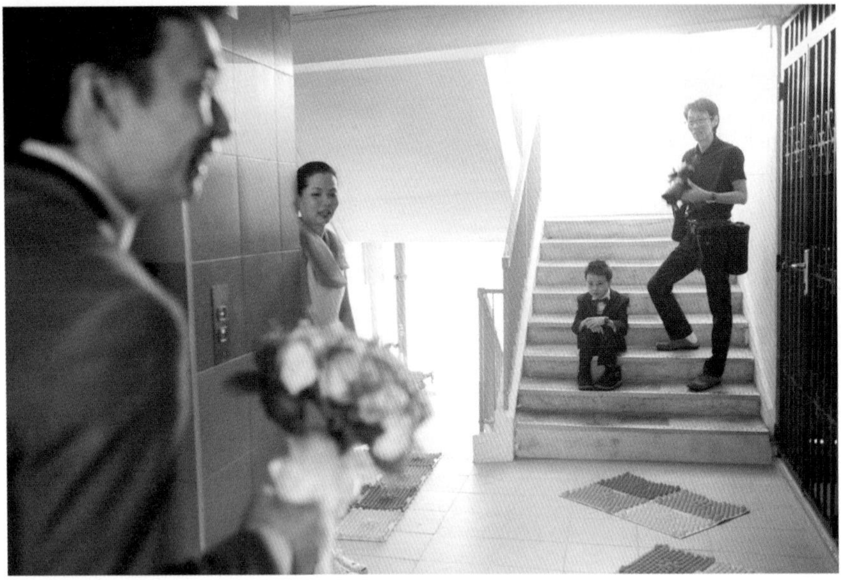

Figure 9.2 A photograph with a spot-meter reading taken off Joseph's face (seated). Benjamin in the foreground has arrived to engage Valarie's bridesmaids in games of forfeit, played so that he may gain entry into the home.

the background and overexpose it, causing clipping (see Chapter 11) in the highlights. Such clipping occurs very often when there is a strong backlight, a use of the spot-meter, and with the flash turned off.

Spot-metering and exposure lock

However, spot-meters can be prone to errors, owing to their very small width, and if used incorrectly can result in gross over- or underexposure, defying the intentions of the photographer. In Figures 9.3a and b, I show two photographs of the same scene, both shot using a spot-meter on my camera. The first photograph has me erroneously using the spot-meter to take a reading directly off the bright window in the centre of the frame. The second photograph was much more like what I had intended. I moved my reading to be taken off Valarie (the bride in the centre of the group on the left) so that the group, Sam the photographer and other details would be correctly exposed.

To do this, I used a technique that is known as *exposure lock*, which is similar to a *focus lock* in Chapter 5. Exposure lock with a spot-meter involves moving the camera so that the centre of the frame (where the spot-meter is) is placed directly on the subject that you want the meter reading to be taken from, pressing a button to lock it (depending on cameras, this might be the shutter release or a dedicated button), then

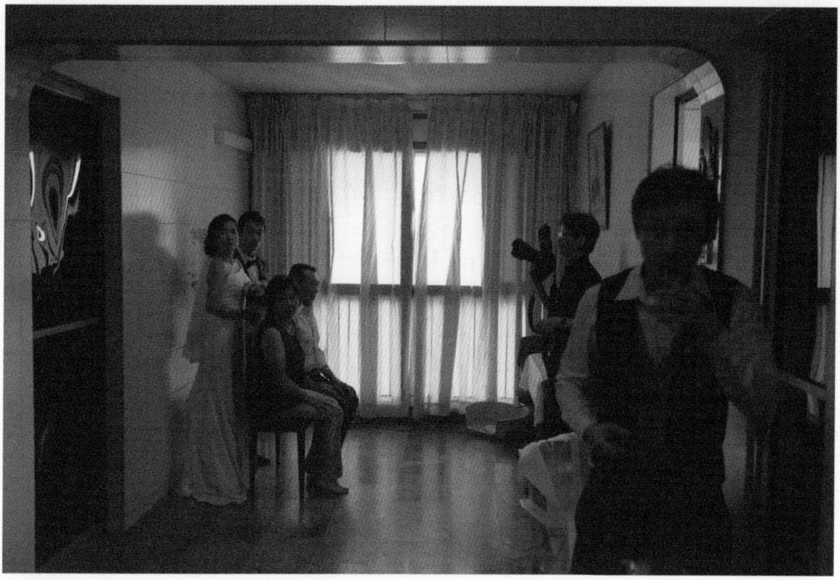

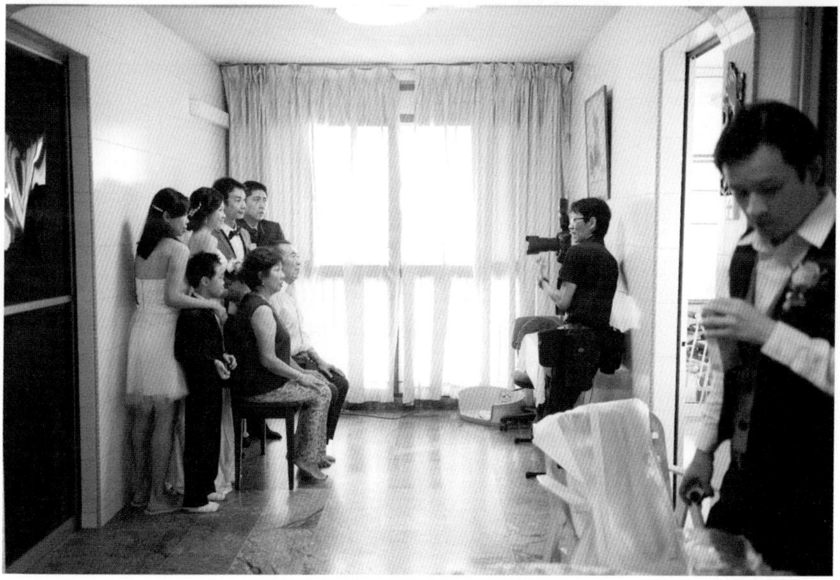

Figures 9.3a and b After the games, the groom heroically retrieves his bride and the post-game ritual of photograph-taking happens. Socially, this segment signifies a certain sense of reconciliation between the groom's and bride's entourage, and they then move together to the next location.

recomposing to the original frame and taking a photograph. In Figure 9.3b, I moved my camera left, to centre and focus on Valarie, took a reading, pressed my AE-L button to lock the exposure, then recomposed so that the group was back on the left before I pressed the shutter release.

Exposure lock works equally well for other metering modes, although the amount that you move your camera varies depending on your mode. For example, if you were using multi-metering, in which almost all parts of the frame are taken into consideration by the camera, you would have to make sure that little to no parts of the frame had aspects that might fool the camera's meter. In Figure 9.3, this would mean moving the camera's frame all the way down to the floor to eliminate the bright window, taking a reading off the floor, locking that reading then recomposing to take the photograph.

Useful tip: Spot-metering is useful for all sorts of situations, especially when you need to ensure that a particular subject is properly exposed. This includes stage or concert performances, when the spotlight is on a performer but all around him or her is darkness, or scenes at the beach or in the snow, where the reflectiveness of sand/snow can fool the meter into underexposing.

Exposure compensation

For the most part, camera meters are becoming increasingly sophisticated and able to judge lighting scenes well, but in difficult lighting conditions they can erroneously expose an image in an attempt to get the "correct," averaged exposure. In other situations a photographer may wish to increase or decrease a suggested exposure setting so as to change the look and feel of a photograph. In either case, it is possible to manually override a camera's meter reading without having to use a spot-meter and exposure lock, by using your camera's *exposure compensation*. This is useful in situations where a subject or scene is constantly backlit, and you do not want to continually recompose for every shot, nor do you want to keep your camera on full manual setting.

Exposure compensation is a feature that allows a photographer to force a camera to increase or decrease exposure based on the current meter reading. This means that additional over or underexposure is always of a set magnitude over whatever the camera's meter suggests is the correct exposure. Exposure compensation is measured in steps of exposure values (EV), where 1 EV corresponds to 1 stop, or a standard-power-of-2 exposure step. What this means is that increasing exposure by 1 EV will double the exposure on a reading, and decreasing exposure by 1 EV will halve the exposure on a reading. For example, if a reading was f/2.8 at 1/800 sec, increasing by 1 EV would result in f/2.8 at 1/400 sec and decreasing by 1EV would result in f/2.8 at 1/1600 sec. Most cameras will offer a scale of approximately 1/3 EV, meaning one can increase or decrease exposure by 0.3, 0.7, 1.0, 1.3 EV and so on.

Photographing in low/very-low light conditions without a flash

Camera shake and the reciprocal rule

During my fieldwork on weddings, I marketed myself as a photographer who took photographs like a photojournalist, i.e. my work attempted to develop a particular visual narrative of the bridal couple's journey on their wedding day, from preparation to ritual to celebration and conclusion. My style was "fly-on-the-wall"; I would often keep a distance and not interfere with the interactions of my subjects as they went about the wedding, only doing so when I wanted to include a posed photograph. As such, much of my work was done without the use of a flashgun, as is also the case with my other fieldwork projects in Chinese spirituality. As Chinese weddings take place in a variety of locations (see Chapter 5 as well), I would, throughout the day, experience a very wide range of lighting conditions as well. Low-lighting conditions were often apparent at the start of the wedding day morning rituals, which could be as early as 4a.m. according to certain regional Chinese customs (as well as the availability of the make-up artist), especially in HDB flats, where individuals tend to keep their room lights off, allowing for natural light to stream in through the windows. Light levels were also low at the evening banquet, where restaurants and hotels tend to use warmer, dimmer lighting to create a certain level of romantic ambience.

These situations, all else being equal, will result in lower shutter speeds in cameras where the aperture and ISO settings remain constant (see Chapter 3 for the exposure triangle). When hand-holding a camera, *low shutter speeds* are a key factor in blurry photographs caused by *camera shake* – where the camera and/or lens makes enough micro-movements during the shutter opening and closing that it will result in that movement being captured in a photograph. Figures 9.4a and b show the effect of low shutter speeds and camera shake. In this photograph, Billy (groom) and Elaine (bride) are making an offering of incense to their family deity in Billy's home, whilst Billy's father watches on and his best man and the maid-of-honour converse in the background. The home, an eclectic mix of sacred and profane, was too small for me to photograph at eye-level.

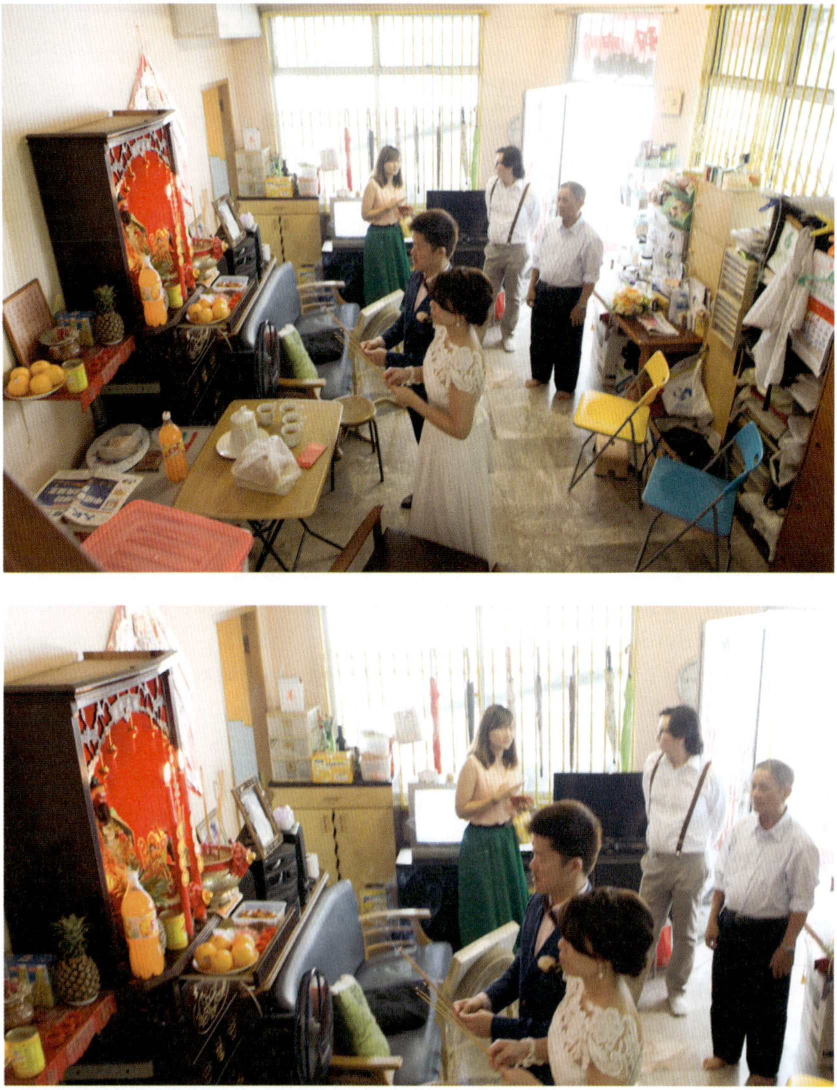

Figure 9.4a and b Unlike photographs where blurred subjects are deliberately introduced (see Chapter 8 on "faceless portraits"), photographs that have camera shake do not have any aspect of the image sharp, i.e. the blur is universal. Whilst this is less obvious on a small photograph, like the one in this book, once the image is enlarged, so is the blurriness, as can be seen in 9.4b.

Hence I climbed the stairs and positioned my camera between the staircase railings to capture this image.

Billy's home was also quite dark, even with the room lights on; the bridal couple were largely cast in shadow. In order to capture the detail of their ritual, I took a meter reading from Billy's face. With my aperture set at f/4.5 and ISO at 1250, my camera calculated a shutter speed of 1/15 sec, or one-fifteenth of a second. The lower shutter speed resulted in a blurry photograph, even if it was in focus (notice that the top of the altar's cabinet is slightly sharp).

According to the exposure triangle, low shutter speeds can be compensated for by either widening the aperture or increasing the ISO sensitivity, either of which would cause a corresponding increase in shutter speeds. But what shutter speed is enough to prevent camera shake? The answer lies in the *reciprocal rule* – which states that the minimum shutter speed to prevent camera shake for stationary objects is the inverse of the camera lens's current focal length. So, as I was shooting at 24mm, my shutter speed should have been at least 1/24 sec to ensure a removal of camera shake.

The reciprocal rule has two implications. One, the longer the focal length of your lens, the faster the shutter speed you would need to prevent camera shake. Hence, if you are shooting from a distance and you are using a telephoto lens of, say, 200mm, you would need a shutter speed of at least 1/200 sec when hand-holding, which explains why many sports photographers rely on monopods when photographing events, as many of them rely on long telephoto lenses of 300mm to capture the action. Two, as the converse is true, that shorter focal lengths means greater leeway with shutter speeds, it is easier to photograph using wide lenses in low-light conditions when not using a flashgun, which is why many street photographers and photojournalists make use of shorter, faster lenses that have large apertures.

There are three more factors that one needs to take into consideration when calculating the reciprocal rule and thinking about camera shake. Previously, with film cameras, all lenses corresponded to their declared focal length when attached to a DSLR, i.e. a 200mm was a 200mm, unless one was using a teleconverter. With digital cameras today, the size of the sensor does affect the resultant focal length of the lens attached to it. The smaller the sensor, the greater the magnification of the focal length (or what is known as the equivalent field of view). This is most obvious when one attaches the same lens to two cameras with different sensor sizes, for example, a Nikon 5200 with an APS-size sensor and a Nikon D810 with a 35mm, "full-frame" sensor. The former will create a magnification of 1.5x, thereby turning a 35mm lens into a 50mm lens, 200mm to 300mm and so on. This means that with the reciprocal rule, the corresponding shutter speeds also need to be the inverse of these effective focal lengths. For more information on this, see Mansurov (2015) and Malan (2015) for a longer explanation of this phenomenon.

The second factor involves automatic stabilisation technology. Cameras and lenses, especially those that have smaller maximum apertures (f/5.6 and above), are increasingly introducing features that compensate for camera shake. Image stabilisation is marketed under different names by different manufacturers, including Vibration Reduction (Nikon), SteadyShot (Sony) and Image Stabilizer (Canon), and can work in slightly different ways (some are built into the lens, others use micro-movements in the sensor), but they are all intended to achieve the same effect. Such technologies claim to allow shutter speeds of anywhere from two to four or more stops of light, where each stop "doubles" the amount the light that is falling on the sensor. In other words, if you have two stops of image stabilisation, your shutter speed can be four times slower when handholding a camera – 1/200th sec for a 200mm focal length goes down to 1/50th sec, and 1/20th sec for a 20mm focal length becomes 1/5th sec. As such, if you are using a camera or lens with such a feature, you will typically have more leeway when it comes to shutter speeds, assuming too that your subject is not moving.

Finally, with the use of digital cameras, photographers are now given a chance to instantly review images they have just taken by using the LCD/LED screens on the back of their cameras. This has several advantages, in that you are able to tell if you did indeed capture the photograph as intended, and also to check for focussing and, in this case, camera shake problems. However, it is important to remember that the smaller the screen, the smaller the image and the less likely that errors or problems will be immediately noticeable – this is the same reason why photographers who use slide film tend to use a loupe to magnify their slides to check for errors. In the case of a digital camera one should use the zoom function when replaying an image to check for camera shake. Some cameras also allow for you to customise a button to automatically zoom to a preset size for quicker reviews.

Useful tip: Despite lenses and cameras having image stabilisation features that give them the ability to shoot in low light as if they had wider apertures, their image quality still remains below professional lenses with wide maximum apertures (f/2.8 and below).

Working in low/no-light conditions

Spot-meter and pre-set settings

Whether or not you have a camera/lens with automatic stabilisation technology, it is still useful to be aware of various techniques that enable you to photograph in situations where lighting conditions are even more challenging. In this section I will move away from my work in weddings and consider fieldwork done in Bukit Brown Cemetery, which had the most challenging lighting conditions in any of my case studies. Bukit Brown, as I noted in Chapter 6, was closed to new burials in the 1970s. Such a closure meant that although the space continued to function as a cemetery, it was no longer maintained by the state, which effectively left it to lie fallow. There is thus no artificial light in Bukit Brown at night, and, being near a catchment area, the cemetery is now overgrown with trees and vegetation, making it near pitch-dark in many areas at night.

At the same time, much of my fieldwork in Bukit Brown happened in low/no-light conditions. Many rituals, including some exhumations and events during various festivals (including the Hungry Ghost Festival, for which see Chapters 4 and 11), needed to have their performance and/or celebration at night. In some cases, like exhumations, I avoided the use of a flashgun, as, unlike a constant video light, the suddenness of a flash was overly blinding, intrusive and annoying for participants. I thus limited myself to whatever ambient light was available. Most of the time this included candles lit by gravediggers for their own use, flashlights from other participants, and, if I was fortunate, the presence of a video light from a colleague who would be given permission to film the ritual. Figure 9.5 shows such a scene.

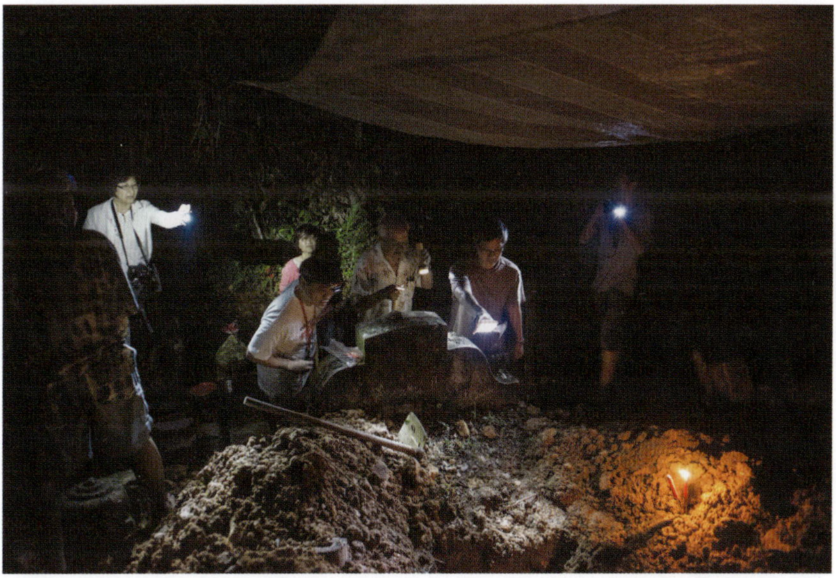

Figure 9.5 Participants and researchers looking into a freshly exhumed grave, using a mix of candles and flashlights. Rather than constantly having to take readings off a candle or particular LED light, I performed one spot-meter off a spotlight and then used those settings on full manual mode. In this case it was f/2.8 at 1/30 to 1/40 sec at an ISO of 5000.

The first step in photographing such conditions is to ensure that one's camera settings are relevant to the scene. General settings for daylight are less useful here, and when photographing at night, I would do one of two things. If the lighting conditions varied greatly from pitch-black to occasional full-illumination (for example, moving from indoors to outdoors and then back again), I would set my camera to aperture-priority (see Chapter 3) with a spot-meter rather than matrix metering. This would allow me to take constant and precise readings of each scene to ensure I got my desired exposure. However, if I was in a particular scenario where the lighting levels were consistent but patchy (as in the case of these images – a few candles and flashlights throwing out a constant level of light, but only illuminating parts of the scene erratically), I would set my camera on full-manual, with a shutter speed fast enough to avoid camera shake. For me, this would be about 1/30 sec for a 24–70mm lens on a full-frame DLSR, although I would incur motion blur when photographing individuals moving. Doing the latter would mean I would be able to spend less time taking readings off small portions of the scene, doing an exposure lock and then re-composing again, which would happen a lot if I had used the former technique.

When shooting in difficult lighting conditions, it is also important to take more photographs than you normally would, especially if your

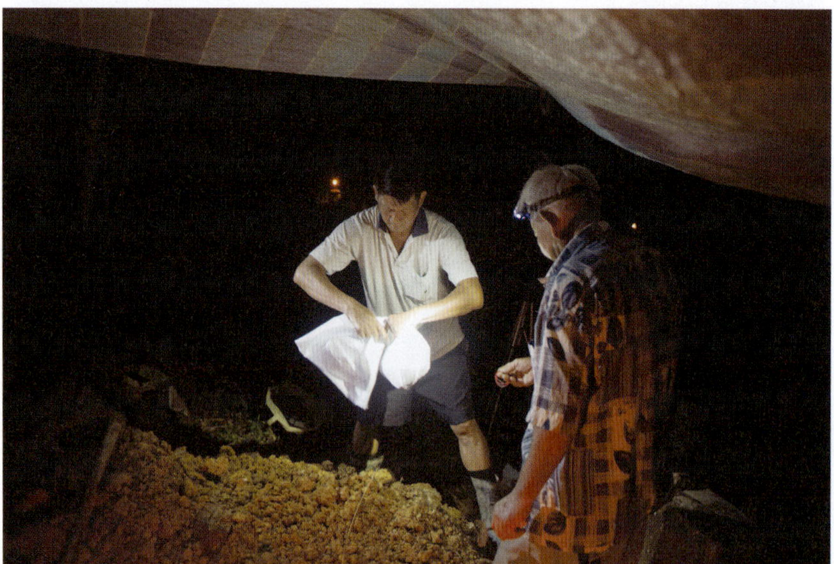

Figure 9.6 Mr Peh (left) ties up a standard white plastic bag holding the remains of the exhumed individual, with Mr Lew holding out some rubber bands to secure the bag. At 1/40 sec f/2.8 Mr Peh is correctly exposed in the photograph.

subjects are moving. In Bukit Brown, it was not always easy predicting what would happen next and when, unlike a wedding where many events were scripted. In Figure 9.6, I photographed Mr Lew, the gravedigger in charge of exhuming this particular grave, assisting Mr Peh, a contractor, with the final stage of the exhumation. After retrieving all possible remains from a grave, the remains are rinsed in rice wine as a symbolic bath, before being placed in a white plastic bag to be transported (in this case by Mr Peh) to a state crematorium for cremation. With a videography light shone directly onto Mr Peh, my manual setting of f/2.8 and 1/40 sec captured him correctly, but overexposed the reflective white plastic bag. Mr Lew, who stood further away from the light, was illuminated only by candlelight. As they finished securing the bag, Mr Peh opened up a ritual umbrella, meant to protect the remains during this transitory period, and walked out of the video light towards the exhumed individual's descendants. In Figure 9.7 I managed to catch Mr Peh's sudden change of direction without having to spot-meter and recompose, but only because I was shooting the ritual steadily without lowering my camera to wait for the next moment.

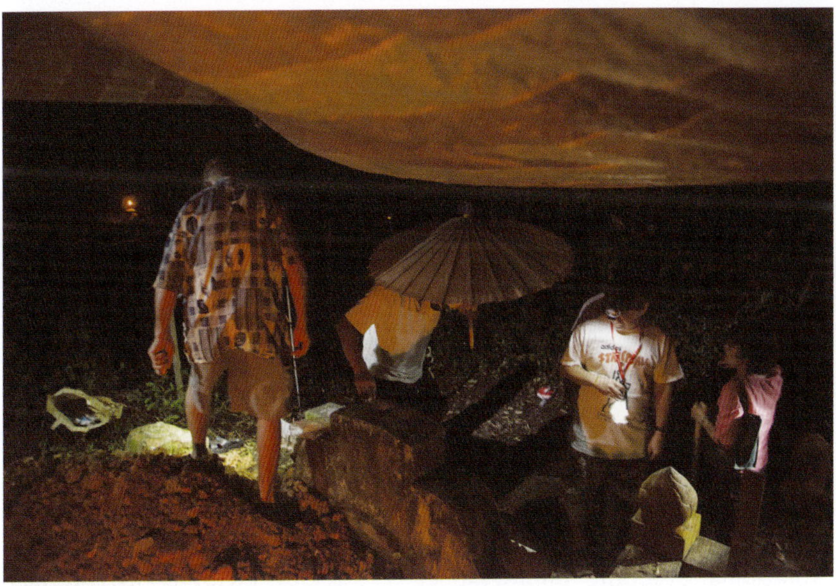

Figure 9.7 Mr Peh moves out of the video light and towards the waiting family. If I had to meter again, I would have to take the reading off Peter, second from right, who had a similar illumination as the video light. However, doing this might have missed Mr Peh at this position. If I had metered off him in the centre, the shutter speed would have been too low to freeze him.

Camera-holding techniques

When shooting in low/no-light, I would often encounter shutter speeds much slower than daytime, which created the potential for a significant amount of camera shake. Since I was mostly shooting handheld, I had to rely on certain hand-holding and breathing techniques to steady my camera. Firstly, I relied on the same principle I learnt when shooting a rifle during my military conscription – I would time the taking of a photograph with my breathing. In general, the human body is at its most still when breathing out slowly, and not when one is holding one's breath or breathing in. When holding your breath you are likely to make micro-movements from the lack of breathing, and when breathing in your chest expands and rises, also causing micro-movement. I would thus take a breath, and as I breathed out, I would press the shutter release button.

The second is the way I held my camera. If using a DSLR, it is always important to hold it with two hands, one gripping the camera body and the other supporting the attached lens. In low/no-light situations I would also employ additional techniques, based on the principle of making the camera as immobile as possible. I would first look for something to lean against, and in doing so would be able to immobilise at least one of my arms to steady my camera. If there was nothing to lean against, and this was often the case in Bukit Brown, I would wrap my left arm across my body, using my left hand to grip my right shoulder. This allowed me to create a bridge upon which I could rest my camera (while still holding and using it with my right hand) – this was steadier than using my left hand to hold the camera as my arm was "locked" against my chest. Finally, if shooting from a lower angle, I would rest the camera on an object whilst using the LCD screen to compose (some DSLRs have a "live view" function that allows this).

Conclusion: working with flashguns

In this chapter, I largely focussed on the use of cameras *without* the help of artificial light in the form of flashguns. However, there are moments in research where a flashgun and other accessories are useful and sometimes even "mandatory," depending on one's role. For example, in my role as a professional wedding photographer, I was also expected to produce perfectly exposed posed photographs of groups of wedding guests and the bridal couple. To do this I would often also mount a flashgun onto my camera. Most compact, prosumer cameras, enthusiast and semi-professional DSLRs tend to feature a built-in flash that is either mounted on the top right of a camera or acts as a pop-up flash. Professional-grade DSLRs tend not to have pop-up flashguns, usually to ensure weather-resistant sealing. Many cameras also feature a hotshoe, which is a mount on which one can add a stand-alone flashgun to help illuminate a scene. But not all of these flashguns are the same. Flashguns are differentiated by both brand and guide number, where a guide number denotes the strength of the flashgun, or how much light it can throw out. Professional flashguns often have a guide number of more than 42, but also tend to be larger and bulkier. Smaller flashguns are more portable, but sacrifice power and may not be able to illuminate your subject adequately.

Flashguns can do much more than just brighten a scene with inadequate light, and although this would require another chapter on its own, I will cover a few possibilities for working with flashguns. The most straightforward way to use a flashgun would be to mount it on a DSLR and allow the camera to trigger and calculate the amount of light thrown out by the flashgun for any particular scene. The flashgun would also be aimed directly at your subject, and this would be known as a *direct flash*. The advantage of using a direct flash is that your scene (subject to the strength of the flash) will likely always be adequately and forcefully illuminated, and because flash shutter speeds can often sync up to 1/200 sec with professional DSLRs, you are also able to avoid problems like camera shake. Direct flash also works in all environments, without the need for surfaces to bounce the flash off – but in doing so it reveals a disadvantage. Subjects and scenes taken with a direct flash tend to come off as very harshly lit, in the spirit of Weegee's paparazzi-style photographs. Direct flash also tends to produce *flash shadows* – short shadows that are cast on a background that is too close to a subject. Such harsh lighting and shadows give a particularly intrusive feel to a photograph, albeit one with much detail.

An alternative would be to use an *indirect flash*, in which the flashgun's head is angled upwards or sideways towards a flat surface like a ceiling or wall. This *bounces* the light from the flash, creating an indirect and diffused light, which also tends to be more evenly spread, rather than concentrated on the subject as in the case of a direct flash. I tend to use indirect flash techniques during weddings, as it gives a softer feel to the photographs, but tend to only do this indoors when there are adequate flat surfaces off which to bounce light.

Useful tip: Some manufacturers sell a variety of light diffusers to attach to the head of flashguns in order to create diffused light anywhere. Some of them, however, are very large and would increase your field presence dramatically.

Besides darkened spaces, flashguns, especially when used as a direct flash, can also act to fill-in shadows left by strong directional light. This is known as *fill-in flash*. For example, in Figure 9.3a, where much of the scene was underexposed because of the strong sunlight coming in from the window, firing a flashgun, despite there being "adequate" light, would illuminate the scene in the same way one would use a spot-meter and exposure lock, or with exposure compensation. Fill-in flash is useful when you want to be sure to capture detail rather than just the form of a photograph. By using a fill-in flash, it is also possible to retain detail in the foreground and background when photographing a subject against a strong light. To understand the intricacies of fill-in flash, see Rockwell (2012) or Rowse (2016).

In order to work in challenging lighting conditions, it is not enough to master one's camera, but one has to develop a style that understands the limitations of the technology in one's hand, as well as the limitations of shooting in different conditions. This is why it is not so much the "quality" of an image but the *studium* with which we seek to encode a photograph. In the next chapter, we will look at devices that offer not only new opportunities but also new limitations to visual research.

Chapter exercises

Challenging lighting situations

Photographing in difficult lighting conditions can be achieved at almost any time of the day. For the most diverse experience, taking your camera out at night, relying only on whatever light is available, creates the most opportunities to learn. However, working indoors in poorly or dimly lit situations can also give you a chance to practise. If indoors, try turning off ceiling lights and use only floor and table-lamps to illuminate a room, thereby creating unevenly lit environments with pools of shadows and highlights.

1 Consider what your relationship with light is like – review photographs in which you used artificial light (like a camera flash) – does this reflect your style of photography? Does artificial light or ambient help you weave your narratives better? In what situations does either kind of lighting suit the way you shoot and relate to your subjects?

2 Practise first with your camera meter and exposure compensation – this will allow you to learn how to make adjustments on-the-fly as you work within challenging lighting conditions. Pick a bright single source of light within a frame – this can be a single ceiling downlight, or a single bright lamp or desk lamp in an otherwise darker room, or if you are outdoors a streetlamp or spotlight might work as well.

   a. First set your camera to aperture-priority with an aperture of f/4 with multi-metering mode (usually the default metering mode in most cameras).
   b. Aim the camera at this source of light, with the source of light directly in the centre of the frame (The source of light should take up no more than 20 per cent of the frame) and take a photograph. After that, change the metering mode to spot-metering and then take the same photograph, making sure that the source of light is again in the centre (assuming that your spot-meter is also centred). You will notice that the shutter speed should be noticeably different when using different metering modes.
   c. Next, repeat the exercise but this time practise increasing or decreasing exposure using exposure compensation (this might be more easily achieved by placing your camera on a tripod to maintain the same framing of light sources). Set your camera back to multi-metering mode, then photograph at 0 EV, then +1/2/3 EV and then −1/2/3 EV. Note how the shutter speed changes to accommodate the increase or decrease in exposure, and how differently the photograph turns out each time.
   d. Finally, practise using the exposure lock. Pick a landscape scene with a bright sky and dark landscape (i.e. the sun is not illuminating the landscape). Photograph the scene using a spot-meter and aperture-priority mode, taking a reading from just the sky. You will notice that the landscape is likely to be quite dark. Now move the camera down so that the sky is not in your frame, and take a reading off the darker landscape and lock the exposure (usually either by half-pressing your shutter release or with the AE-lock

button), then recompose to include the bright sky and take a picture. Notice how the exposure changes when you do this.

3 Experiment with the reciprocal rule (this does not have to be in poorly lit conditions). First, set a focal length of 80mm at f/5.6. Set your camera to shutter-priority mode, then while taking the same photograph (hand-holding the camera), adjust the shutter speeds to 1/20s, 1/30s, 1/40s, 1/60s, 1/80s and 1/100s. Watch for when camera shake starts to affect the sharpness of the image (this might change depending on the available light and presence of any image-stabilising technology). To see extreme examples of camera shake, shoot in a dimly lit room at 50mm, ISO200 on aperture-priority, ensuring that the shutter speed is in seconds rather than fractions of seconds.

4 Practise hand-holding and breathing techniques for low shutter speeds. Set your camera on shutter-priority with a focal length of 50mm and a shutter speed of 1/30s. Try and take a photograph hand-held, breathing out slowly as you press the shutter release. Also try to experiment with different ways of stabilising the camera in the field. Lean against walls when taking photos, or shoot with your elbows placed on a table to create a human bipod.

chapter 10

Smartphone photography

Key technical concepts

- Understanding the opportunities and limitations of smartphones for visual research
- Basic techniques for better smartphone photographs
    - Holding a smartphone for photography
    - Focus lock / exposure lock
    - Exposure compensation
- Working with apps in post-processing
- Conclusion: the future of visual documentation?

Case study keywords: aesthetic markers, urban Singapore, Chinese religion

Introduction

> For many photojournalists . . . the problem is not the iPhone, which is merely a device, after all. The problem is that using it – or any camera, professionally requires an understanding of visual storytelling, which is about sequencing and patience, framing, knowing what to exclude as much as what to include.
>
> (Spinner 2013)

The ubiquity of smartphones means that everyday photography is increasing exponentially. A recent Google Study in 2014 (Low 2014) showed high or increasing smartphone penetration rates around the world – Singapore being the top with 85 per cent ownership, an increase from 72 percent in just one year. Other countries around the world were not far behind, including Korea at 80 per cent and Sweden at 75 per cent. Developing countries, with slower mobile broadband speeds, still saw healthy growth. Coupled with improving imaging technology – the average smartphone has about an 8–14 Megapixel resolution (the iPhone 6s has 12MP) with ever-improving software algorithms for clearer and sharper images – many see smartphones as at least a complementary device to DSLRs in photojournalism and other kinds of visual work in the field. Indeed, Gómez Cruz and Meyer (2012) have argued that the smartphone, particularly the iPhone, has heralded the "fifth moment" in photography.

It is in the field of photojournalism where smartphone technology has had the most ramifications (Alper 2013). With a diversification of channels of communication for news and other forms of media, some traditional newspapers have found it more cost-effective to seek out individuals who are both journalists and photojournalists (Spinner 2013). A greater reliance on mobile devices to experience media has also meant that in some ways, photographs need no longer be prepared for print as much as they used to, as the requirements of computer, tablet and smartphone screens are less onerous than high quality, large-scale prints. Individuals, both amateur and professional, have taken advantage of these affordances, making use of apps like Instagram, VSCO and Snapseed to develop visual stories that are primarily distributed online through social media (Hochman 2014; Keightley and Pickering 2014; Van House 2011).

The social sciences have been largely concerned about mobile photography (and related social media) from the point of view of the consumer, and how the technology has created new ways of understanding memory (Keightley and Pickering 2014), identity (Hall 2015), place-making (Hjorth and Pink 2013), society (Ling 2008) and the presentation of the self (Villi 2015). In many of these studies, the use of mobile phone technology and its implications have taken precedence. For example, Hjorth and Pink (2013) looked at how the use of location-based services (e.g. Instagram geotagging) is almost ritualized into everyday practices of place-making and social-connectiveness. On the other hand, Van House (2011) looks at how mobile phone photography has changed the way personal images are consumed, distributed and mediated between public and private spheres. However, in most of these studies, where the subject is the use of smartphones, few researchers have *used* smartphones as a means of collecting photographic data.

Most ethnographically important visual work using smartphones has thus come from practising photographers, especially in the fields of photojournalism, documentary and street photography. When smartphones were first launched, particularly the iPhone, camera technology had not yet caught up with the needs of photographers. However, many photographers now use smartphones, again more often than not a variant of Apple's iPhone, as part of their photographic practice. Others have completely eschewed the use of larger cameras in favour of smartphones, although these remain in the minority. Well-known documentary photographers and photojournalists include Aik Beng Chia, who performs street photography in Singapore solely through the use of an iPhone (Chia 2015a). Chia's documentary project, *SingKarPor*, combines architectural, spatial, street and portraiture photography into a powerful story of everyday life in urban Singapore – *Rochor Centre* (2015b) is a particularly good example of his surreptitious yet direct approach to his subjects. Also of note is David Guttenfelder, an award-winning photojournalist working for Associated Press, who spent a year documenting North Korea through his smartphone and posting the photographs on Instagram. Guttenfelder's work interrogates the little seen aspects of social and material lives of North Koreans – a place that Guttenfelder admits "is not the kind of place where you can make what photojournalists call good pictures very easily" (Tharoor 2013).

In this chapter, I will consider how smartphones can best be used as part of one's fieldwork. Using examples drawn from all my different research projects, I will show when and where smartphones can best be utilised for maximum efficacy.

Understanding the opportunities and limitations of smartphone cameras

Minimal field presence

Chase Jarvis's book *The Best Camera is the One That's with You* (2009) is a study of art and culture through photographs created by his iPhone. The title of the book has been adopted by other photographers to argue that availing oneself of every opportunity to photograph is essential for capturing the right moment. In Chapter 2, we discussed the issue of field presence, where the size and type of camera can and does affect one's relationships with one's informants. At the top end of the scale were large DSLRs with long lenses, making some perceive photographers as overly intrusive or stereotype them as paparazzi. On the other hand, the ubiquity and size of smartphones means that informants often assume the holder to be simply someone trying to take a few snapshots. Such assumptions made through assessment signals sent out by a smartphone afford one anonymity to capture candid moments without the subject knowing. In genres like street photography, as in Aik Beng Chia's *SingKarPor*, this gives the smartphone photographer more room to work.

When documenting the spiritual aesthetic markers in the Singaporean urban landscape, I would keep an eye out for annual temple celebrations, where larger and more well-off temples had the financial capability and manpower to set up large tentages in empty fields in HDB neighbourhoods. These fields are more common in more mature estates, and like the void decks in HDB flats themselves (see Chapter 4), become a tabula rasa for individuals to create temporary but prominent performances of identity and values. One such field in the north of Singapore is regularly occupied by temples and *sintua* – who establish multiple points of performances within a single space. Two main areas are present here – a large tentage that mimics the layout of a temple, and a smaller stage for *Getai* singers to perform and entertain devotees, passers-by and deities, both present and perceived. The tentages are temporary and often fleeting – professionals are hired to set them up and tear them down in hours. They usually consist of large rectangular wooden planks as flooring, metal scaffolding and heavy tarpaulin drapes that act as shelter. Fluorescent lighting and electric fans are also mounted onto the metal scaffolding, so that the tentages can be used in any weather and at any time of the day.

I had chanced upon these serendipitously – and was unprepared with any camera gear. However, I wanted to photograph this event not just for its elaborate staging, but also because of a convenient contrast with other aesthetic markers of Singaporean identity. This was August, and National Day banners were still erected around the neighbourhood, including a very large one fronting the tentage.

Moving inside, I was also able to photograph the front of the tentage, the main altars, offerings and interactions without any fuss. Many of the celebrants were still setting up, and hence I appeared as a curious bystander (I was) with a simple smartphone camera.

Easy panoramas

Although many cameras now offer this function, smartphones have the most accessible and user-friendly panoramic function. Panoramas have been used to convey a sense of interconnections between disparate events within a particular space, or to show many elements of a space in a single photograph. Panoramic modes in cameras have existed for quite some time, but the software within the camera that stitched different photographs together still proved to be lacking until their developments over

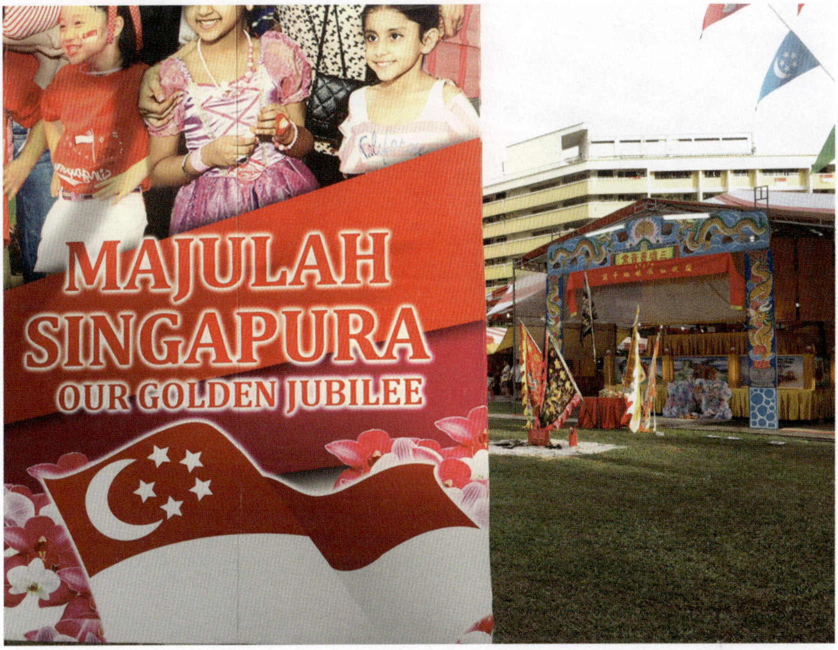

Figure 10.1 Moving close enough to the banner and tentage, I was able to juxtapose the political billboard with religious banners in the background. In the far background are the HDB flats that form the perimeter of the field on which the tentages have been set up. Through images like these, I wanted to show the fluidity of spatial use by political and religious groups in Singapore.

the last five to seven years, owing much to new algorithms developed in smartphone technology. In my attempt to photograph the tentages I saw in Bishan, I also wanted to show how these large open fields worked as a social nucleus for the individuals living close-by, and to do so I wanted to tell the story of the tentage from a higher vantage point (see Chapter 4). Such fields are often bounded by high-rise flats, so I walked the perimeter of the field to the nearest block of flats overlooking the field, and took a lift to the highest possible floor.

Positioning myself at a perpendicular point to the centre of the main tentage, I had two options. One, photograph the tentages from a high vantage, but only showing the tentage and field, or, two, attempt to show how the community of flats cocooned the space as part of their lived everyday places. A concrete path bisecting the field was particularly important because it was the main arterial route from the blocks of flats on the left to the main bus interchange and mass-rapid transit (MRT) train station in Bishan. Taking advantage of the increased traffic from the event, a lone ice-cream seller on a motorcycle with portable freezer set up

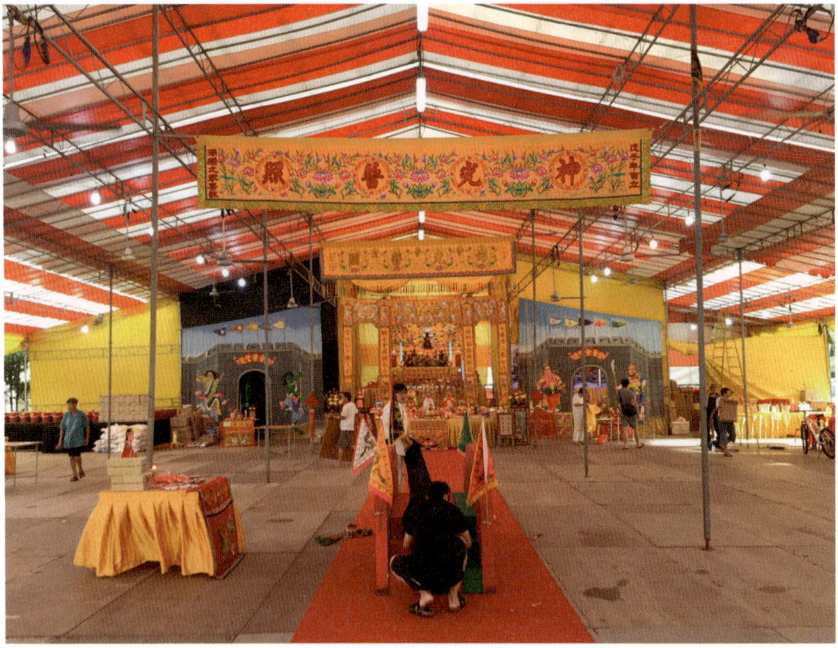

Figure 10.2 The inside of the tentage as devotees are setting up. In front of me is a *Ping An Qiao*, or Peace Bridge, a structure that devotees will later walk across in a ritual whilst carrying paper effigies of lost souls, who will carry their sins for them into the netherworld, and in turn be saved. No one paid any attention to my presence with an iPhone.

shop along the concrete path, his umbrella visibly advertising his wares from a distance.

The panorama was a convenient way for me to create a summary of this space. Within a single photograph I could show the layout and positioning of the flats, tentages, concrete path and the landscape in which all these structures were placed (the less expensive HDB flats are equally juxtaposed against private condominium housing in the top right of Figure 10.3). Oftentimes, when I am trying to show different events in a single space, but where my lens is not wide enough, I will also make use of panoramas to develop a quick way of surveying and summarising multiple things at the same time.

To get a usable panorama, first position yourself roughly at the centre of all the objects that you want to photograph; being too far to the left or right means that you will capture too much of one side and lose information on the other. Practise first by sweeping the camera across the field of vision that you want to capture, taking note of where you want

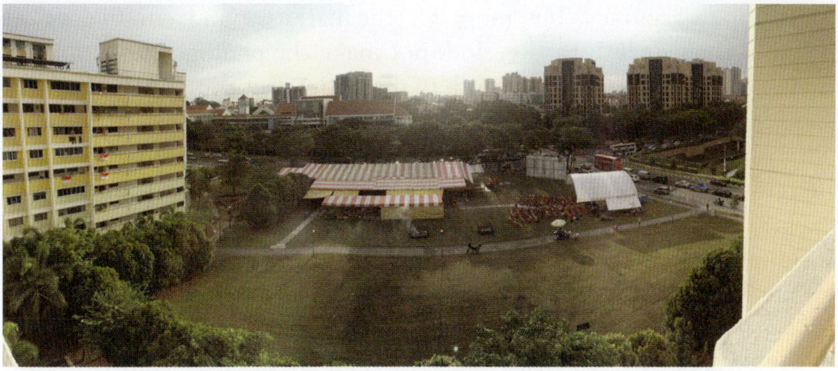

Figure 10.3 A panorama of temple celebrations in Bishan. As this was an impromptu shoot, I was not carrying a tripod, and as such was not able to pan across the field evenly, resulting in a warped concrete path in the centre of the image.

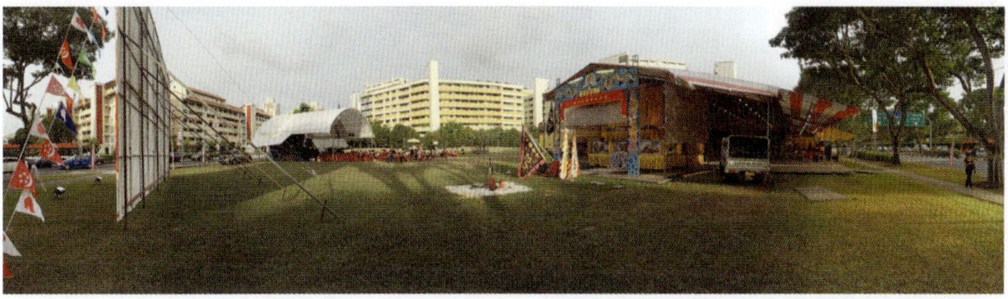

Figure 10.4 The same temple celebrations on the ground, showing the back of the political billboard in Figure 10.1. Notice how in order to bring together so many elements, segments of the images have different lighting conditions and levels of distortion.

to start and stop the image. When you are ready, hold your smartphone with two hands (to steady the smartphone as much as possible), press record and pan the camera across your desired field of vision. When you have reached your end-point, press record again to finalise the panorama.

However, panoramas also introduce a high amount of distortion (see also Chapter 8) because of the wideness of the angles. This distortion is more pronounced the closer the object is to the camera. Notice how also in Figure 10.3 the whole field bends and warps. If you are photographing a large object or building and you are standing close enough to it, the panorama will also cause the building to warp (as is the case for Figure 10.4). It is for this reason that architectural photographers still eschew the use of such functions. But as we are not always photographing for absolute accuracy, but more for the narrative and emotive values of the image, such distortion does not make the photograph completely undesirable. That said, if you wish to minimise distortion, make sure that straight-lined objects are as far away from your smartphone as possible. This can be done by angling the smartphone either up or down by a small margin. In Figure 10.3, I deliberately angled the smartphone upwards to exclude the handrails that were distorting and warping due to my lack of steadiness.

Useful tips: When photographing a panorama, wait for a moment in which everything is relatively still. An individual or object moving across your path as you take the panorama will result in multiple instances of that individual or object. If the movement is slow enough, it may result in an "accordion" effect where the image of the individual or object is repeated rapidly in succession.

Sensor size

In order to fit everything into a smartphone, which is getting slimmer with the introduction of every new model, manufacturers have reduced the imaging sensor to about 1/50th of the size of a 35mm negative frame, or of the size of a full-frame DSLR's sensor (Schiesser 2016). This has two important implications: one is that it is less likely you can make extremely large prints with a photograph produced by a smartphone; the other is that there are repercussions with digital noise (see the next subsection). However, it does have one advantage. With such a small sensor, a smartphone has a much closer minimum focussing distance than a DLSR with a normal, non-macro lens. This means that when confronted with a situation where you need to photograph something up close, a smartphone could conceivably produce a usable image, although, because of its sensor, it would prove more difficult, though not impossible, to create high-quality photographs. Abdul Mutuma has nonetheless done this, using an Android phone and pieces from a broken point-and-shoot camera (Cade 2015).

Best in daylight or with sufficient light

One significant limitation of smartphones is their ability to handle digital noise. In order to create the best-possible quality of photographs, many smartphones, especially the iPhone, reduce the ISO as much as possible. This often means photographing at ISO-32 (for reference, two of the highest quality consumer films in their time were the Kodak Ektar 25,

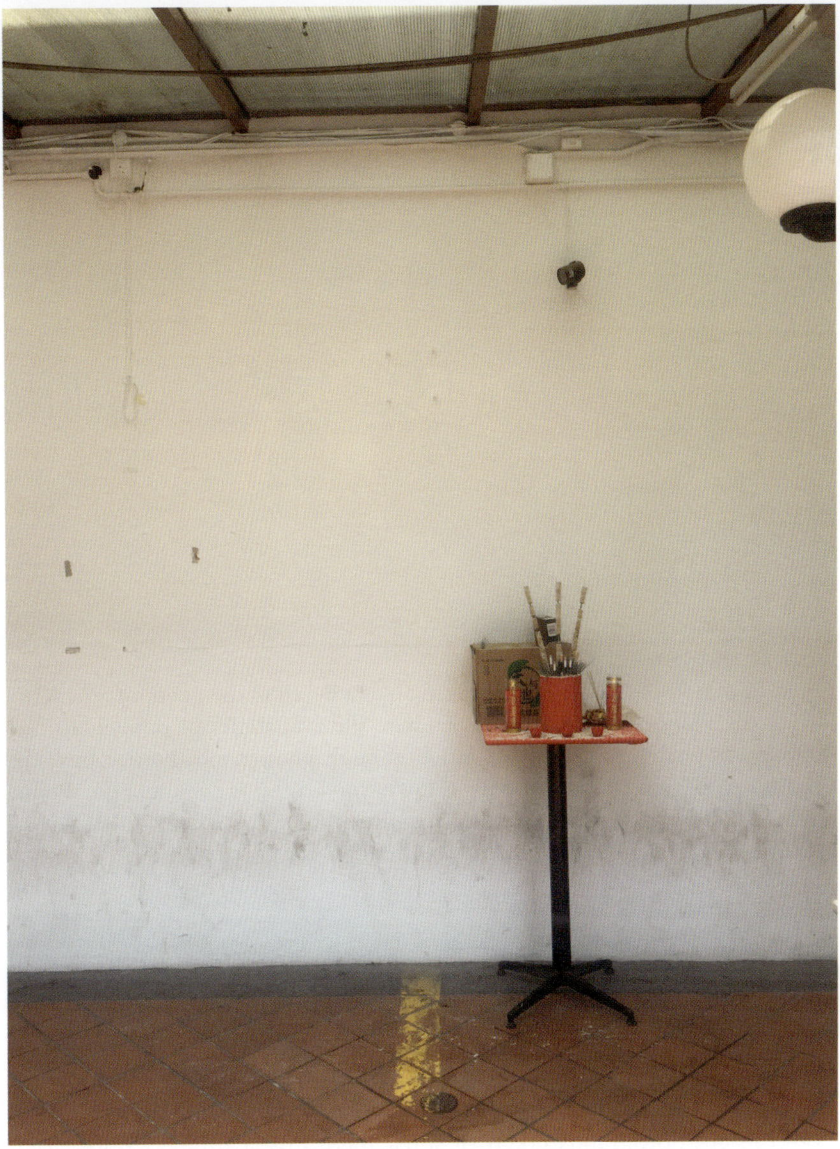

Figure 10.5 Shot in broad daylight without a flash, this photograph clearly captures the nuances of a temporary altar set up for the Hungry Ghost Festival. Photographed in Robertson Quay in central Singapore – a commercial nightspot – the faded yellow marking is a symbol for a "smoking box," where individuals are permitted to smoke. This marking visually divides the photograph into two areas – sacred and profane.

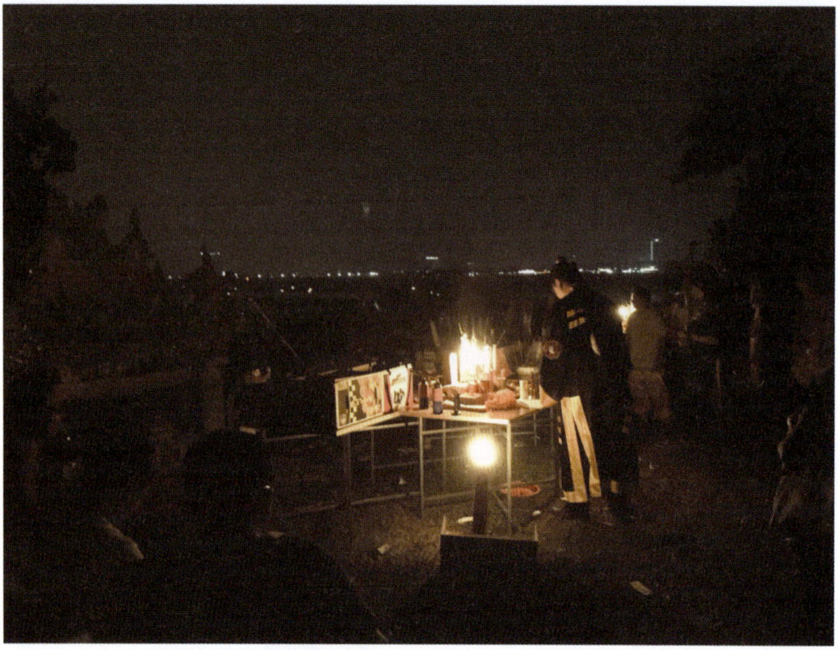

Figure 10.6 A Taoist priest conducts rituals at a beach in the north of Singapore during the Hungry Ghost Festival. Despite the availability of candlelight, my iPhone was unable to create a detailed-enough photograph. Notice how the candles on the altar table are also overblown (too bright) as a result of the iPhone trying to compensate for the dark environment. Notice also how the sky has a greenish-cast, owing to the presence of digital noise.

with an ISO rating of 25, and Fuji Velvia, with an ISO rating of 50), which is fine in broad daylight, but becomes more of a problem when photographing at night (see Chapter 9), in the shade, or in a dimly lit environment. When the iPhone is placed in this situation, it automatically pushes up the ISO in order to retain a fast enough shutter speed. Looking at photographs taken of spirit mediums at night, I notice that my iPhone increases its ISO rating up to ISO-1000. The result is a photograph that is lacking in detail, containing a significant amount of digital noise.

Useful tip: Digital noise looks awful in colour, but when converted to black and white, can create a atmosphere similar to grain in film photography. Grain is traditionally seen in photojournalism and war photography genres, where photographers need high-speed film to ensure faster shutter speeds to caption action.

At the same time, it is also important to understand where and how such images may be used. Despite the photograph being of poor photographic quality (sharpness, detail, colours, etc.), it is still a socially significant photograph in which meaning can be made and analysis done. These photographs can also become more aesthetically pleasing when distributed in smaller formats and using post-processing filters and apps (more on this later). Smartphones have not just become a more dominant way to conduct vernacular photography, they have also become a more dominant way of consuming such images, through social media channels like Instagram and Facebook. As such, when viewed through such channels, especially Instagram, a viewer will see the image at a scale quite different from that of a large, high-quality print (and the same can be said for some kinds of electronic publications). Consider Figures 10.7a and b.

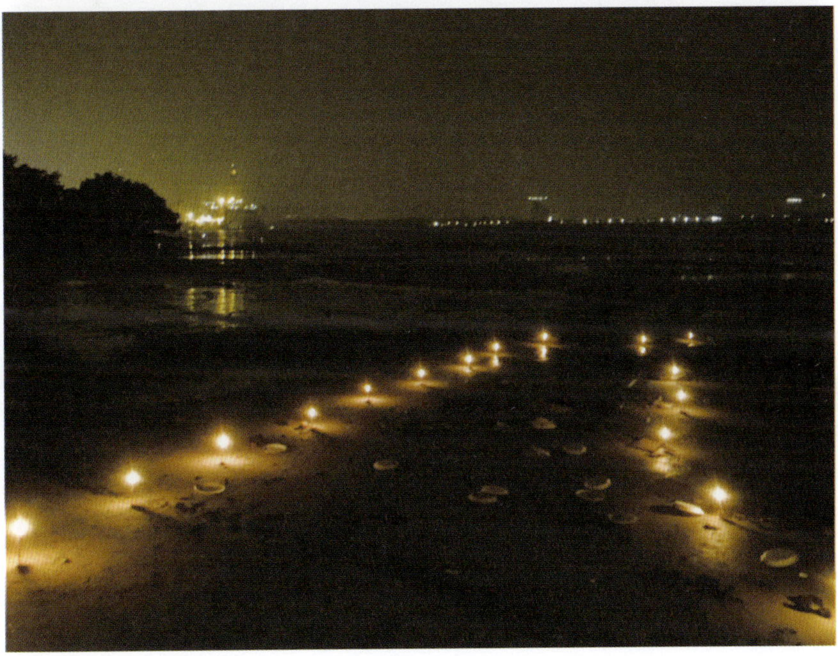

Figure 10.7a Although soft, the image shows an oil rig in the background of the beach where a salvation ritual was taking place. Candles had been set up to guide lost souls from the sea to partake in food and money offerings from devotees. Shrunk down, the image retains an ethereal and ghostly feel, giving a sense of how it felt being on the beach at the time. However, if enlarged, the limitations of my iPhone become much more apparent. 10.7b shows an enlarged part of 10.7a.

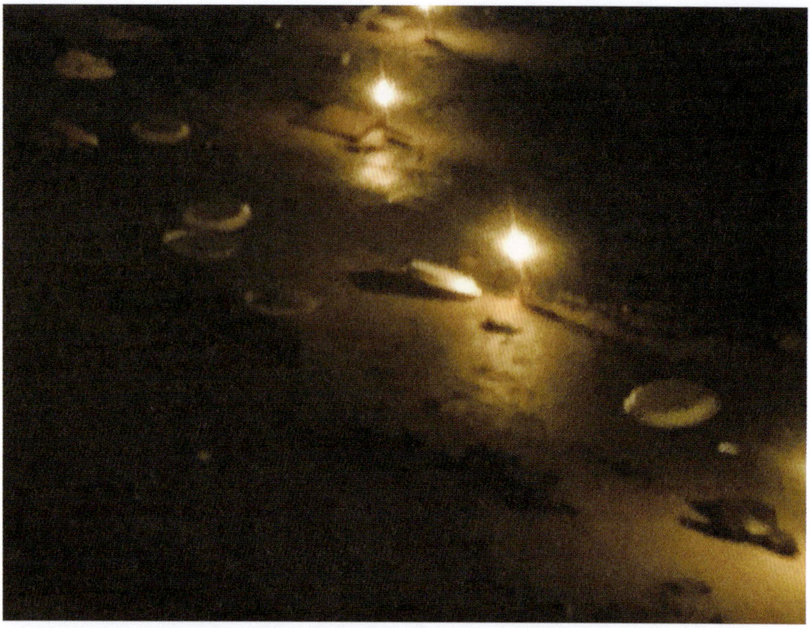

Figure 10.7b Plates of offerings are lined up next to candles, but the noise makes it hard to discern the objects as a visual field note for future reference.

Making better use of your smartphone

Although smartphones often work on a lowest-common denominator paradigm, meaning that manufacturers try to make them as easy to use for as many people as possible, they contain several hidden features by default (meaning that you do not need to download additional apps to use them). In this section I will look at how you can enable focus lock and exposure lock (see Chapter 5) and exposure compensation on a smartphone. For convenience, I will be referring largely to the iPhone 6/6s with iOS 9 installed. However, the principles of these features are similar to other phones with different operating systems – just that user interfaces are regularly updated and fine-tuned.

Holding your smartphone

Many individuals who take snapshots with their smartphones tend to hold it in the same way as if they were making a phone call – with one hand and using the thumb of that hand to press the shutter release button on their smartphone's screen (see Position 1 in Figure 10.8). However, this is the least stable way of capturing an image, as the pressure of the thumb will also often cause the smartphone to tilt slightly forward (depending on the individual's grip on the phone). In very bright lighting conditions, this is less of a problem, but in situations that require a stable camera, for example moving subjects or low-light conditions, there are other and better ways of holding a smartphone.

The first is to hold it as if you were texting with two hands. Doing so will allow you to place more fingers behind the camera (Position 2) and steady the camera as you press the shutter release button. This is advisable when you wish to photograph in portrait orientation, and/or when you are photographing on the street and want to remain anonymous and hidden, as this gives the impression of texting. You could also place one hand at the top of the smartphone when holding it in a vertical position, so as to steady the camera even further. Whilst this is effective, it also makes the act of photography more obvious, and increases the chance of a stray finger obstructing the lens. The second way, if you want to capture your subject in a landscape orientation, is to hold the camera at both ends with both hands, as if you are texting with your thumbs (Position 3). Not only does this provide stability, it also provides anonymity as in Position 2. Again however, this does mean that a stray thumb or finger might obscure the lens, which is not always obvious on a smartphone screen when photographing in bright sunlight.

Focus lock and exposure lock

As a refresher, focus lock occurs when you want to ensure a particular subject in your frame is in focus, regardless of where it is in the frame. In Chapter 5, I explained how using a half-press on a shutter release button would usually allow you to lock both focus and exposure. It is also possible

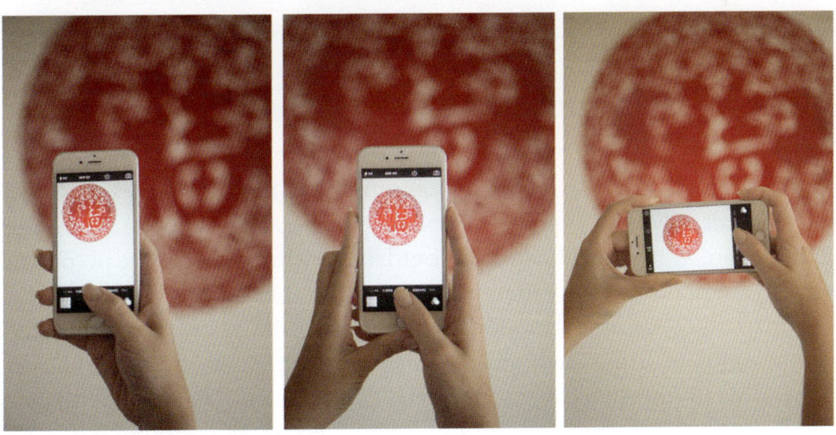

Figure 10.8 From left to right: Position 1, 2 and 3 of holding a smartphone when taking a photograph.

to enable focus and exposure locks on a smartphone, and in some ways is easier than doing this with a DSLR. First aim the smartphone at your subject, and decide on the point on which you want the camera to lock its focus and exposure setting. On an iPhone, use your finger to tap and hold on the subject until a focussing square animates, and a label that says "AE/AF Lock" appears. The lock is now present and can be cancelled by tapping anywhere on the screen; whilst locked, the focussing square will remain present to remind you of where on the screen the camera is locked.

At the same time, you will also see a brightness symbol next to the focussing square that looks like the sun. By moving your finger up and down the screen, you can then adjust the exposure setting of the smartphone without changing its focus. This is the iPhone's version of exposure compensation, which I covered in Chapter 9. To adjust the exposure, move your finger up or down the screen to increase or decrease the current exposure setting on the smartphone, thereby either brightening or darkening the image. As is the case with other cameras, this way of adjusting the camera's metering is very useful for lighting situations that might trick a camera, or where you wish to override the "correct" settings to show more details in parts of photographs with shadows. Figure 10.9 shows an example.

Useful tip: Avoid zooming in on a subject using a smartphone's digital zoom – this is because the smartphone is not actually increasing the focal length of its lens (the lens is fixed) but rather enlarging and "cropping" the image to the desired portion of the original composition. This results in highly pixelated images. It would be better to photograph as per normal, then crop it in post-processing.

Working with apps and add-ons

Apps

With the speed at which technology is moving in mobile devices, it would be difficult to recommend or explain particular apps in an academic publication, which will be quickly outdated within a year. Instead, in this section I will discuss the different categories of apps currently available on the market, what affordances they provide to the photograph, and the implications of using such apps. Apps for photography on smartphones generally fall into two categories – one, there are apps that assist, enhance or customise your photography *whilst* you are taking a photograph; and, two, there are apps that edit the photograph that has already been taken. Amongst the latter there are also apps that assist in distributing the image

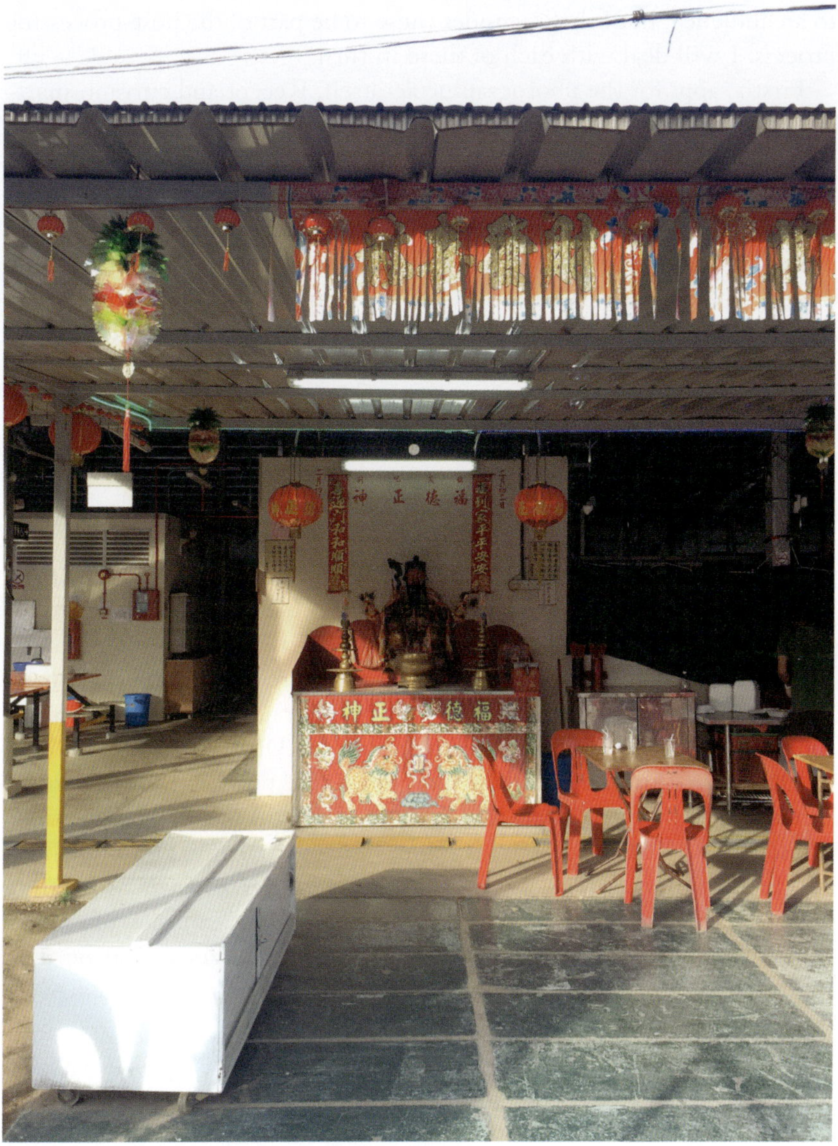

Figure 10.9 A makeshift altar in a makeshift structure. The hawker's market in Ghim Moh, a suburb west of Singapore, is undergoing refurbishment, and both Man and God must move. This altar is dedicated to *Fu De Zheng Sheng* (福德正神), or *Tua Pek Gong*, the Earth God of Wealth. At the time of photographing, a large part of the altar was shrouded in shadow, despite a fluorescent lamp hanging over it. I focussed and exposure locked my iPhone on the part of the altar in shadow, then increased the exposure till I was able to see the altar's details. This resulted in the sky overhead (top of the photograph) being overexposed, but I judged that to be acceptable as it was not my primary object of concern. This, however, has also created an interesting effect of the residual power cables overhead.

to an audience, but I shall consider these to be part of the post-processing process. I will deal with each of these in turn.

Firstly, apps for the photographic act itself. Recent and current smartphones are always improving their default camera app. For example, Apple's iPhone's default camera app now allows for exposure compensation, High Dynamic Range (HDR) mode, customised flash and focus/exposure lock, as I showed in the sections above (Android's default camera app also includes similar features). However, many experienced photographers find that the controls are limited, and make the camera app similar to that of a compact camera on almost fully automatic mode. Hence, many apps, both free and paid, offer photographers more latitude and customisation when taking a photograph. These often mimic the functions on DSLRs, such as white-balance (correcting for artificial light), separation of focus and exposure locks (so that you can focus on one object and measure exposure on another), and the ability to save one's photographs at higher resolutions or as uncompressed TIFF files (see Chapter 11 for more information). Many of these apps also claim to include improved software algorithms that process the taken image for better clarity and sharpness and some, like Camera MX offer unique features like "shoot the past," which is to capture a few frames automatically just prior to you actually taking a photograph. Popular apps in this subcategory include Camera+, CameraPro and DSLR Pro.

Other apps for enthusiasts include those that purport to mimic older cameras or develop a "film effect" on photographs taken. These include Hipstamatic, VSCO and Instagram. However, many of these filters also tend to give an impression of over-processing, so if you are aiming to present photographs to at least approximate what you saw physically (in terms of colour, saturation, sharpness), these filters should be used sparingly and selectively (some do indeed boost colours without over-saturating the image).

Secondly, apps for post-processing. With the increase in the processing power of smartphones and tablets, these apps offer a cheaper and easy-to-use interface that also approximates the basic functions of professional post-processing software like Adobe Photoshop. (In fact, Adobe themselves offer a tablet-centric app for photo-processing on a freemium model – the basic app is free whilst premium features come at a price.) The advantages to these apps are obvious – they provide basic features of more expensive software for a fraction of the cost with a user-friendly interface. Adobe themselves in recent years have admitted that Photoshop is becoming increasingly difficult to learn, owing to its numerous incarnations and iterations.

Such apps offer a myriad number of functions that are either increasing or improving with each version. These include the ability to straighten horizons, crop, and adjust for hues, brightness, shadows, contrast and highlights. More advanced features include the ability to transform and warp a photograph (to correct for distortions), select parts of a photograph to adjust (rather than the whole image), and heal spots on an image (for example, the removal of wrinkles or blemishes on an individual). Apple's default iOS software has a number of these features as well, but popular add-on apps include Snapseed (by Google), Camera+ (which combines a camera app and post-processing app), Darkroom, Photor and Afterlight.

Useful tip: Photography and app websites regularly review and rate photo-editing apps, constantly keeping an eye out for the newest and best to download and/or buy. Such websites also summarise these app features so that you know what you're downloading. Popular ones include iPhone Photography School,[1] Creative Bloq[2] and Wired.[3]

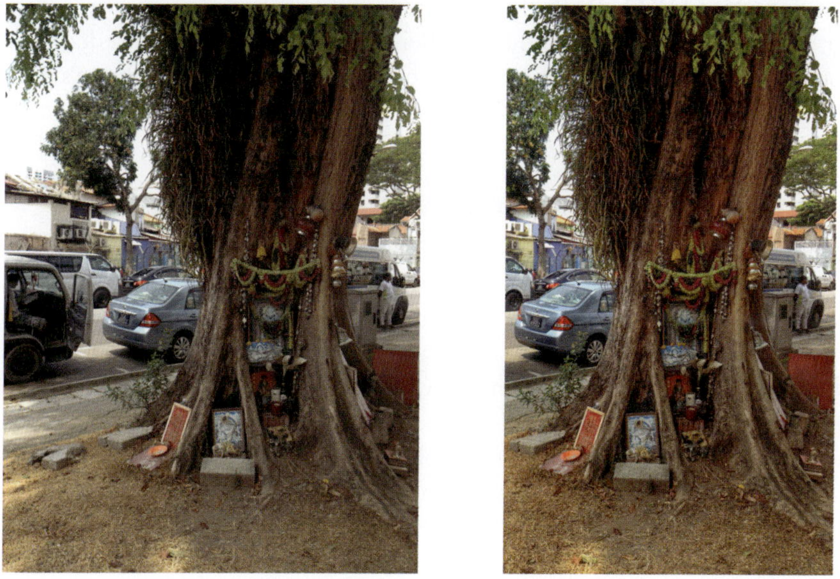

Figure 10.10a and b The photograph on the left is the original taken in 2013 in Little India, an historical ethnic quarter in central Singapore. The tree appears to be sacred to more than one faith, having both Hindu and Chinese religious altars and artefacts. However, I photographed the tree whilst it was shrouded in the shade, resulting in dull colours and a lack of detail. The photograph on the right has been edited in my iPhone's Snapseed app – it shows how I cropped out a distracting element on the left, and increased the contrast and saturation of the image using Snapseed's HDR filter. The result is a greater focus on the tree, along with a better description of its hybridic elements.

Physical add-ons

The popularity of smartphones has also led to entirely new industries set up to support these devices. Enthusiasts can now choose from a wide variety of accessories that complement and extend a smartphone's capabilities. One useful accessory is the add-on lens. Add-on lenses are small lenses that are attached to a smartphone and placed in front of the smartphone's lens. This usually allows the user to either magnify or widen the smartphone's focal length, which is typically between 27 and 30mm (the iPhone 6 has a 35mm equivalent focal length of 29mm, similar to a wide-angled lens). By using a (normally magnetic) mount, one can attach a telephoto lens, wide-angled lens or even a macro lens to a smartphone. This does allow for much more flexibility in shooting styles, but such lenses also tend to increase a photographer's field presence, and certainly give assessment signals to one's subjects that their photographs are being taken. Other manufacturers also take add-ons even further, transforming the smartphone into a control device rather than an imaging device, and moving the imaging work to a separate connected camera, as in the case of Sony and DXO. With these accessories, the smartphone's screen acts as the LCD viewfinder and controller, whilst the lens is superseded by a standalone camera and sensor, connected either through the phone's port or via Bluetooth.

Conclusion: the future of visual documentation

Will smartphones replace DSLRs? In the short term, this is highly unlikely, as the quality of smartphones, owing to their smaller sensors, cannot compare to that of a large sensor DSLR. DSLRs are also more versatile and can draw from a much wider range of high-quality lenses. As such, it is better to acquaint yourself with both a DSLR and a smartphone, so that you will be able to use either depending on your situation. As mentioned in Chapter 2, smartphones are best used when you prefer to remain as inconspicuous as possible, and also when you need to have a camera on you at all times. If your informants are comfortable with you photographing them, you might then wish to consider using at least a point-and-shoot, or a smaller micro four-thirds camera to work, giving you much more leeway in post-processing and printing.

Apart from smartphones, manufacturers are constantly innovating in portable imaging devices. One exciting development on the horizon (and already showing up on social media) is 360-degree still photographs and videos. From 2016, there appears to be an increasing number of devices that allow individuals to photograph all around them with a single shot, reducing the need to post-process a number of images together. This might have some implications for the future, and raise further theoretical questions about the value of photographic composition – i.e. if everything can be photographed simultaneously, do we then still need to worry about what and how we photograph? Of course, the answer for now is yes, but as cameras become more portable, smarter, feature-rich and ubiquitous, one can never be sure how much automation will replace the human eye.

Chapter exercises

Smartphone photography

As smartphone cameras grow in complexity and quality, we can expect to see many more visually intensive social science research projects being carried out using this technology, especially in situations where such cameras are ubiquitous amongst participants, for example in photovoice projects.

1 It is important to first understand in what conditions smartphones are best utilised. As of 2016, smartphones still perform at their best in bright daylight conditions, and are best displayed on smaller screens. That said, it is useful to push the limits of what your smartphone can do. Start by photographing different situations and subjects in different lighting conditions – indoors, outdoors, daytime and night. Export these images that you take to a computer and view them on a larger screen – errors and limitations are not so obvious on smaller smartphone screens – and watch for how the noise quality (see Chapters 3 and 11) of the image changes.

2 Next, practise steadying your smartphone through handling techniques. Try photographing a still scene (not a moving object) whilst holding your smartphone in the different positions covered in this chapter. At the same time, turn on the gridlines of your smartphone's camera and try to align one of these lines to a static horizon. You will notice the differentiating levels of difficulty experienced in trying to keep that line aligned with different handling positions.

3 Attempt to create a panorama of your neighbourhood. Panoramas are best created in static environments, i.e. when there are no moving elements like people walking

or vehicles moving. Stand in the midpoint where you want to create a panorama, noting important elements to your left and right. Pan slowly in either direction, and note how the level of distortion increases the closer an object is to you. Also try this technique *with* individuals moving across the screen, as this will also let you know how to compensate for unexpected moving objects – i.e. you will have to pause and ensure they are not captured by the camera when moving, else you will have multiple instances of the same individual in the photograph.

4 Many exposure and compositional techniques covered in this book are also applicable to smartphones, especially those in Chapters 4 to 9. Start off here by learning how to focus lock (Chapter 5) and spot-meter / exposure lock / exposure compensate (Chapter 9) your smartphone – this will differ depending on the smartphone make, model and operating system. Practise the same exercises in Chapters 5 and 9 for these techniques. Of particular importance is learning (by practising) where one should tap to take a spot-meter reading on a smartphone, and what elements of a photograph may sometimes need to be "sacrificed" (through over- or underexposure) to correctly expose your subject.

Notes

1 http://iphonephotographyschool.com/. Retrieved 30 Jan 2016.
2 http://www.creativebloq.com. Retrieved 30 Jan 2016.
3 http://www.wired.com. Retrieved 30 Jan 2016.

chapter 11

The visual researcher's workflow (basic digital darkroom techniques)

Key technical concepts

- Post-shoot procedures – transferring, saving and storing, backing-up
- Software: digital asset management / workflow vs photo-editing
- Basic editing concepts
    - Colour levels
    - Exposure, highlights and shadows
    - Clarity, vibrance and saturation
    - Noise reduction
    - Batch processing
- Ethics and further editing in Photoshop

Case study keywords: wedding rituals, aesthetic markers, urban Singapore, Chinese religion

Introduction

In this technical chapter, I will be discussing the various ways and means by which one manages, edits and disseminates photographs taken in the field. This chapter is not meant to be a definitive chapter on post-processing, as entire books can be dedicated to learning the software for the management, editing and storing of digital photographs. And there are such books, like that of Evening (2015) for Adobe Photoshop, Bradley (2015) for Adobe Lightroom and Fox and Smith (2016) for a general introduction to digital post-processing. Instead, I will be covering specific elements of digital post-processing that can enhance photographs typically taken in the field, without delving too deeply into the detailed technical aspects. In other words, this chapter should give you enough information to prepare and submit photographs for publication in academic journals and publications.

The digital darkroom has often been a source of study, debate, discussion and controversy for photographic work in both professional (Lowrey 2003; Russial and Wanta 1998) and academic circles. Buse (2010), for example, considered how the concept of instant-ness has changed from the time of the printed instant (Polaroid) to the digital instant, in some ways effectively eliminating certain steps within a darkroom (in-phone editing, as we saw in Chapter 10, further contributes to this phenomenon). With the advent of the digital darkroom, there has been an increasing level of attention attached to the issue of image manipulation, even from as early as the 1990s (Harris 1991; Shapter 1993). Others have considered the implications of image manipulation from various perspectives. One, fashion: Reaves et al. (2004) looked at audience reception to the use of digital manipulation of models. Two, newsroom structures: Greer and Gosen (2002) explored public attitudes towards the credibility of a manipulated image. And three, social science research: Jordan (2013) considered the very definition of image manipulation when it comes to protecting the identity of informants.

Image manipulation has thus resulted in debates about the ethics behind photography and whether or not photographs should tell all of the truth, tell some of the truth or simply imply some kind of truth (Ritchin 2010; Tagg 2009). Various academics have discussed this in the context of the social sciences (see Becker 2008; Harper 2012; Knowles and Sweetman 2004), asking how then we should read or use photographs in presenting our findings. As such, I will not be contributing to this discussion, except to agree with Knowles and Sweetman (2004) and others that photographs are like, and can be read as, texts with their own metaphors, rhymes and layers. Post-processing, or image manipulation in this chapter, does not seek to alter that text dramatically, that is, to change the story through the deliberate removal or addition of elements into an image (cropping is a grey area) or make other changes that most photojournalism codes of ethics find troublesome.

This chapter is centred on the idea of *workflow* (Alper 2013; Cobley and Haeffner 2009; Zavoina and Reichert 2000), i.e. the processes that one can go through when taking a photograph from a camera's memory card to a publication, whether that is print or online. In professional photography, workflow refers to the photographer's sequence of processing and managing images. Here, I offer a simplified workflow for the visual researcher.

Post-shoot procedures – a lesson in backing-up your photographs

The years 2012–2015 proved to be the most intensive for me in terms of fieldwork. Not only was I photographing Bukit Brown Cemetery almost every two weeks, I was also conducting my own research on the spiritual landscape of Singapore. These two projects alone generated more than 75,000 images, amounting to several terabytes of data. There were days when shoots happened consecutively, such that I had to develop a process of quickly emptying my memory cards once I had finished shooting in order to prepare for another shoot the next day. Such incidents also happened during the time I conducted fieldwork as a professional wedding photographer, in which some weddings would span two days over a weekend, or I might be asked to photograph two different weddings over two days.

These circumstances were further exacerbated when technology failed. In 2006, after a wedding shoot, I transferred one set of wedding photographs to my desktop's secondary hard drive, before formatting my memory card for a second, different shoot the next day. Two days after, that secondary hard drive crashed, and having overwritten the memory cards with the second wedding, I had no choice but to spend a large amount of money to partially retrieve the photographs using a specialist data retrieval company. The incident taught me that more important than equipment or good photographs is that photographs need to be preserved. In a digital environment this is both easier and more risky. Film negatives cannot be replicated as easily, yet at the same time are more durable in some ways, owing to their physical nature.

Copy, don't move

Digital files can be easily copied from one medium to another, and they should be. Thus the first thing to do after a shoot would be to first *copy* all images to a hard drive. I emphasise the term *copy* because some may choose to move files directly from memory card to hard drive, or use an importing software that will automatically delete the files on one's memory card. I recommend copying, then verifying that the files are readable on the hard drive, before doing anything to your memory card.

Create master folders

If you are using digital asset management software (DAM) like Adobe Lightroom (more on this later), this may not apply to you. However, many researchers often use the basic file systems in Windows or Mac to arrange their files. If you fall into the latter category, it is sometimes useful to create a master folder denoting the event and date of your shoot, then subfolders within that folder for different file types – one for Raw images, one for JPEGs, one for lower resolution web JPEGS and so on and so forth. This allows you to keep all relevant photographs within the same folder for future analysis and retention.

Make a backup, then make another backup

Once I have copied the files to my hard drive, I would then make a copy of these files on a separate hard drive, usually one that is external to my computer. My main working computer has two hard drives working in tandem in a Raid-0 configuration, i.e. data is written to both drives simultaneously in the event that one hard drive fails (which has happened twice in the last three years). This means that once I make a backup, I will have copies of these photographs on three different physical hard drives. Only when I have verified that the backup is readable as well, will I delete the files on my memory card in anticipation of my next shoot.

Towards the end of a project, I would also archive my photographs, both unedited and edited, onto an optical disc, as these tend to be more stable and less likely to deteriorate over the longer term. It is generally unadvisable to use flash media like memory cards to store data in the long term as studies have shown that memory cards will eventually lose that data. Optical media like CDs, DVDs and Blu-Rays are the most stable source for consumer-level use – although the quality of these discs tends to vary widely. The key principle to purchasing optical media is to first find brands that have a reputation for quality, like that of Sony, Verbatim and third-party manufacturers who use Taiyo-Yuden, and then to store the discs in a dry and cool location – preferably a dry-cabinet to prevent disc rot.

Useful tip: External hard drives are a quick and relatively inexpensive way of backing-up your data – don't rely on a single hard drive on a desktop or laptop because there is always a risk of drive failure. Looking at websites like Backblaze,[1] one can get an inkling of different brands' reliabilities.

Software: digital asset management vs photo-editing

Which software should you use when engaging in visual research to organize and edit your photographs? Firstly, it is important to understand the difference between digital asset management and simply photo-editing software. Digital asset management, or digital workflow software is designed to take you through the entire process of importing, organizing, basic editing and export/dissemination of photographs. Some of these, like Adobe Lightroom, create databases of photographs stored on your computer and arrange and organize them for easy referencing and finding. In Lightroom, photographs do not move physically (for example, some could be on your external hard drive and others could be in your desktop hard drive) but are instead catalogued within the programme. Digital Asset Management software is generally more useful under four conditions. One, you are the only individual accessing the photographs and do not need to collaborate with other photographers or editors, as these programmes tend to be standalone. Two, you have on hand a large amount of photographs and want some kind of cataloguing system (I prefer to do my own cataloguing and archiving). Three, you prefer an automated system of handling your files and basic editing needs. Finally, you tend to work only with photographs rather than a mixed set of media and files. Popular programmes include the aforementioned Adobe Lightroom, which is the industry-standard software for this category, Apple Aperture (which is being discontinued), ACDSee Ultimate 9 (but for Windows PCs only), and CaptureOne Pro (which is more for medium-format camera digital files).

In contrast to this, photo-editing software works by itself, or in tandem with Digital Asset Management programmes. If one uses Lightroom to engage in basic editing like exposure, contrast, tones and noise reduction (more on this later), then Photoshop would be employed for the finer details like dodging and burning, blurring or sharpening specific parts of a photograph, or more complex image manipulations like liquefying or extracting a subject from its background. In other words, neither programme completely replaces the other, and professionals often use both for different segments of their workflow. Adobe Photoshop remains the industry-standard for photo-editing, but for many enthusiast photographers, it is expensive and has many features that remain unused. With the introduction of Creative Cloud, Adobe has moved to a subscription-based business model, forcing users to pay monthly or annually for access to the latest versions of their premium software. As such, many alternatives to Photoshop are becoming more popular – these include Affinity Photo (but for Macs only), Corel Paintshop Pro, and, surprisingly, Microsoft Paint.net, which comes free with Windows.

Useful tip: Lightroom and Photoshop, the industry-standards, attempt to be as comprehensive as possible in offering features to professional photographers, but because of that are also priced at a premium. There are many programmes that specialize in doing specific tasks very well, like batch processing Raw files into JPEGs, or managing images, and are offered at a fraction of the price. See Coleman (2015) for a list of recommended titles. At the same time, remember that if you are a student or academic, you qualify for educational discounts on many manufacturers' titles.

Because of this plethora of titles, it would be impossible to explain how each one works and how to use them. Instead, I will be showing the basic principles of photo-editing and image workflow, which can be found in many titles. For the sake of convenience, I will be using references and screenshots from Adobe Photoshop, Adobe Bridge and Adobe Camera Raw, of which the latter two come free with Photoshop and are integrated into a workflow process. These are installed on a Windows 7 PC, and I manage my images manually in a Windows folder environment. Adobe Bridge is a programme that sits between all other Adobe programmes, acting as a digital asset browser, going beyond photographs to include PDFs and other proprietary file formats that Adobe programmes create, like InDesign and Illustrator files. Bridge allows users to browse and process all kinds of photograph formats using Photoshop and Adobe Camera Raw, the latter sitting within Photoshop as a basic Raw file editing tool.

Understanding histograms and tonal ranges

Photographers often argue that it is vital to understand how a histogram works in digital photography, particularly so that one understands how to ensure a photograph is "properly" and "correctly" exposed There is such a thing as technically correct – in that a photograph is not over- or underexposed, and that its tonal range is not clipped (which is when a region of the photograph has been exposed to the point that it becomes a solid white and details cannot be recovered). However, in this chapter I will be discussing how to achieve usable photographs that may or may not be absolutely perfect in terms of exposure.

A digital photograph comprises pixels – tiny digital dots that are themselves composed of a combination of the primary colours of red, green and blue. In a typical 8-bit photograph, each pixel can have a numerical brightness value that ranges from 0 (darkest) to 255 (brightest). A programme can scan a digital photograph and count the number of pixels at different levels, then visualise these distributions into a chart which is the histogram, where the y-axis denotes the number of pixels and the x-axis denotes the brightness level. The x-axis is further subdivided into three regions – Shadows (the darkest third of pixels), Midtones (the middle third of pixels) and Highlights (the brightest third of pixels). This last point is particularly important because it shows how photo-editing programmes change the way a photograph looks.

By inspecting a histogram, photographers will be able to tell what the tonal range of a photograph is (see Meyer 2013 for a comprehensive overview of histograms). A tonal range is the region in which the highest number of brightness values exists. Whilst there is no such thing as a perfect tonal range, more enthusiastic individuals may argue for the contrary, insisting on an even spread (this is not true). Photographs on either end of the histogram tend to give more dramatic results in terms of lighting – low key images have most of the tones in Shadows, and high-key images have most of their tones in Highlights. As you continue to photograph you may come to prefer one of the three over the others, or adapt your style to suit the subject.

Basic editing functions

In this section I will assume that you have captured your images in your camera's Raw format and will be doing basic editing using a Raw editor. (However, it is also possible to edit JPEGs and TIFFs in Adobe Camera Raw, by right-clicking on any image in Adobe Bridge and selecting "Open in Camera Raw").

Double-clicking on a Raw file in Adobe Bridge will launch Adobe Camera Raw in Photoshop, as shown in Figure 11.1. Users are typically greeted with a screen that looks like this – a preview of the selected photograph and a panel of sliders on the right, with additional tabs giving more editing options. For the purpose of this chapter I will be focussing

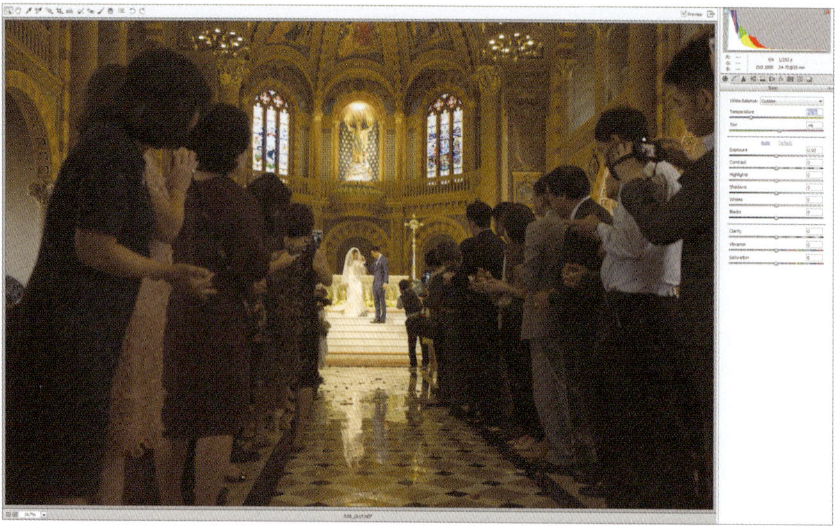

Figure 11.1 Adobe Camera Raw interface – original, unedited photograph of a Catholic Thai-Chinese wedding in Bangkok.

on the "Basic" tab. For a more comprehensive tutorial on all the features of Adobe Camera Raw and Photoshop, see Evening (2015).

The basic tab (Adobe Camera Raw, Adobe Lightroom)

White balance, temperature and tint

The basic tab contains sliders that affect the general feel of a photograph, and whilst some sliders (white/black) tend to be unique to Camera Raw, others can be found in other Raw editors. These sliders are relatively blunt instruments compared with the finer tools of Photoshop, and are meant for quick edits. However, for a visual researcher these controls tend to be sufficient for the majority of images taken as part of one's fieldwork. Starting at the top, we can see a drop-down box called *White Balance* and two sliders called *Temperature* and *Tint*. These three options affect the overall colour balance of a photograph. White balance can be defined as the degree to which white light is perceived by the camera in a photograph. Although our human eye is very good at defining coloured and white light, both film and digital sensors are not as accurate or nuanced. Hence in tricky lighting situations digital cameras can often produce images with a colour cast that the naked eye does not perceive. For example, Tungsten light is very warm, and produces photographs that have a yellow or orange tint. Fluorescent light also tends to give a greenish cast on film. Adjusting the white balance on a photograph (either in a camera or in post-processing) is one way of getting rid of these colour casts.

In Camera Raw you will start with white balance in "As Shot." This is how the camera has perceived the scene when the image was captured. Clicking on the drop-down box will reveal several options, including "Auto" (Camera Raw will attempt to rectify any colour casts) and scenarios that one may choose that best define under what conditions the photograph was taken, whether it was in daylight or under tungsten or fluorescent light. Such options are equivalent to the manual white balance options that can be found in many digital cameras and some smartphone photography apps. These modes will tell the camera how much to correct the colour cast of the photograph.

Alternatively, and this is my preference, I would edit the *Temperature* and *Tint* separately and manually, largely because some photographs are better off with a colour cast. In Figure 11.1, we see a Catholic ritual in Bangkok, the groom, Chuang, leading his bride, Pearpilai, down the altar's steps. Guests form a ready line in the pews with their smartphones, revealing the ritual as part media consumption, part spectacle and part performance, and demonstrating how much mobile devices now mediate our experience of ritual and visual consumption. My camera had done a good job of controlling colour casts, but in Figure 11.1 I have deliberately increased the *Temperature* of the photograph to show the effect of tungsten lighting and the presence of warm tones. In professional wedding photography this is optimum, as warm tones are inviting and give a feel of romance. But warm tones also cause photographs to lose detail because of their softer cast. Hence to correct this I drag the *Temperature* to the left to "cool" the photograph down, resulting in Figure 11.2.

The second slider, *Tint*, remains untouched as the photograph does not need correction in this aspect. However, there are times where photographs contain too much of either a green or a magenta cast, sometimes because of gas-emission lighting like fluorescent or neon lights, or sometimes because of other corrections made to other colours in the photograph. Some photographers would sometimes also deliberately introduce a magenta cast to give a certain feel of old-ness to a photograph (mimicking the cast of consumer photographic prints from the 1970s).

Exposure sliders – exposure, contrast, highlights, shadows, whites, blacks

The next set of sliders deal with the exposure of the photograph. These allow you to correct for exposure errors made in-camera, to recover

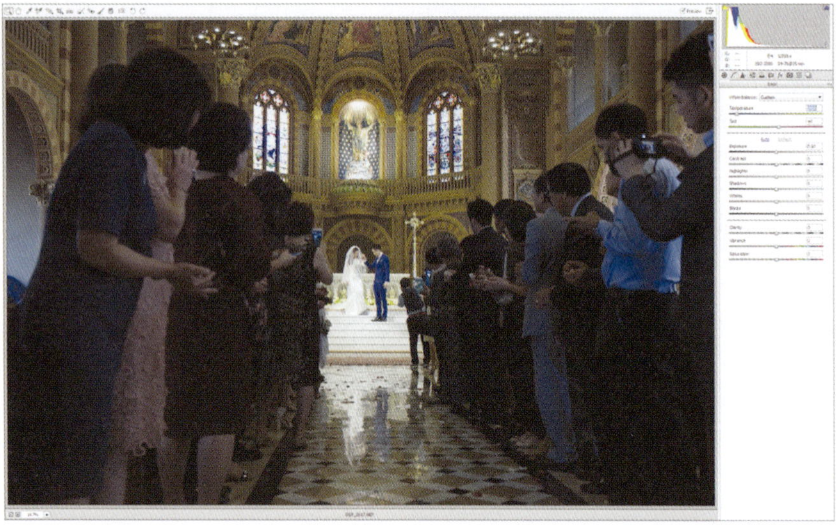

Figure 11.2 Temperature corrected to remove warm colour cast.

details or to add impact to a photograph. Just above the sliders you will notice two words, *Auto* and *Default*. Clicking on *Auto* will make Camera Raw attempt to correct the photo to the most even exposure possible, as seen in Figure 11.3.

In Figure 11.3 you will notice that to make this correction Camera Raw has automatically moved several of the sliders left and right, and this is a good example of what each slider does. The first slider, *Exposure*, controls the light levels of all parts of the photograph. In other words, increasing or decreasing the *Exposure* causes all parts of the photograph to become brighter or darker, regardless of their relative initial exposure. Using the exposure slider can brighten a dark area, but at the same time might cause a correctly exposed segment to become overexposed. Hence, it is better to use the *Exposure* slider sparingly and in tandem with the other sliders. The second slider, *Contrast*, controls the amount of *difference* between the brightest and darkest parts of a photograph. The more contrast, the greater the difference. In Figure 11.3, Camera Raw decided that there was too much of a difference between the individuals in shadow and the bridal couple in the spotlight, and attempted to equalise the difference by reducing the *Contrast* slider.

The next two sliders, *Highlights* and *Shadows*, are used to recover details that may be lost in photographs that have too much or too little exposure respectively (and is the reason that you should shoot in Raw formats rather than JPEGs, because in a Raw format much more information is

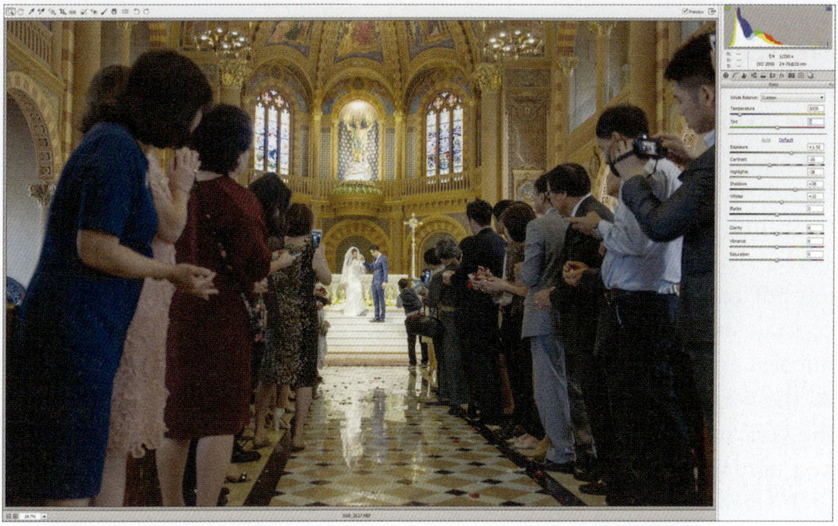

Figure 11.3 Full automatic correction.

retained, despite over/underexposure). Moving the highlights slider to the left/right reduces/increases the exposure of the photograph, which can bring back details lost to overexposure. In Figure 11.3, Camera Raw increased the overall exposure, which would have caused the windows, bridal gown and stairs to all become overexposed, resulting in a white-washed segment. So, in order to compensate for this increase in *Exposure*, Camera Raw also reduced the *Highlights*. Similarly, pushing the *Exposure* slider too far would also have caused the entire photograph to be over-exposed, but as Camera Raw wanted to show the detail of the rest of the participants, it also increased the *Shadows* slider, making the darkest areas brighter and allowing us to see the nuances of clothing worn and technology used.

At first glance, the *Whites* and *Blacks* sliders appear to do similar things to the *Highlights* and *Shadows* sliders. But as Kelby (2013) and Sheppard (2013) have pointed out, these sliders are meant to control for the absolute brightest and darkest *points* in a photograph, i.e. the white and black point. These help to improve contrast in a photograph by setting a true white point and a true black point. For practitioners seeking the highest image quality, these points are important. However, visual work in the field may or may not demand that level of precision – and this is often up to the personal preference of the researcher. That said, "murky" images that feel muddied tend to benefit from the use of these sliders.

Clarity, vibrance, saturation[2]

The last three sliders in the *Basic* panel deal with the "presence" of a photograph – its clarity, vibrance and saturation. *Clarity* adjusts for the mid-tone contrasts of an image (Carey 2010), i.e. the aspects of a photograph where the tones are between the brightest and darkest points. Moving the *Clarity* slider to the right, as I did in Figure 11.4, increases the contrast of these mid-tones and has an added advantage of making the photograph appear sharper without the use of a sharpening tool (which does the same job but has other side-effects). Moving the slider to the left reduces that contrast, but also has an effect of soft-focus, which is useful for weddings but also gives the appearance of lost detail. The *Clarity* slider can be pushed all the way to either side for dramatic effect, but one should be cautious of the very harsh lines between objects it can create at +100 value. Clarity is best used as fine-tuning tool in conjunction with the *Contrast* slider.

Vibrance and *Saturation* are related sliders that affect the depth of colour of a photograph by enhancing or reducing the presence of colour. Like *Contrast* and *Clarity*, *Saturation* and *Vibrance* work together, where one is a much broader tool that affects all tones in a photograph whilst the other focusses on the mid-tones. *Saturation* adjusts all colours, and is useful in situations where the camera was unable to capture the full spectrum of colours in a scene, perhaps because of available light, or when you want to give an over-saturated or de-saturated effect (the latter being very

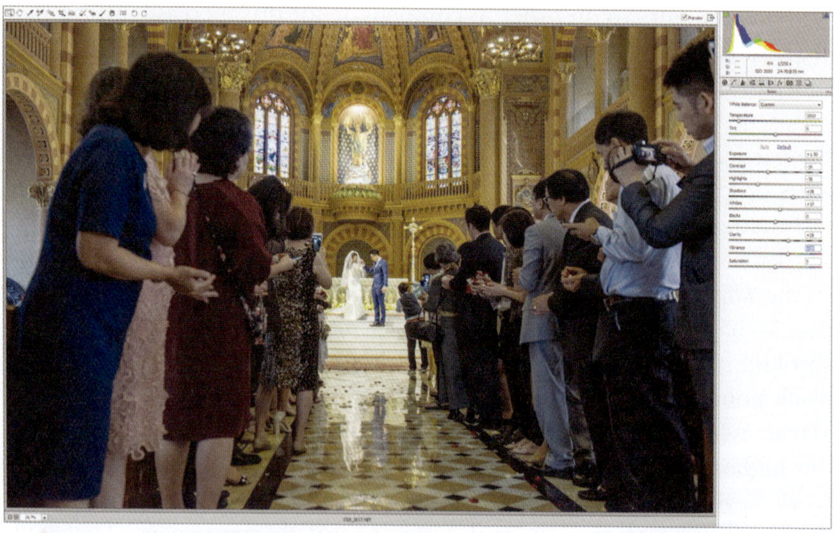

Figure 11.4 Clarity and vibrance: the photograph now appears sharper and more colourful, but retains the natural skin tones of the subjects.

popular in Instagram filters). If you want to convert a photograph to greyscale quickly and easily, you can pull the *Saturation* slider all the way to the left and this will remove all colour. Some photographers like to use *Saturation* exclusively to either create punchier colours, or give a more subdued, pensive feel to a photograph. However, one should note that in doing so *Saturation* also affects skin tones, and in photographs with individuals this can either give the effect of "orange skin" (over-saturated skin tones) or a deathly pale look (under-saturated skin tones). With the latter, this is sometimes compensated for by correspondingly increasing the *Temperature* of the photograph.

Unlike *Saturation, Vibrance* adjusts the colours of mid-tones in a photograph. This is a more subtle approach to enhancing or reducing colour, and as a photographer I use it in tandem with *Saturation* and *Temperature.* I would first desaturate the photograph gently to create a more pensive feel, then increase the *Vibrance* to bring some colours back but with more subtlety, then finish off with a warmer tone.

> Useful tip: Oftentimes, academic journals will print photographs in greyscale but keep colour photographs for electronic versions. Whilst it is common to simply submit colour photographs and let the printer convert them to greyscale, you may wish to submit a greyscale version yourself, to ensure that details are not lost in the conversion process. The simplest way to convert a photograph to greyscale is to reduce the *Saturation* of a photograph to 0. However, this is also a blunt instrument, and some photographers advocate a complicated procedure of removing a LAB channel, which helps to retain tonal variation.[3]

Cropping and straightening a photograph

In Chapter 4 I discussed the importance of ensuring level horizons in a photograph. Whilst many tutorials online give excellent training on straightening, it is important to at least mention it here (together with cropping). Cropping a photograph involves the removal of elements on the edges of a photograph in order to create more focus on what remains. For example, a photograph might be too wide, including irrelevant objects, or an individual might have accidentally stepped into the edge of your frame when you were taking a photograph. Cropping helps one recompose and increase impact, but should be done with care to avoid overcropping – i.e. removing too many elements.

To crop a photograph in Adobe Camera Raw or Photoshop, select the Crop Tool, which looks like two right-angles crossing over the other (in

Camera Raw, it is the sixth button on the top row from the left). Pressing and holding down on the button reveals the different crop dimensions – 2×3, 4×6, 16×9 and so on. If you are sending an image that will be printed out like a 35mm negative, it is better to choose a typical crop, like 2×3. However, if you want to be creative and are not restricted by paper sizes, you can choose *Normal* and this will allow an unconstrained crop.

In Figure 11.5, I have clicked on the crop tool and dragged the resulting cursor over the image while holding the left mouse button down. This creates a box over the image, which tells me which parts of the photograph are included or excluded. Once I double click anywhere on the included portion, Camera Raw will crop the image. However, unlike other programmes, the excluded sections are always retained (see non-destructive editing below) and pressing the crop tool button again reveals the excluded portions.

Useful tip: Straightening is effectively a rotated crop in Camera Raw. To straighten an image, pick the straighten tool to the right of the crop tool, and drag the resulting cursor in a line along the horizon that you want to straighten, this will result in a similar cropped image, but with a rotation to bring that horizon level.

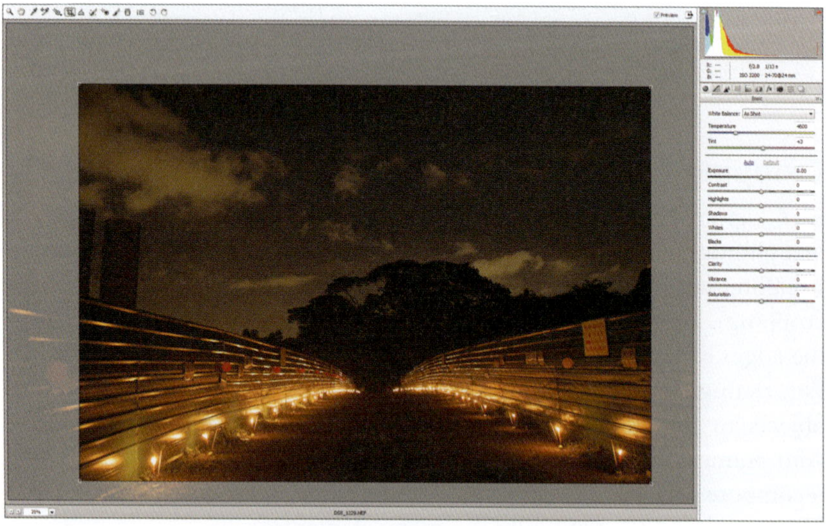

Figure 11.5 Landscape image of Bukit Brown Cemetery, roughly two months before the road was demolished.

Exporting a photograph

Once you are done editing an image, you can choose to export it in a format that is more easily disseminated than Raw (see *Batch Processing* later on in this chapter). On the bottom left hand corner of Camera Raw is a button that reads "Save Image." Clicking on it will give you options to save the photograph in a chosen format, compression and name. There are two typical formats that are submitted to academic publishers, TIFF and JPEG. TIFFs are uncompressed, lossless and higher in quality overall, but tend to be larger in size, making submission more difficult. JPEGs are compressed, lossy and lower in quality compared to a TIFF, but are very often more than sufficient for academic publication in a social science journal (medical and other scientific journals sometimes have higher image requirements). For TIFFs, it is recommended to save with an LZW compression (to reduce it in size without compromising quality too much). For JPEGs, saving at a quality level of 8 is usually sufficient, as anything beyond 10 simply increases file size.

Other important functions

Noise reduction

Whether you are photographing at night or indoors, you may eventually produce photographs that have a significant presence of digital noise, which in Chapter 3 I discussed as grainy, coloured specs that can distort the colour (Chroma Noise) and details (Luminance Noise) of a photograph. Noise has always been an issue at higher ISO levels, and camera manufacturers and software developers are continually working to reduce the presence of noise in digital images. These efforts range from better sensors in cameras, to better in-camera algorithms to reduce noise just after an image is created, to specialised software and processes to reduce noise. Specialist programmes like Noise Ninja have existed for more than 10 years, but you will also find noise reduction functions in most photo-processing programmes.

In Adobe Camera Raw, you will find that function by clicking on the *Detail* tab, which is the third tab that looks like two triangles. There are two categories on sliders in this tab – *Sharpening* and *Noise Reduction*. *Luminance* sliders reduce luminance, or greyscale noise, the kind of noise that makes photographs appear grainy and reduce detail, whilst *Colour* sliders reduce colour noise, which can be seen as coloured artefacts in a photograph.

The two main sliders, *Luminance* and *Colour*, control the amount of noise that is reduced in a photograph, whilst the other three sliders have specific functions. *Luminance Detail* controls the threshold of luminance noise – higher values preserve detail but leave more noise and lower levels remove more noise but lose more detail. *Luminance Contrast* controls the level of contrast preserved – the lower the level, the less contrast is preserved, but the smoother the image will appear. And *Colour Detail* controls threshold of colour noise – the higher the value, the more coloured edges are preserved. In Figures 11.6, 11.7a and 11.7b, I was photographing the activities of a temple in Bukit Brown Cemetery during the Hungry Ghost Festival. It was my first encounter with collective ritualistic action for the Hungry Ghost Festival, and I was carrying an older camera using a telephoto lens. The group allowed us to take some photographs, but not to talk to the *tang-ki,* and not to use any artificial light. Instead, we relied on available candlelight. As I was using a telephoto lens, I set the ISO to 5000 to ensure a high enough shutter speed, which allowed me to document the ritual, but also generated a significant amount of noise. At the same time, I wanted to retain as much detail of the ritual as possible, so, as is the case in Figure 11.7b, any attempts at noise reduction were conservative, with an intention to retain elements like the shape of the wisps of smoke coming from incense sticks. To reduce noise, zoom into a part of the photograph where noise is most apparent.

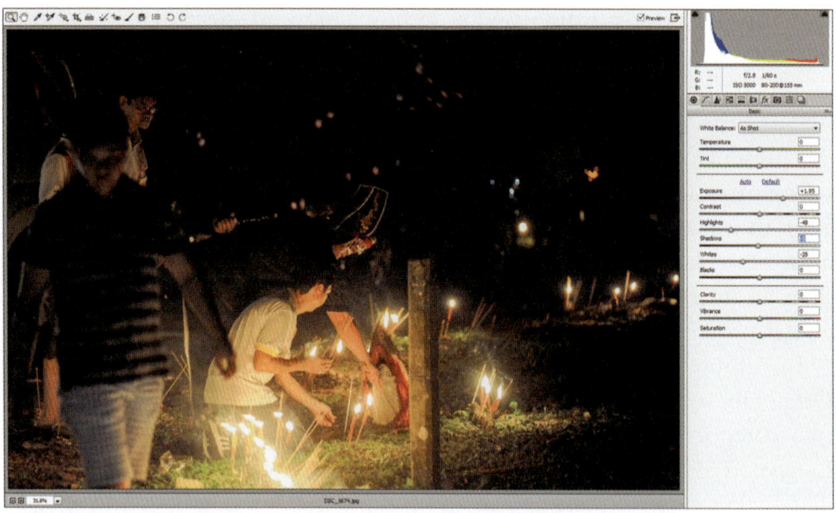

Figure 11.6 Shot at ISO-5000 on a Nikon D700, this photograph of a *tang-ki* guiding his followers in Bukit Brown Cemetery contains a heavy amount of noise, accentuated by an increase in exposure. The noise is even more apparent when zoomed in (Figures 11.7a and b).

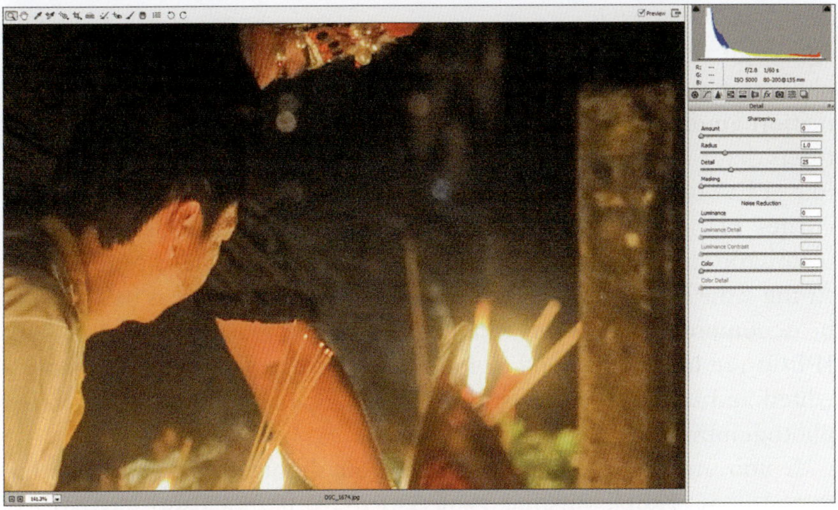

Figure 11.7a (above) and b (below) 11.7a shows a close-up of the photograph. Notice how there appears to be a fine texture over the photograph, both in the appearance of grain and in the discoloration. The grain is luminance noise and the colour is colour noise. By shifting the luminance and colour sliders to the right, I am able to reduce the discernible presence of noise and achieve a smoother and more accurate image (11.7b).

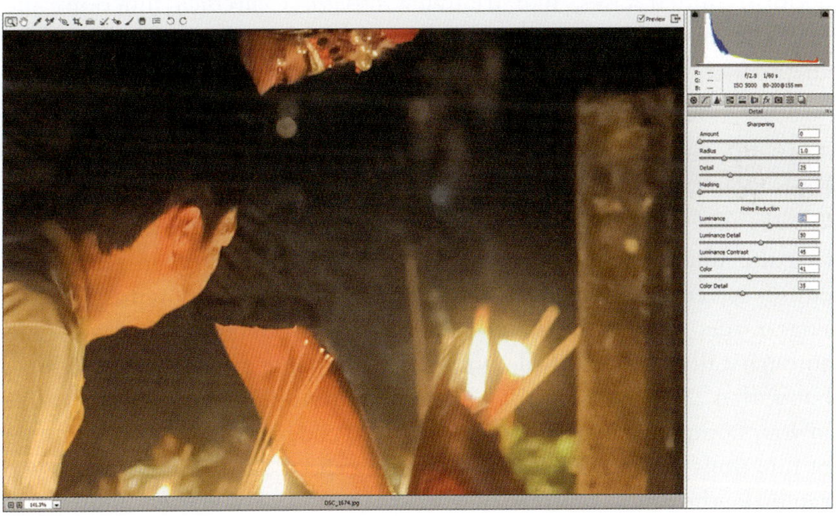

Figure 11.7b

Batch processing

Although the Raw format is an excellent way of storing and editing photographs, it is far less flexible when it comes to viewing and dissemination amongst a wider audience. Because different camera manufacturers have different Raw formats, there is no one universal format like JPEG or TIFF. Hence Canon cameras create .CR2 images, Nikon creates .NEF and Olympus creates .ORF. This often means that one has to download additional plug-ins in order to view these files on a computer. At the same time, Raw files tend to be larger than JPEGs as they tend to be uncompressed and contain more information than a JPEG. Although JPEGs are lossy (they tend to lose quality every time they are opened, edited and saved), they are still the most popular way of disseminating photographs online and offline.

If you are shooting in Raw (and you should be to make editing easier), it is possible in some cameras to save both a Raw and a JPEG file at the same time. Some photographers have also pointed out that certain cameras have better in-camera Raw processing than the software they are bundled with. However, at one point or another you will probably need to process a large number of files from one format to another, usually either from Raw to JPEG or Raw to TIFF. Rather than opening each file one by one, it is possible to batch process Raw files by running scripts within photo-processing software. Adobe Bridge makes use of Photoshop's *Image Processor* script,[4] but other programmes can perform similar tasks, like Irfanview's *Batch Conversion* function[5] and RawTherapee's Batch Processor,[6] both of which are free to download and use.

XMP sidecars, develop settings and multiple edits

Both Adobe Camera Raw and Adobe Lightroom employ what is known as non-destructive editing. This style of handling images means that the image itself is not edited, but rather information relating to edits is stored in a separate file. In Camera Raw this is known as a .XMP sidecar file. When you edit a photograph in Camera Raw, you will automatically create this file with the same name as the file you edited, but with a .XMP extension. This will be invisible in Bridge, but visible in your computer's file browser. The .XMP sidecar is useful for a number of functions. One, by deleting or moving the file to another folder, you can make the image revert back to its original, unedited state. This allows you to make multiple sets of edits to the same image without having to save multiple copies. Two, you are able to apply these sets of edits to multiple images, thereby saving you time from editing them one by one. This is particularly useful when you have many photographs of a similar subject, or with a similar colour temperature, that you want to correct *en masse*.

> Useful tip: To apply the same setting from one edited photograph to several in *Adobe Bridge*, first right-click on the edited photograph and choose Develop Settings → Copy Settings or press Alt + Ctrl + C. Then select the photographs you want the same settings applied to, right-click and choose Develop Settings → Paste Settings or press Alt + Ctrl + V. This will then open a dialogue box that lets you customise the exact settings you wish to apply (by default crops are omitted).

Conclusion: ethics and further editing in Photoshop

Adobe Camera Raw began around 2002 as a simple plug-in to bring Raw files into Photoshop (O'Neil Hughes 2015). But since then it has expanded to become an important workflow tool in its own right. It is important to stress that Camera Raw and other similar tools do not completely replace Photoshop. Rather, they exist to work in tandem with Photoshop's more detailed tools, like its brushes and filters. Conceiving this chapter was difficult because I was torn between showing a detailed how-to for Camera Raw, or trying to show how both Camera Raw and Photoshop worked. I chose the former because the latter would have meant a superficial treatment of some very convenient tools and concepts that are also available in Photoshop. Furthermore, many of the basic editing tools in Photoshop create some ethical dilemmas for visual researchers – for example, the use of the clone tool to deliberately remove elements in a photograph for better aesthetics, or a healing brush designed to make a subject look younger, slimmer or in some cases, larger. As such, this chapter has focussed on workflow and *enhancing* images that would have been taken while reading the preceding chapters. It has been deliberately basic and introductory, so as not to overwhelm the reader with functionality and concerns. In other words, this chapter also only skims the features available in Camera Raw (and Lightroom).

However, some editing tools in Photoshop are particularly useful for sensitive situations in which a participant or participants need to remain anonymous. In the final chapter, I will consider the technical things we can do in post-processing that allow us to stay ethical as visual researchers.

Chapter exercises

The digital darkroom

The digital darkroom is much more complicated than has been shown in this chapter, with editing options far exceeding the simple sliders I have covered. The exercises listed here thus only attend to the very basics of editing a photograph to correct for "mistakes" made while shooting, and to prepare photographs for publication. These exercises also assume you are running Adobe Photoshop and Adobe Bridge and Camera Raw.

1 First capture photographs that would benefit from heavy editing – these would typically be images that are over and underexposed by several stops, or are composed in a way that would require cropping and/or levelling (uneven horizons). Also create some photographs at a very high ISO rating so that you can practise with noise reduction techniques. If possible, make sure that these photographs are captured in your camera's Raw format, as opposed to JPEG or TIFF.

2 If you prefer to manually categorise your photographs (as opposed to using an automatic file system like Lightroom), start to think about designing how you name and store your files and folders. This could be by project, date, keyword, person, subject or event. Also, start immediately considering how to ensure your files are safely backed-up – this could be as simple as a secondary external hard drive, or increasingly popular cloud-storage solutions like Google Drive, Dropbox, iCloud or OneDrive.

3 Start by transferring your photographs to your computer to work with. Open this folder using Adobe Bridge, and select a photograph you want to edit by double-clicking on it (if Raw format) or right-clicking and selecting "Open in Camera Raw." This should typically launch Adobe Photoshop and the Camera Raw Plug-in. Based on this chapter, move the sliders in the "Basic" tab to the left and right to see how each slider affects your photograph. If you have also created photographs with a high

ISO rating, click on the detail tab to adjust for noise reduction as well.

4 After editing a photograph, try removing the *develop settings* from outside of Bridge. Go to your file browser and navigate to the folder holding your photographs. Search for the .XMP sidecar file that has been created: it should be the same filename as the photo you recently edited, but with a .XMP extension. Move this file to another folder, then return to Adobe Bridge to view the photograph. The develop settings should now be gone. To reintroduce these settings, simply move the .XMP file back into its original folder.

5 If you have taken several photographs in rapid succession, chances are you want to be able to apply similar editing settings to them. You can either use the technique covered in the chapter, or synchronise the develop settings. First select multiple files at the same time by holding the Ctrl key as you select each file. While still holding the Ctrl key down, open the file in Camera Raw – causing all files to open in a side-scrolling window. Edit one file as normal, then select all the other files in the side window and click on "Synchronise." This should copy and paste the develop settings to all other files.

6 Practise exporting your photographs for publication. In Camera Raw, there will be a "Save Image" button on the bottom-left of the screen. Click on this to launch a "Save Options" screen that will give you options to save the image in a variety of filenames and formats. For maximum quality, save your Raw image as a TIFF file, with LZW compression, although this will create a file that is relatively larger in size than other formats. If you wish to save for portability, select JPEG with a quality between 8 and 10. In most instances, saving above a quality of 10 will only result in larger file sizes with no discernible increase in quality.

Notes

1 https://www.backblaze.com/blog/hard-drive-reliability-stats-for-q2-2015/. Retrieved 31 Jan 2016.

2 A useful guide on these three sliders can be found here https://helpx.adobe.com/lightroom/how-to/lightroom-clarity-vibrance-saturation.html. Retrieved 4 Feb 2016.

3 http://www.photoshopessentials.com/photo-editing/black-and-white/lab-color/. Retrieved 4 Feb 2016.

4 https://helpx.adobe.com/photoshop/using/processing-batch-files.html. Retrieved 7 Feb 2016.

5 http://www.bleepingcomputer.com/forums/t/50519/simple-batch-conversion-using-irfanview/. Retrieved 7 Feb 2016.

6 http://rawtherapee.com/. Retrieved 7 Feb 2016.

chapter 12

Technical aspects for ethical visual research

Key technical concepts

- What kind of photo-ethics are we discussing?
- Gaining consent – field presence and your camera
- In-camera techniques for ethical visual research
    - Framing to conceal
    - Shutter speed to anonymise
- Post-processing blurs

Case Study Keywords: aesthetic markers, urban Singapore, Chinese religion

Introduction

The discussion of ethics is inevitable in visual methods, and many scholars have spent a lot of time and effort in working out the ethical implications of our visual practice in academia (Bates 2014; King and Levin 2006; Pink 2007; Wheeler 2002). Matthews (2005:200) defines ethics in photography as "*the principles of best practice* that any photographer should adopt in carrying out their practice." Professional image-makers have also weighed in on the debate, with numerous individuals and organisations establishing codes of conduct for photographers and/or photojournalists. For example, the Association of Photographers, based in the United Kingdom, publishes a guidebook, *Beyond the Lens* (Thomas and Ibbotson 2015), for ethical practices amongst photographers, providing a comprehensive overview of ethical concerns including copyright, accounting/book-keeping, contract law, professional standards, professional practice and digital and moving images. Likewise, the National Press Photographers Association in the United States also provides a condensed set of guidelines in the form of a code.[1]

In the field of Visual Sociology, both the International Visual Sociology Association (IVSA)[2] and the British Sociological Association's Visual Sociology Study Group[3] have placed online a statement of ethics for researchers who seek to use visual methods in their fieldwork. The Society for Visual Anthropology also hosts regular ethics forums, "aimed at nurturing debate and critical reflection on the ethical dimensions of anthropological imaging."[4] Other scholars have also considered the ethical implications of professional practice, such as Lester (2015), who applies philosophical approaches to practice, considering ethical frameworks like the golden rule and Kant's categorical imperative in photojournalism, and Kobre and Brill (2004), who provide interviews, case studies and video documentaries of how professional photojournalists work.

There is thus no shortage of texts, textbooks and arguments surrounding what could be and what might not be ethical in image-based research (Clark, Prosser and Wiles 2010; Jordan 2013; Langmann and Pick 2013), photographic practice (Van House 2011; Wheeler and Gleason 1995), smartphone photography (Blaagaard 2013) and post-processing (Buehl 2014; Greer and Gosen 2002; Lowrey 2003), both professional and academic. This chapter thus does not seek to add to the debate, but rather to introduce techniques that follow the best practices of *consent* and *confidentiality*. I will again, using case studies, consider the issues of field presence and the comportment of the photographer, and how, depending on one's relationship with one's informants, this can aid or reduce consent. Looking at the basic principles established in preceding chapters, I will show how the use of compositional methods, like framing, and camera techniques, like shutter speed and depth-of-field, help to anonymise individuals. Finally, I will take a quick look at Adobe Photoshop and specific tools that can help with post-processing and anonymisation.

Getting consent in the field

Some of the most difficult moments in getting consent in the field were when I was dealing with *casual* informants – individuals whom I had not met before, but stumbled upon in Bukit Brown Cemetery. It was impossible to arrange pre-meetings because we did not know who they were or when they would show up in the cemetery during the Hungry Ghost Festival. Thus it meant having to stake out the cemetery, waiting for vehicles to pause at *Tua Pek Gong's* shrine at the gates to offer prayers, before following discreetly in a car as they travelled into the cemetery. More often than not, these groups would prove to be incredibly friendly and receptive, and would be more than happy to allow me to photograph and record their rituals.

In these situations, we benefited from a number of factors. The first was a lack of what some term to be "research fatigue" (Clark 2008; Mandel 2003) amongst this section of the Singaporean demographic. Our presence as researchers / educationalists was both novel and respected, and our informants had not yet been interviewed, surveyed and observed to the point of irritation. As such, we were often welcomed as quiet and unobtrusive observers, which we achieved by maintaining a respectful distance using longer lenses at times. The second factor was the increasing acceptance of imaging devices in Chinese religious activities owing to the profusion of smartphone technologies in Singapore. If we were not there with cameras, it was very likely (and more often than not this was actually the case) that one of the devotees had a camera or smartphone. I would also occasionally encounter temple groups who appointed one follower as the official photographer, and he would often be carrying a full set of camera gear. The final factor was social – many saw it as an opportunity for publicity, others as a form of evangelism for their faith, especially because of declining figures in individuals who self-identified as "Taoists" according to state categories of faith, where these branches of Chinese religion belonged, with many middle-class Chinese moving towards megachurch faiths (Chong and Hui 2013). As such, our presence and documentation were sometimes interpreted as a legitimisation of their spiritual work.

Some occasions, however, proved to be more difficult. At the height of the Hungry Ghost Festival in 2012, I and my colleague Yew-Foong followed a group into the Paupers' section of Bukit Brown. Unlike other temple groups, these individuals were clad entirely in white, and from their speech, appeared to be of a different socio-economic status from most other devotees. Their pre-preparation rituals were different – instead of loose offerings, everything was carefully and meticulously arranged on a blue tarpaulin sheet, with a perimeter of white string bounding the food and drink. A small temporary altar had been set up with a deity whom I had never (and until now have not again) encountered. Their body language upon our arrival appeared to show a certain level of suspicion.

Our first step was to establish trust, and this meant not alarming them with our field presence. I was carrying my full complement of camera gear – two DSLRs, one on each shoulder with one mounted with a large

80–200mm f/2.8 lens. With my field outfit I looked either like a photojournalist or a very enthusiastic tourist. So I hung back in the shadows whilst Yew-Foong, carrying only a small prosumer camera, approached the group to ask for permission to observe and photograph them. After a number of minutes of somewhat tense negotiations, we were allowed to watch and observe but not photograph anything until the end of their rituals. Yew-Foong and I dutifully stood silently in front of the group for an hour while they chanted and prayed.

When the ritual was over, the leader of the group, with what looked like a faux leopard skin draped across his shoulder, approached us to explain the uniqueness of his rituals and the differences in beliefs that he and his followers held in contrast to other groups. He claimed to worship a pre-Buddhist holy man, and that the white string was meant to prevent the spirits from partaking of any offerings until they had been preached to by this group. All this while we still had not taken any photographs, instead choosing to listen and ask questions about his belief system. When he was satisfied that he had briefed us, we then asked if it were possible to document aspects of their rituals, to which he gave his permission, but only for artefacts and offerings, to which we agreed.

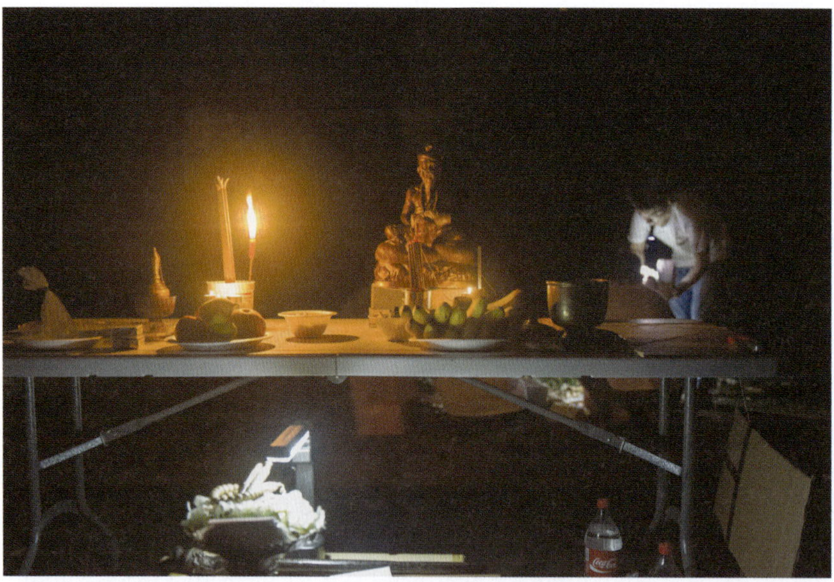

Figure 12.1 We were given permission to photograph only the group's artefacts and not their identities. In this image I used a wide aperture of f/2.8, no flash, and an ISO rating of 6400 to photograph in almost pitch darkness. The wide aperture had the added benefit of anonymising one devotee in the background through a shallow depth-of-field.

In other words, it took us about 1.5 hours of conversation and discussion before any visual work occurred. Even then, I deliberately restricted myself to a conservative, distanced style of photography in this situation, shooting with a wide angle to avoid zooming in on any one individual's identity, and avoiding the use of a flashgun, all so as to remain unobtrusive and to capture the sense of darkness in which this group worked.

Whilst the group had become accustomed to our presence, and especially my photography, by the end of this encounter, I still made it a point to maintain that trust that we had established. Instead of simply thanking and promising to send copies of the photographs to them, I also offered to show them the images I took on my camera through its LCD screen, to assure them that no one was identifiable. This is similar to building rapport with a Polaroid camera – some photojournalists often carry a Polaroid camera that can create instant prints in the field to give to informants, so as to establish a relationship necessary for photography. In doing this one is able to affirm one's ethical stance in the field. Simply offering to show the photographs can establish rapport – groups or individuals may decline, satisfied with the gesture as an act of sincerity.

Useful tip: The type and size of your camera can often influence consent, but this is also dependent on who your informants are. As mentioned in Chapter 2, individuals looking for publicity (perceived or otherwise) might judge your "professionality" by the brand and size of camera you carry (the larger the better). In other situations the reverse is often true.

In-camera techniques for ethical visual research

In the preceding chapters of this book I alluded to various ways in which we can maintain an ethical stance in visual research, through not just *what* we shoot, but *how* we shoot. In this section I will specifically look at what can be done at the point of taking a photograph to ensure anonymity for our informants. Anonymity has been an often-discussed point in visual work by social researchers – Sarah Pink (2012b) pointed to John Perivolaris's work on migrants and how the choice of photographing only their backs ensured that they could not be identified (see an example in Pink 2012b:132). But at the same time, other researchers like Wiles, Coffey, Robinson and Heath (2012) have found there to be ongoing tensions between an informant's desire to be seen and heard, and the ethical duties of a researcher to protect said informants. Likewise, Langmann and Pick (2013) consider the issue of dignity when collecting data through photographic means – arguing, like me, for the application of selective camera angles in ensuring a mutually beneficial ethical outcome for informant and researcher. Jordan (2013) has also proposed a set of guidelines where image manipulation, management and research integrity can be approached when doing social science research, and this is worth considering in tandem with the techniques I am presenting. Here, I wish to show how the use of frames, exposure and depth-of-field can creatively anonymise an individual without restricting the way they face our cameras.

Framing and blocking

Framing, as discussed in Chapter 5, is a way for us to centre the reader's attention onto a particular element in a photograph. However, frames and other objects can also be used to *block* and *obscure* identifying features through the careful positioning of subject and object. In my fieldwork in Teck Ghee Court (Chapter 4), I had adopted the role of wandering ghost, choosing to experience and sense my way around the spiritual place-making activities of residents and stallholders. During the *Chao Du* ritual, I found myself perched at the top of an amphitheatre whilst the burning of *kim zua* took place at the bottom, with celebrants throwing stacks of *kim zua* into two large wire-mesh burners. The wire-mesh burners were large steel structures supported by a thicker frame and wrapped in porous steel mesh, allowing me to see through the burner to the participants.

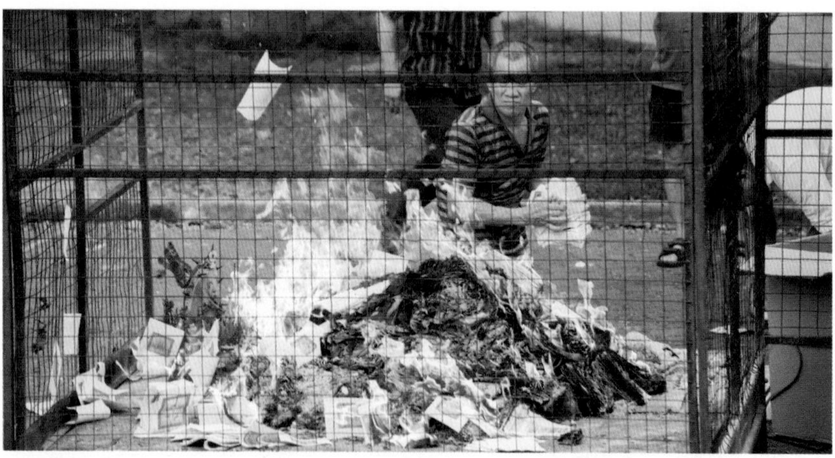

Figure 12.2 A celebrant tosses *kim zua* into a wire-mesh burner. By cropping the photograph I was able to anonymise the two other celebrants in the background, but careful timing and positioning allowed me to use the wire-mesh burner's frame to obscure this individual's identity without resorting to post-processing.

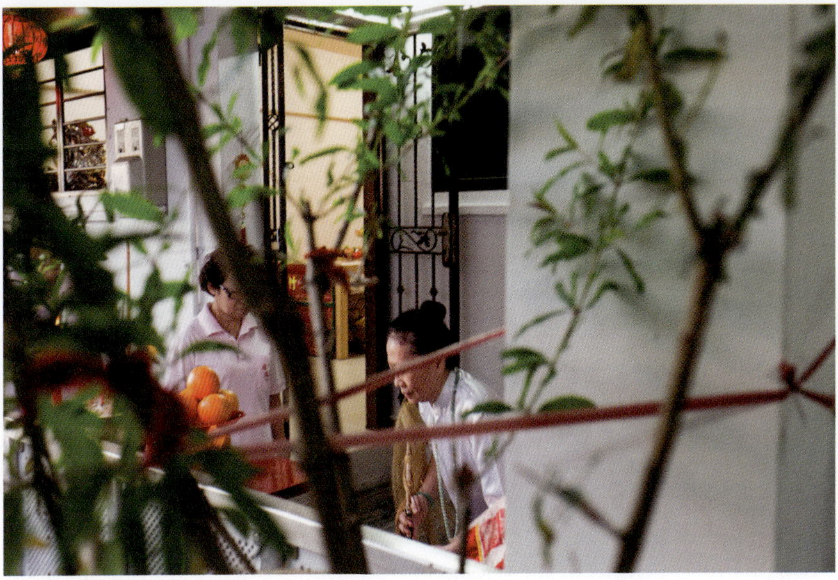

Figure 12.3 Madam Lim, a *tang-ki*, has her house temple positioned just outside a lift-landing in this block of flats, creating an L-shaped corridor where I could position myself. Here, I make use of a plant to block her assistant's identity on the left, while using the raffia string to anonymise the *tang-ki* herself as she knelt in ritual.

Almost any object or subject can be used in this way to either fully or partially obscure another subject that you want to anonymise. Instead of inanimate objects photographers have also used the hands and other body parts of other subjects in the photograph to help anonymise their subjects. In Figure 12.3 I had obtained Madam Lim's permission to photograph her and her followers, but had also chosen to include some anonymous photographs in the event I needed to keep her identity secret. In general, it is useful during your fieldwork to develop a range of photographs that show differing levels of identity of your subjects for different purposes, whether that is in academic or more commercial publications.

Exposure

Typical technical settings: spot-meter or exposure compensation

Rather than using an object to hide a subject's identity, it is also possible to make creative use of light, both ambient and artificial to achieve similar effects. This can be done through underexposure and the use of silhouettes, but often requires a strong source of light, usually directly facing the camera. In other words, for this to work you need to shoot *into* the light. Where you meter will determine if you underexpose or overexpose the photograph. This can be achieved either by spot-metering (see Chapter 9) off a particularly bright (to underexpose) portion of the frame, or by adjusting using the exposure compensation function on your camera to deduct about 1–2 stops of light (see Chapter 9 as well).

In Figure 12.4, I relied on the positioning of Taoist priests during a *Yew Keng* ritual (see Chapter 8) to get a semi-silhouette. I did not underexpose fully as I wanted to retain some detail of their vestments, but could easily achieve full anonymity by adjusting the *Shadow*, *Exposure* and *Blacks* sliders in Camera Raw (see Chapter 11).

In Figure 12.5, I took advantage of the presence of a very strong light source set up by the state in Bukit Brown Cemetery, as both a security and a safety measure. Ah Heng and his devotees were already making use of the angle of the light to set up their main altar (to the left of the photograph) which allowed them to work in the pitch-darkness of Bukit Brown. The spotlight in the background was so strong that I did not need to take a spot-meter reading. Rather, I let the brightness of the light determine the exposure using a standard multi-metering mode, which was correct for objects upon which the light fell, as can be seen in the altar for children in the midground of the photograph.

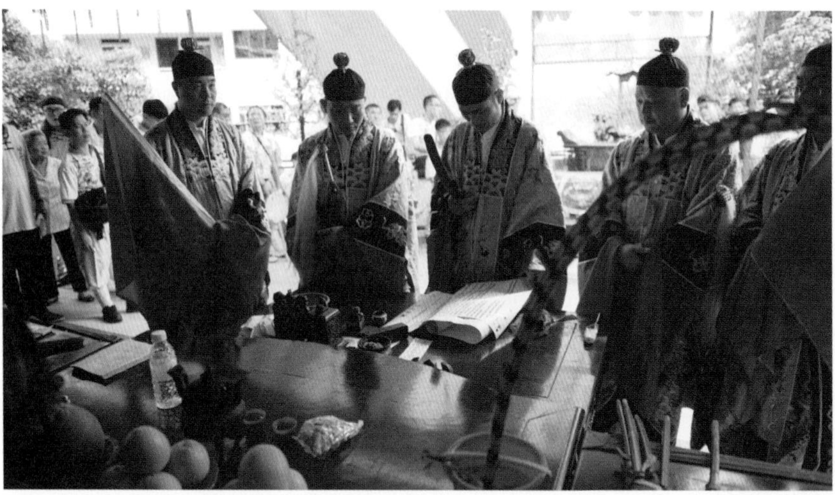

Figure 12.4 With their backs to the light and standing in the shade, these five Taoist priests from China, specially hired to perform rituals in Singapore, could be easily anonymised by taking a spot-meter reading off the brighter background behind them. The camera will expose correctly for the individuals at the back (notice the limitations of this technique if you have subjects where there is light falling onto them) and underexpose the subjects in the front.

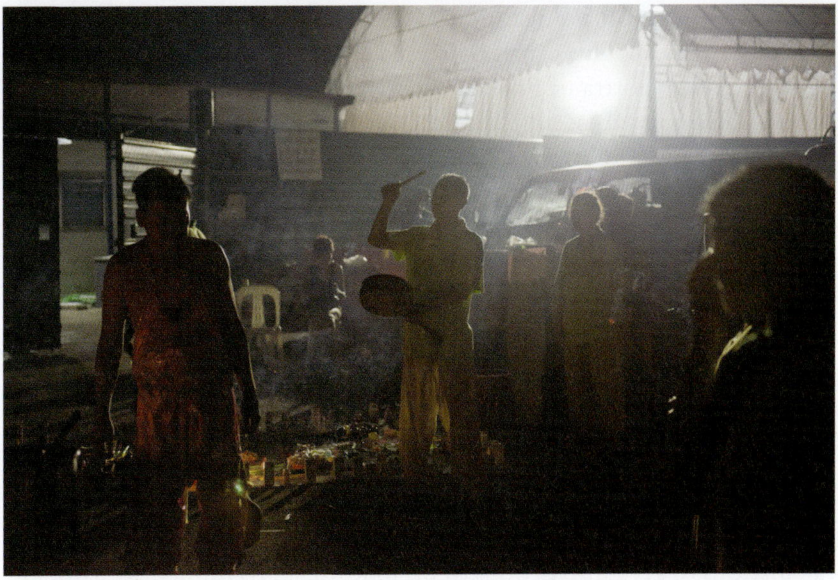

Figure 12.5 In Bukit Brown Cemetery, just before this section was landscaped, devotees from *Xuan Jiang Dian* gather to perform their last *Han Yi Jie* (寒衣节), or Winter Clothing Festival in this space. Led by Ah Heng (see Chapter 8), the group set up altars for both adult and child ghosts (see Chapter 4). The light behind is a spotlight cast by a tentage set up by the state in preparation for mass exhumations to clear the land.

Longer exposures can also mask identities in different ways. In Chapter 8 I discussed how slow shutter speeds, when combined with moving subjects, can blur the identities of informants enough that they remain anonymous. At the same time, significant overexposure in some lighting conditions can create interesting photographs in their own right while at the same time fulfilling their primary purpose of confidentiality. In another *Chao Du* ritual, this time at a beach in the north of Singapore, I had the opportunity to photograph a group of devotees as they made their way onto the beach to pray (Figure 12.6). As this was close to 10p.m., there was little ambient light, but with the use of a tripod borrowed from a videographer colleague, I was able to reduce my shutter speed to 10 secs – an impossible time if handheld.

Depth-of-field

Although this has been implicitly suggested throughout the book (especially Chapter 7), depth-of-field can also be a very useful tool in anonymising one's informants. In Chapter 7, I discussed how a shallow depth-of-field can make features on an object imperceptible due to the level of blurriness. This can also be used to your advantage when you are photographing portraits of individuals and you wish to keep certain facets anonymous. This may not necessarily be the individual themselves – it could be their followers / onlookers in the background, or a sensitive location that you do not want to so easily disclose. Either way, a shallow depth-of-field, best achieved with a longer telephoto lens and wide aperture, can create a selective view of your informants.

Oftentimes in my fieldwork with *tang-ki*, I find myself photographing them with a number of devotees in the background, attending to their every need. And although I have general consent to be present with a camera, this situation presents similar circumstances when I need to selectively anonymise individuals in the background. In Figure 12.7, I find myself kneeling in front of an altar table chaired by Nick, a young *tang-ki* preparing for his group's *Chao Du* ritual (the same group I photographed in Figure 12.6). Nick is already in a trance, and making divine calculations to give instructions to his followers. His immediate assistant,

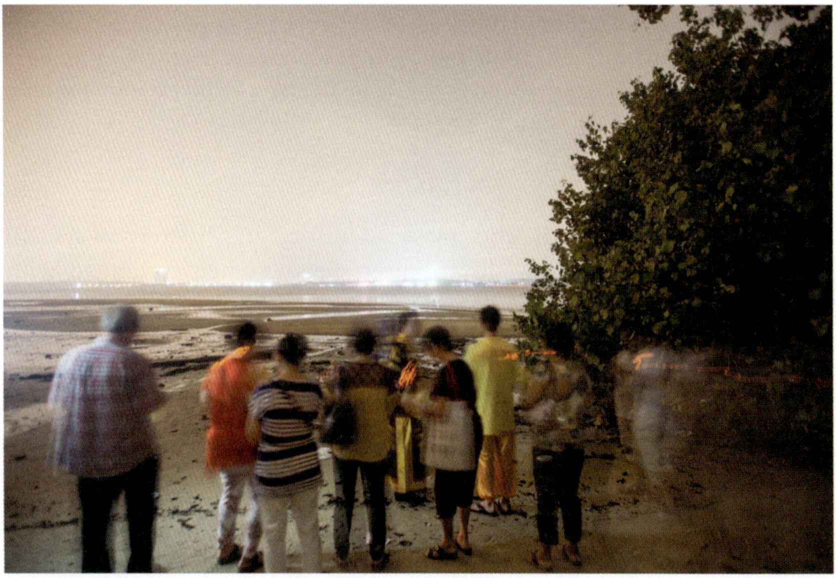

Figure 12.6 In a pitch-dark environment, a 10-second exposure on a tripod reveals the hidden spiritual landscapes of night rituals. Notice that the leaves on the tree to the right are still sharp, indicating a lack of camera shake (see Chapter 9), but the movement of my informants on the beach, along with the incense sticks that they hold, creates light trails and ghostly images. Such trails and leftover images from moving subjects are much harder to replicate in post-processing than in-camera.

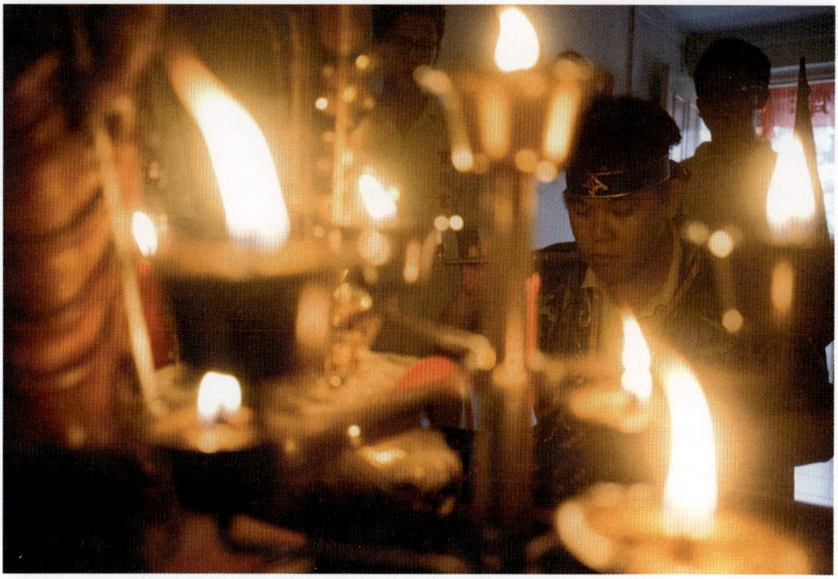

Figure 12.7 Nick is framed within the candle flames (see Chapter 5 on framing) while I both make use of framing to obscure one assistant on the left and anonymise the other through underexposure and depth-of-field.

Eugene, stands directly behind with his flag, an object said to hold Nick's soul whilst his deity inhabits his body. Eugene is backed by the evening light streaming into the HDB flat's door, and, using the brightness of the candles, I combined the use of silhouettes with a shallow depth-of-field, hiding many of his features. (A similar effect can also be seen in Figure 12.5 in the foreground, for one of Ah Heng's followers, and in Figure 12.1 in Bukit Brown Cemetery.)

Post-processing and anonymity

As noted by Pink (2007), other scholars like Lomax and Casey (1998) and Dant and Bowles (2003) have used post-processing software to blur and cover the faces of their informants. Likewise, in a visiting seminar to Singapore, Joanne Punzo Waghorne displayed photographs taken of Hindu devotees in HDB flats by obscuring their faces with a large white disc, superimposed using Photoshop. While this added a very interesting dimension to the photograph, it also changed the feel of the image from primarily ethnographic to artistic (not that the both cannot co-exist together). In this section I will examine technologies available in post-processing that can offer subtle ways of offering more anonymity to one's informants.

The use of blurring and anonymity in photography has evolved as technology has improved. Rather than pixelating or obscuring a face using drawn objects, post-processing software is increasingly able to mimic "natural" blurs caused by camera dynamics, i.e. depth-of-field. One such innovation is the use of an *Iris Blur* in Photoshop, where one is able to mimic a shallow depth-of-field whilst keeping parts of a photograph sharp, allowing researchers to blur not just individual faces but also entire environments if so desired. In Figure 12.8a, I am documenting the moment in which Jonathan, a young *tang-ki*, enters into a trance to be possessed by the spirit of *Tua Ya Pek*. Using a wide aperture, I was able to blur the foreground but not the background of his followers, as they were too close to him.

Figure 12.8b shows an application of the Photoshop filter *Iris Blur*, which creates a blur surrounding a radius set and customized by the user. The tool is a shortcut of sorts for other techniques in Photoshop, which could either involve using the *Lasso* tool to draw around the area one wants to keep sharp, *Inverting* the selection and then applying a *Gaussian Blur* filter (see Sponaugle 2013), or selecting the subject using the *Quick Select* tool, *Refining Edges* and using *Lens Blur.*[5] Whichever technique you choose to use, the potential results create natural blurs capable of anonymising subjects, backgrounds and foregrounds.

Other kinds of blurs are also offered in Photoshop that reduce the appearance that a photograph has been overly artificially altered. The problem with blurring an individual's face, especially if he or she is the primary subject in a photograph, is that the blur (or even pixelation) is often awkward and clumsy, sometimes giving the impression of censorship and obscurity, even if the intention was to protect. Although this technique results in photographs that look as if they have been erroneously taken, they do provide some degree of anonymity in exchange for technical excellence. This involves the use of the *Motion Blur* filter, which blurs a photograph in a way that looks as if the subject was moving when the photograph was taken. The downside as I mentioned is that it could also be interpreted as camera shake, but at the same time can mimic the use of slower shutter speeds.

Conclusion: ethical grey areas in post-processing

I wish to conclude this chapter by reflecting on the implications, but at the same time opportunities, of other popular post-processing tools, in particular tools that are able to "airbrush" objects and subjects out of a photograph. These include the *Healing Brush* tool, which intelligently copies pixels from areas around the brush to remove spots, wrinkles and other small artefacts; the *Clone Stamp* tool, which copies a pre-designated area of a photograph onto another area, and is often used to the same

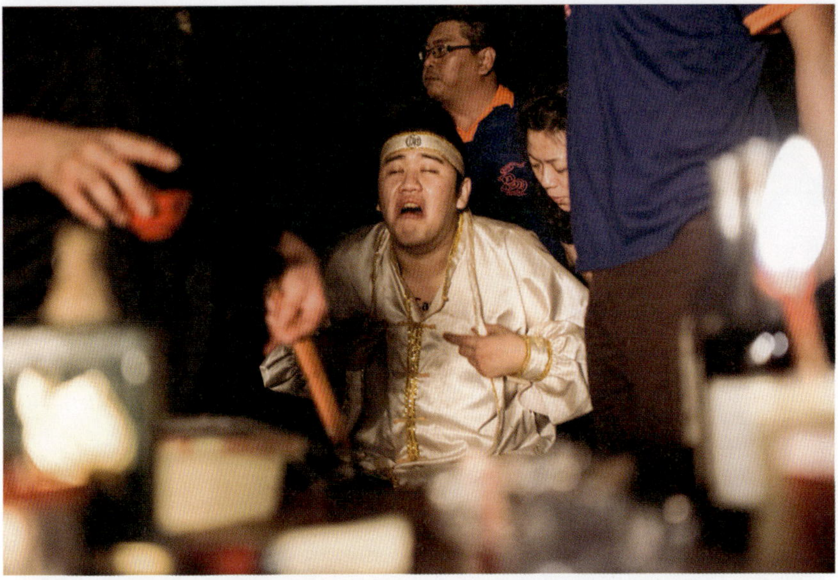

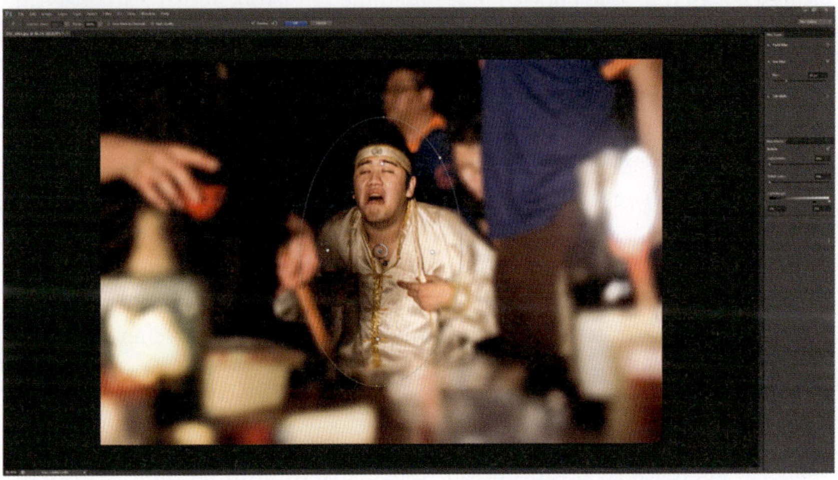

Figure 12.8a (above) and b (below) Jonathan entering into a trance. In circumstances involving many by-standers, it might become necessary to anonymise those who did not explicitly give their permission, while keeping your informant recognizable. The solution lies in post-processing.

effect as the *Healing Brush* tool; and most recently a *Content-Aware Fill* tool, which is similar to the *Clone Stamp* tool but is faster and used to remove larger artefacts in photographs. Such tools are not always used to deceive or alter a photograph's initial portrayal. For example, it is common for digital cameras to accumulate dust on their sensor, resulting in black

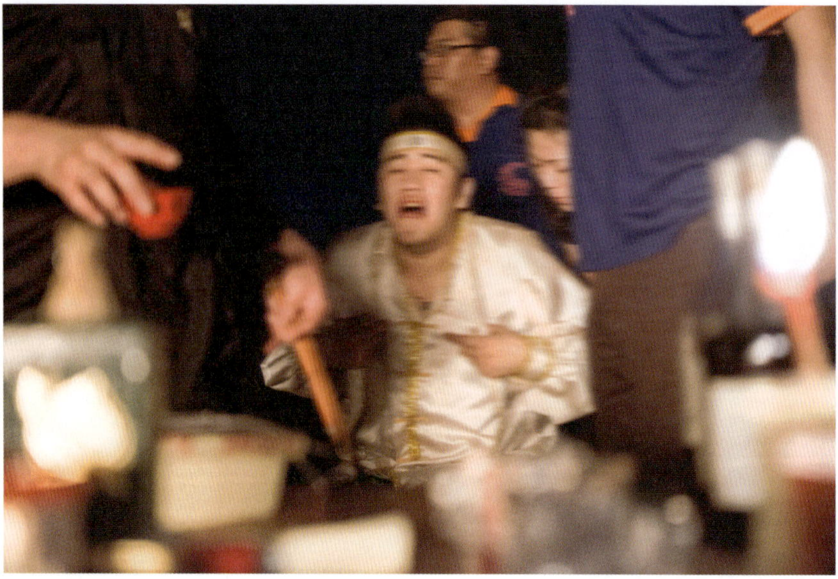

Figure 12.9 In the same photograph, I used the *Lasso* tool with a feather setting of 100 pixels to draw around Jonathan and his two followers in a wide arc. I then used the *Motion Blur* filter a number of times in small increments to gently blur out their identifying features. In order to create a more natural blur, I deliberately selected a much larger area than just Jonathan's face, including his body and hands. To learn how to use the *Lasso* tool, see Adobe's Help page.[6]

specks when photographing the sky or bright/light-coloured surfaces, particularly when using a narrower aperture – *Clone Stamp* tools can copy parts of a bright sky to effectively remove these spots. However, they also present a particular ethical grey area in the presentation of our photographs when we choose to use such tools to remove distracting elements or individuals – making the photograph more aesthetically pleasing, but prone to accusations of deception, especially in ethnographic work that demands a certain level of specificity (Pink 2007).

With the prevalence of digital photography and post-processing, photojournalists have often fallen foul of ethical guidelines that hold photographs to the strictest of "truths," in that nothing should be added or taken away from a photograph. For instance, Zhang (2016) noted how a photojournalist, Stepan Rudik, was disqualified from the World Press Photo competition for removing an inconsequential foot in the background from a photograph of a man having his hand taped. The photograph itself was also cropped very tightly and heavily post-processed, but the ethical issue came in the removal of a foot, probably through the use of a tool like Photoshop's *Clone Stamp*.

But such standards vary between different genres of photography. Editorial and commercial photography, especially weddings and fashion, make heavy use of such tools to achieve the particular vision of the photographer and/or art director. As a wedding photographer, I would sometimes be asked by clients to make them appear slimmer, have more hair, or adjust the shape of a trouser leg. One subject (whose photographs I never used in my research) demanded that a deliveryman be removed from the background because it spoiled the festivity of his photograph, but such demands are few and far between. When such things occur and clash with the ethical demands of my work as a visual researcher, I often maintain two sets of images (hence the importance of backing-up) which are edited and prepared for different purposes, applying different filters and tools for client and research.

As I mentioned at the start of this chapter, ethics are often debated, and will continue to be debated in the field of professional photography and visual research. With the technological landscape ever changing, and the introduction of algorithms and cameras designed to make every photograph a "good" photograph, we will find ourselves constantly challenged with deciding just *how* ethical we want to make our photographs.

Chapter exercise

Technical aspects to ethical visual research

As this chapter focusses on maintaining anonymity in photographs, the exercises will also concentrate on how you can make use of everyday environments to anonymise your subjects. There are two ways of going about practising. One is to conduct traditional street photography in public, deliberately trying to capture portraits of individuals without revealing their identity. The second is easier but offers less of a challenge – approach a friend or classmate and use them as a model to practise framing, cropping and blurring techniques in a controlled situation. This allows you to see how your camera would work when attempting to anonymise in the field.

1 The easiest way to anonymise an individual is of course to only photograph their back, but it is not always possible to position yourself at that angle. Thus more creative

ways need to be found. First begin by trying to use everyday foreground objects to obscure facial features. In the city these could be lamp posts, fences, doorways or other urban architectural features. Also try using non-physical options – for example, pools of shadow cast at eye level that can hide facial features. Finally, experiment with composition where only your subject's torso/ body is in the frame (i.e. crop it in a way that does not include parts of or the whole face).

2 Secondly, make use of exposure techniques to anonymise. Position yourself such that your subject is between you and a strong source of light. Either use a multi-metering mode, or take a spot-meter reading off the strong source of light so as to create a silhouette of, or an underexposed instance of, your subject. Ensure that your subject is facing you, so that you can practise with sufficient levels of underexposure to hide his or her facial features.

3 Make use of aperture and shutter speed to create instances of anonymity. Experiment first with depth-of-field. Position your subject in the foreground, with another object or subject in the background, and open your aperture as wide as possible (the lowest f-stop you can given your chosen focal length). Focus on the object in the background such that the shallow depth-of-field will cause your subject to become blurred. If possible, progressively shorten the distance between your foreground subject and background object as you photograph to see how the blur is affected.

4 With shutter speeds, use a tripod for practice and set your camera to shutter-priority with a low ISO rating. Get your subject to move or make movements or gestures. Photograph these movements at progressively lower shutter speeds – 1/100s, 1/60s, 1/30s, 1/15s, 1/4s and so on and so forth. Pay attention to how slower shutter speeds can blur movements, but also how they can affect overall exposure, depending on lighting conditions. This exercise is best practised indoors where you can control the amount of light in a room.

5 Finally, experiment with post-processing in Photoshop to blur your subject's face. Apart from using the Iris Blur tool

covered in this chapter, you can also use a Lasso Tool and Gaussian Blur for a more customised (non-elliptical) shape of blur. Open a photograph of your subject (TIFF or JPEG) in Photoshop and select the Lasso tool. Set the Feather to 100px and then roughly draw around your subject's face. Whilst the face is selected, go to Filter → Blur → Gaussian Blur, and use the sliders to preview the amount by which the selected area is blurred. Click OK to complete the application of the filter.

Notes

1 https://nppa.org/code_of_ethics. Retrieved 8 Feb 2016.
2 http://visualsociology.org/about/ethics-and-guidelines.html. Retrieved 7 Feb 2016.
3 http://www.visualsociology.org.uk/about/ethical_statement.php. Retrieved 7 Feb 2016.
4 http://societyforvisualanthropology.org/about/ethics/. Retrieved 8 Feb 2016.
5 https://www.youtube.com/watch?v=iTYamYkDn04. Retrieved 12 Feb 2016.
6 https://helpx.adobe.com/photoshop/using/selecting-lasso-tools.html. Retrieved 12 Feb 2016.

chapter 13

Final remarks and an annotated photo essay

Introduction

To what extent then is "technically good" photography important or useful to us in social science research? This is an odd question to ask, especially when throughout the book I have advocated for a degree of technical prowess in conducting photographic research. As Bush (2016) noted of the winning photograph of the World Press Photo award – much technical coherence was sacrificed for the sake of the image. Taken by Warren Richardson (2015), the photograph shows an exhausted refugee passing a child through a mesh of razor wire. Shot at 3am in the morning, with no flashgun for fear of being discovered by patrolling police, Richardson had no choice but to shoot in this way – the image is noisy (ISO 6400) and blurry (camera shake and/or motion blur of 1/5 sec shutter speed on a focal length of 24mm), appearing to undermine the very things this book purports to call important. But this is also proof of technical ability – of being able to see photographically. The photograph is technically both strong and weak – it betrays the difficulty of the circumstances in which the subject was photographed but is also testament to the ability of the photographer to create and visually narrate in such a situation. It also shows how *studium* (Barthes 1981) works – to inform, signify and surprise all at the same time. For those of us who feel that pinprick of emotion when seeing the image, perhaps it is because we can relate to the sacrifices that parents make for their children; we could also experience what Barthes calls the *punctum* of a photograph.

In the age of what Bush (2016) calls the "superabundance of photography" and the ubiquity of digital photography (Ritchin 2010), researchers must find ways in which their photographs work harder than to just depict and describe. They must expose different *kinds* of truth. Again, scholars and writers have long argued, and continue to argue, about how truth is shown and understood in photographs, and it is not in the purview of this book to consider these arguments from any particular disciplinary angle. To understand such debates, it would be useful to read Barthes (1981), Benjamin (2008), Berger (2008), Ritchin (2010) and Sontag (1977, 2013), and for a good summary of critical photographic theory, see la Grange (2005) and Bate (2016). Instead, I want to close this book by musing on the ways of truth-telling in photographic practice, and how we want to show this work, regardless of the disciplines that we work in.

As Franklin (2016) argued in a well-written article on truth in documentary photography and photojournalism, the latter is a subdiscipline of the former. Photojournalism has its own code of ethics, its own adherence to the truth (Newton 1998; Wheeler and Gleason 1995), and its own unique practices (Yaschur 2012), and in recent years has increasingly stuck to that idea of absolute truth – punishing photographers found to have staged or manipulated their photographs in the slightest way. Documentary photography, however, appears to have more leeway in staging and manipulation. Franklin (2016) pointed out how portraiture photography remains as one category in the World Press Photo awards to be exempted from staging rules, since, quoting Paolo Verzone, "all the portraits in the history of mankind have been staged." I propose that one of the reasons for this is the expectation of and the ability to provide transparency through captions and preambles, something that photojournalists are not always able to do.

Visual researchers, I would argue, have that same kind, if not more, of a luxury in transparency when we use photographs in our work. Our articles, books, book chapters and other kinds of writing are longer in form (Mabe 2010; Steele 2014), giving us the time to explain clearly how our photographs are meant to work within the wider body of a study. As such, it is possible for us to use photographs in almost any way we can imagine, as long as we locate them within our own practice, and are clear about our intentions. In these situations theory is as important as practice, because theory helps us to contextualise our images for the reader. Truth, in other words, is not simply what we see and show in a photograph, it is also how we see and show what is in a photograph, and how we create a narrative around our images (Tagg 1988), especially in the digital era

(Mitchell 1994). As Tagg (2009) also points out, what we see as the truth in a photograph is also framed by its circumstances and distribution (and who distributes it, for which see also Taylor 1998:52). For example, how do we show and share a sociological imagination (Mills 2000) through photography? Is it simply the interaction of human beings, or can we express the wider social themes we identify through our observations? Or how do we photograph the *sensations* and *sensory experiences* of a particular space – the ways in which people have made a space a place? The answer lies partly in what we photograph, but also in how we photograph. To this extent, I have tried in several conclusions in chapters in this book to encourage you to experiment with different ways of telling – to go beyond documentation and explore expression (Edwards 1997).

Throughout this book I have used examples from all aspects of my fieldwork, such that no single chapter was able to show a sustained visual investigation into any social phenomenon that I have been investigating. As such, I would like to close this book on photography *with* photography – and present a visual essay of the Nine Emperor Gods Festival, an annual celebration popular amongst adherents of Chinese religious practices in South-East Asia (Cheu 1993; DeBernardi 2004). Known also as the annual Vegetarian Festival in Phuket (for the vegetarian fast that devotees undergo prior to the festival), the Nine Emperor Gods Festival is said to commemorate the deity *Dou Mu*, the mother of the Northern Dipper constellation, and her sons, sometimes referred to as the Nine Dipper Lords. Held on the Ninth day of the Ninth Lunar Month (usually September), the festival lasts for three days, during which devotees engage in performative place-making around the island, beginning and ending their journey at the sea, where they invite and send off some or all of the nine Emperor Gods.

In 2014, as part of a wider project to document an area in North-East Singapore known as Punggol, I set out to photograph the Nine Emperor Gods Festival as celebrated by *Hougang Dou Mu Gong* (Temple). This was said to be the oldest temple dedicated to *Dou Mu* and her nine sons, established in 1902 through an amulet imported from Penang in neighbouring Malaysia. The temple itself is now surrounded by houses, shopping malls, viaducts, roads and religious institutions, and thus in order to carry out the rituals for the festival devotees make their way make their way to Pulau (Island) Punggol Timor, a small island adjacent to Punggol. The island itself is completely industrial, with no residential buildings existing; its landscape is one of yard cranes, temporary housing for migrant labour, cement mixers and trucks. But for the three days of the festival the island is transformed into a sacred place, complemented by a boisterous parade of floats, lion and dragon dances, spectators and fireworks. I followed the devotees at strategic points of the festival, photographing to tell two narratives. One, the hierophanic (Eliade 1961) act of sacred place-making through structure and aesthetic markers (Heng 2016; Knowles 2003), and, two, the story of religion and their performative identifications in Punggol. The photographs I have chosen are also meant to reflect as many as possible of the principles identified in this book – and I will be specifying them in the captions of each image.

Through this book, I hope that you the reader will also start (or continue) on your journey of excellent photographic grammar. But no book, website, online-learning course or programme can on its own make you a good photographer and a good visual researcher. Instead, constant practice, reviewing your images and peer support are the keys to better, more meaningful photographs.

Annotated photo essay: when gods come to Punggol

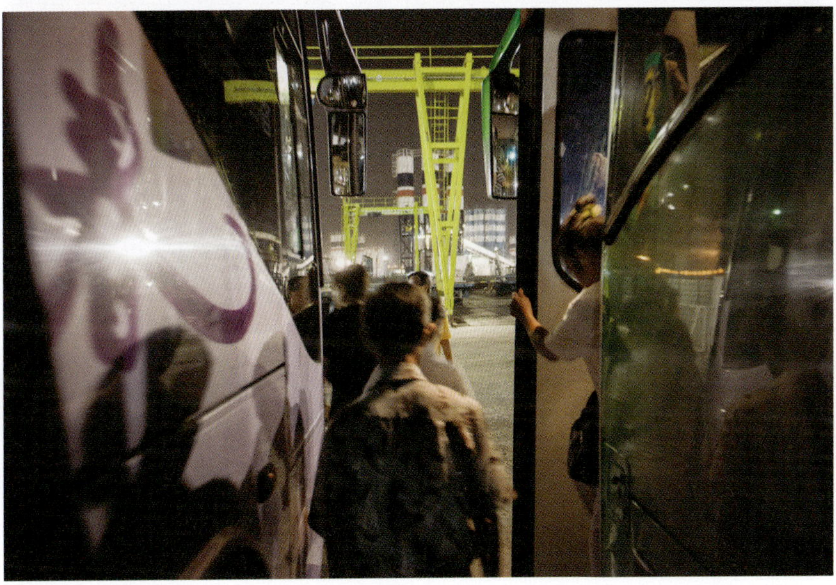

Figure 13.1 Devotees from Hougang *Dou Mu Gong* arrive on buses at Pulau Punggol Timor.

Technical details	*Techniques used*	*Post-processing*
Aperture f/2.8 Shutter speed: 1/15 sec ISO: 3200 Metering: Matrix Focal length: 24mm	Framing (Ch 5) Rule-of-thirds (Ch 5) Juxtaposition (Ch 4) Faceless portraits (Ch 8)	• Crop / straighten • Decreased shadows and highlights (-) • Decreased saturation (-)

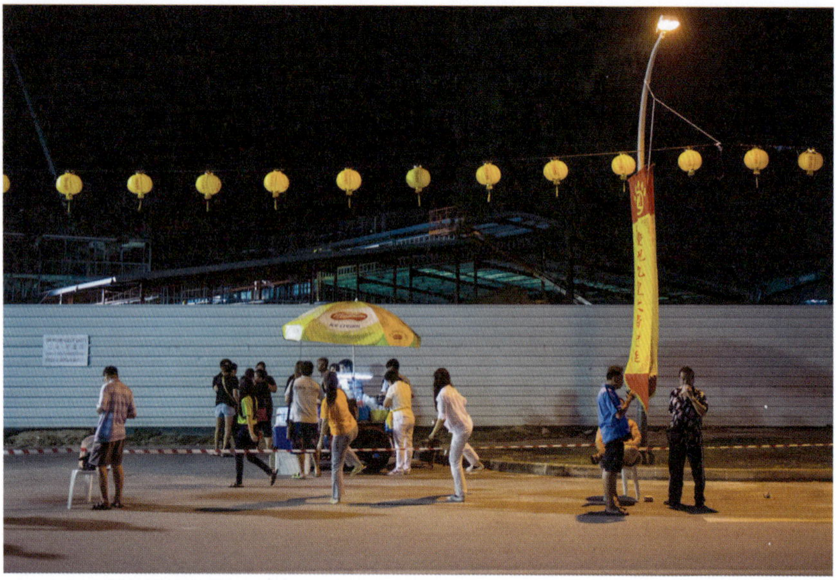

Figure 13.2 "Official barriers" are no impediment to ice-cream.

Technical details	*Techniques used*	*Post-processing*
Aperture f/2.8 Shutter speed: 1/320 sec ISO: 3200 Metering: Spot Exp comp: -0.3 Focal length: 35mm	Rule-of-thirds (Ch 5) Juxtaposition (Ch 4) Depth-of-field (Ch 7) Structure (Ch 4)	• 30% crop / straighten • Increased shadows (+) • Increased clarity, vibrance, saturation (+)

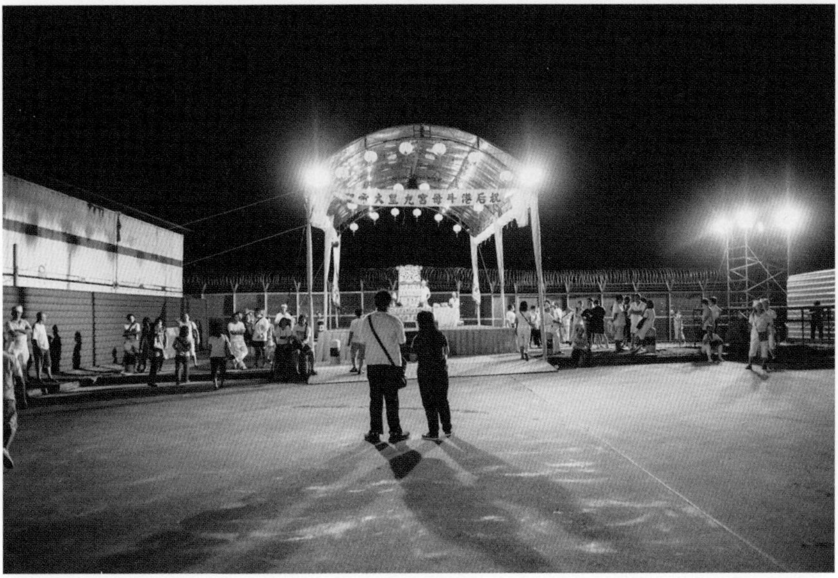

Figure 13.3 A couple ponders preparations at the main ritual stage.

Technical details	***Techniques used***	***Post-Processing***
Aperture f/2.8 Shutter speed: 1/1250 sec ISO: 3200 Metering: Spot Exp comp: 0 Focal length: 24mm	Low vantage point (Ch 4) Spot-metering (Ch 9) Environmental portrait (Ch 8)	• Straighten • Increased contrast (+) • Decreased blacks (-) • Desaturate (-)

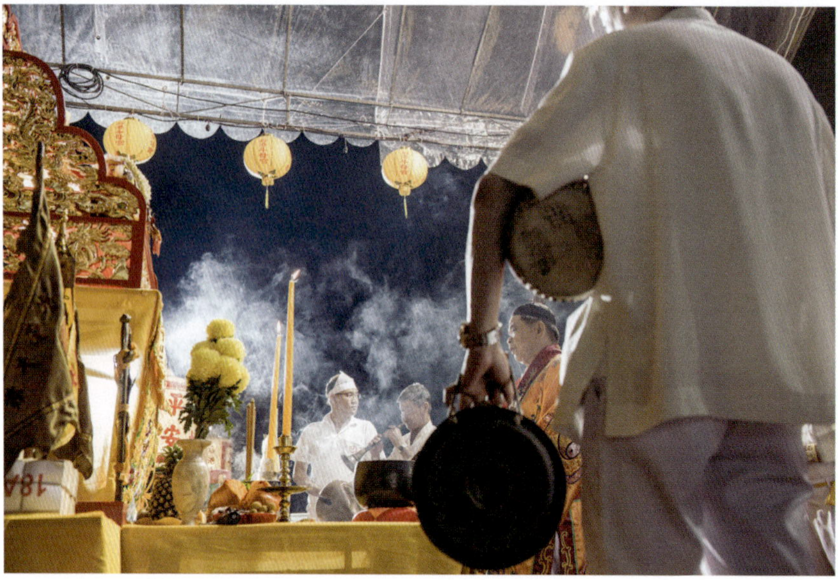

Figure 13.4 With the arrival of the main contingent of devotees, a Taoist priest calls upon the nine Emperor Gods.

Technical details	***Techniques used***	***Post-processing***
Aperture f/4 Shutter speed: 1/100 sec ISO: 1250 Metering: Matrix Exp comp: -0.3 Focal length: 40mm	Framing (Ch 5) Low vantage point (Ch 4) Environmental portrait (Ch 8) Focus lock (Ch 5)	• Decreased whites (-) • Increased clarity (+) • Decreased saturation (-)

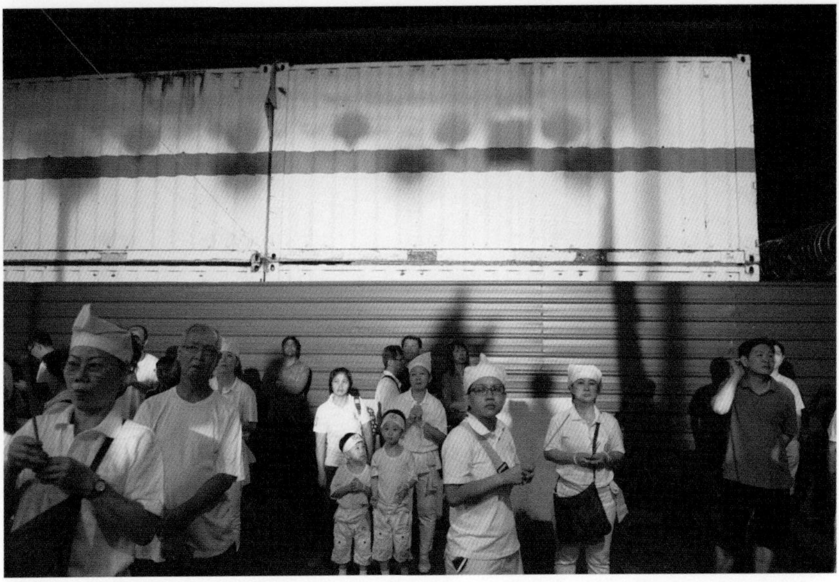

Figure 13.5 Devotees wait for the Gods to arrive.

Technical details	***Techniques used***	***Post-processing***
Aperture f/4 Shutter speed: 1/200 sec ISO: 1250 Metering: Matrix Exp comp: +0.3 Focal length: 24mm	Structure (Ch 4) Focus lock (Ch 5) Exposure lock (Ch 9) Exposure comp (Ch 9)	• Decreased shadow (-) • Desaturation (-)

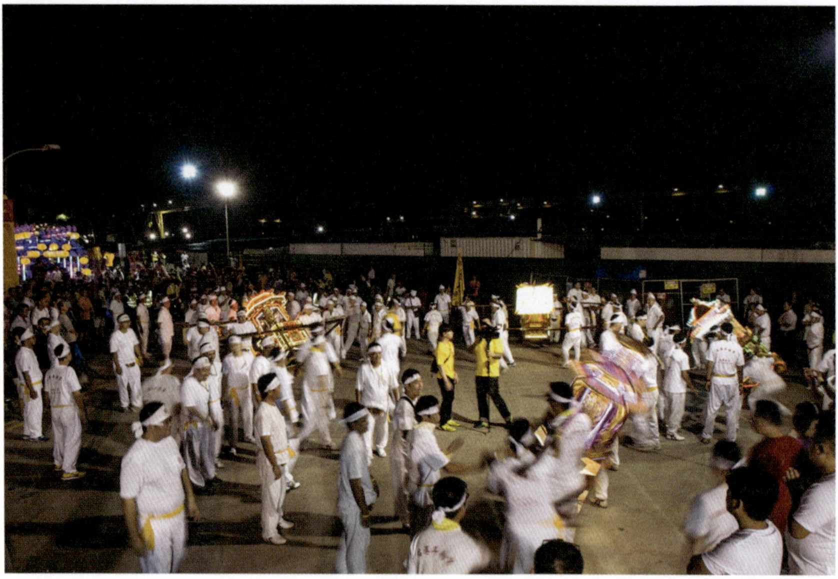

Figure 13.6 The Gods arrive, inhabiting idols and urns that are placed in *kio* (palanquins) that rock back and forth.

Technical details	***Techniques used***	***Post-processing***
Aperture f/10 Shutter speed: 1/6 sec ISO: 500 Metering: Matrix Exp comp: 0 Focal length: 24mm	Slow shutter speed (Ch 8) Exhale and shoot (Ch 9) High vantage point (Ch 4) Level horizons (Ch 4) Deep depth-of-field (Ch 7)	• Increased shadows and whites (+) • Increased clarity and vibrance (+) • Decreased saturation (-)

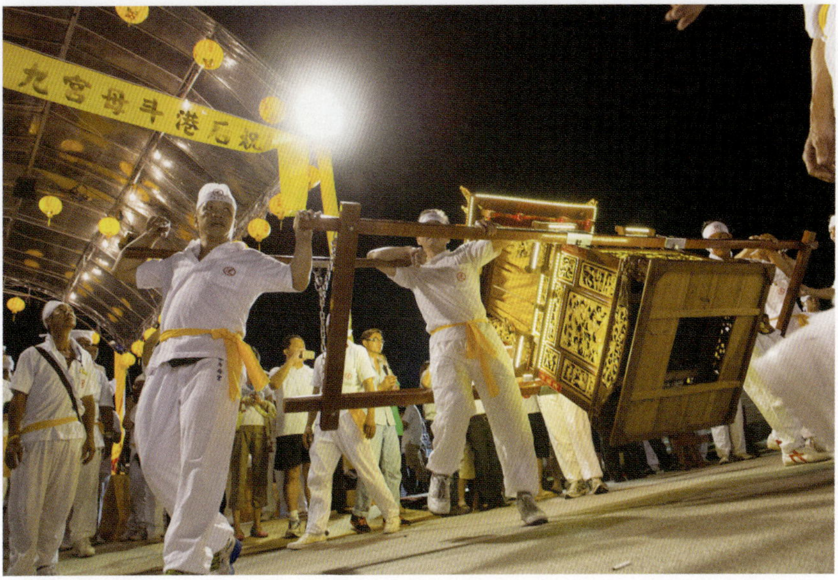

Figure 13.7 Another view of a *kio* as it is paraded around the ritual stage.

Technical details	***Techniques used***	***Post-processing***
Aperture f/5 Shutter speed: 1/200 sec ISO: 2000 Metering: Matrix Exp comp: 0 Focal length: 24mm	Low vantage point (Ch 4) Rule-of-thirds (Ch 5) Uneven horizon for impact (Ch 4) Environmental portrait (Ch 8)	• Increased contrast (+) • Increased shadows (+) • Increased vibrance and saturation (+)

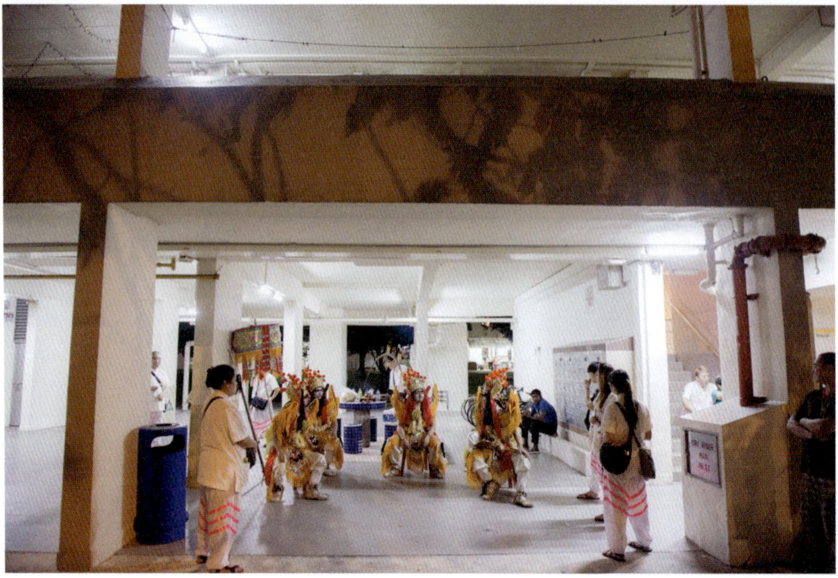

Figure 13.8 Devotees taking the role of *Ba Jia Jiang* (八家將, Eight Home Generals), a cultural form commonly seen in Taiwan and gaining popularity in Singapore. Waiting for the *Dou Mu Gong* procession to arrive in a sister temple.

Technical details	***Techniques used***	***Post-processing***
Aperture f/3.2 Shutter speed: 1/40 sec ISO: 4000 Metering: Matrix Exp comp: 0 Focal length: 24mm	Framing (Ch 5) Environmental portrait (Ch 8) Exposure lock (Ch 9)	• Increased exposure and contrast (+) • Decreased highlights and whites (-) • Increased vibrance (+) • Decreased saturation (-)

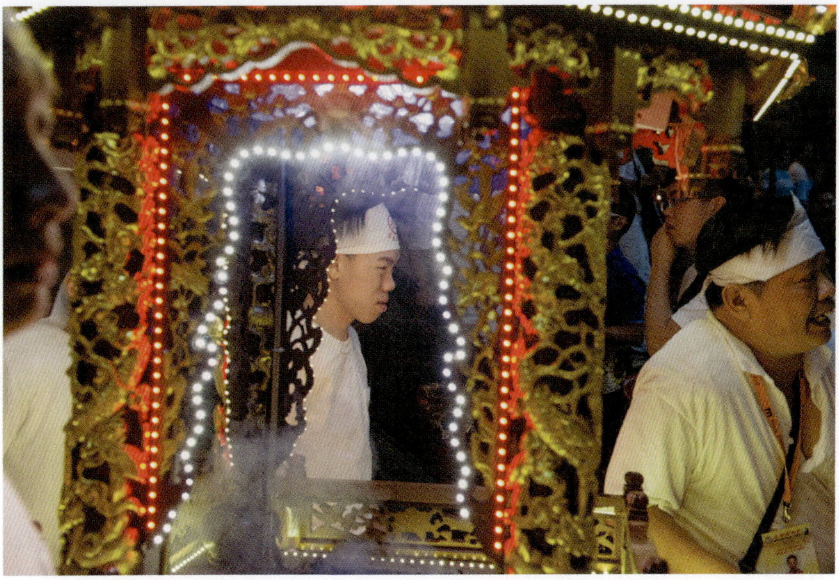

Figure 13.9 The Gods arrive at the *Gao Lin Gong* (槔林宫) in Bishan.

Technical details	***Techniques used***	***Post-processing***
Aperture f/5.6 Shutter speed: 1/125 sec ISO: 2000 Metering: Matrix Exp comp: +0.3 Focal length: 48mm	Framing (Ch 5) Half-body portrait (Ch 8) Exposure comp (Ch 9) Depth-of-field (Ch 7)	• Increased whites (+) • Decreased blacks (-) • Increased clarity (+)

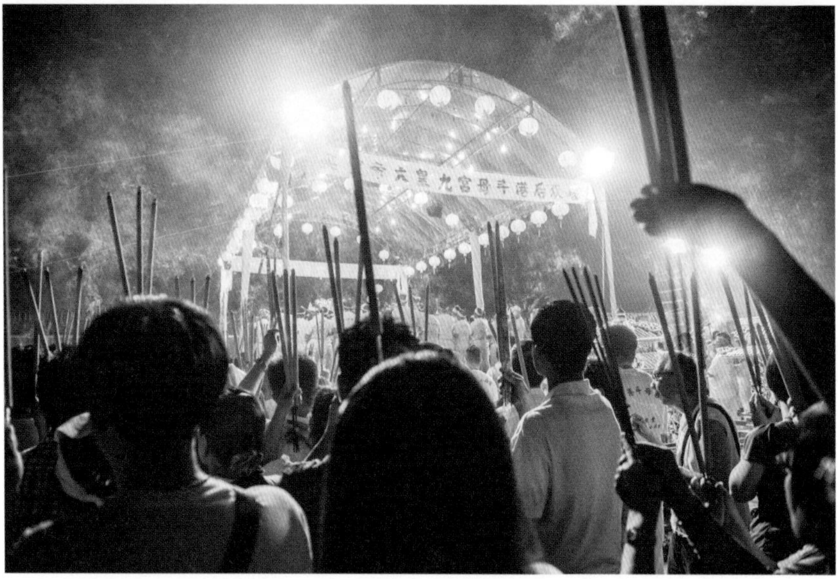

Figure 13.10 The Gods return to Pulau Punggol Timor for their send-off. The event is repeated around the island and is one of the few Chinese religious events in Singapore well-attended by politicians.

Technical details	*Techniques used*	*Post-processing*
Aperture f/3.2	Depth-of-field (Ch 7)	• Increased contrast (+)
Shutter speed: 1/640 sec	Focus lock (Ch 5)	• Decreased highlights and blacks (-)
ISO: 3200		• Significantly increased clarity (+)
Metering: Matrix		• Decreased saturation (-)
Exp comp: 0		
Focal length: 24mm		

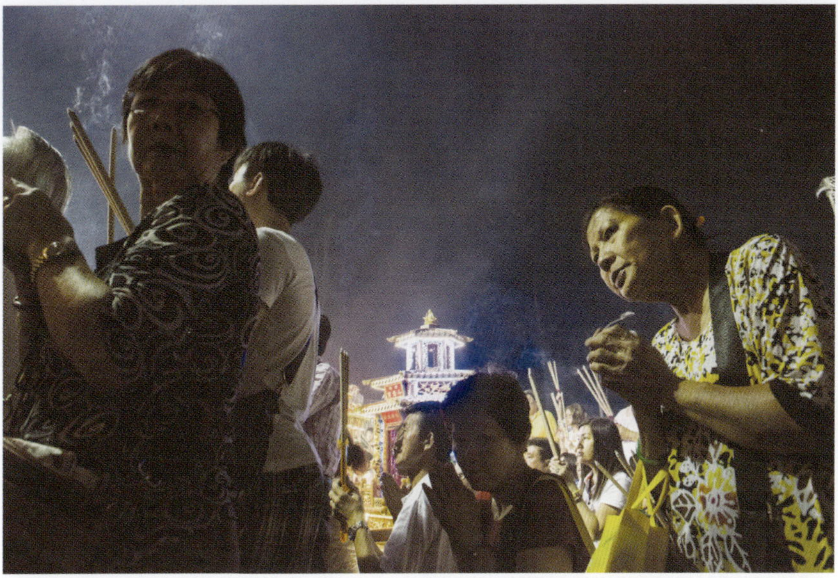

Figure 13.11 With a *kio* in the background, devotees offer their prayers, requests and respect to the Gods.

Technical details	*Techniques used*	*Post-processing*
Aperture f/7.1 Shutter speed: 1/100 sec ISO: 3200 Metering: Matrix Exp comp: 0 Focal length: 24mm	Depth-of-field (Ch 7) Focus lock (Ch 5) Anonymity (Ch 12) Framing (Ch 5) Low vantage point (Ch 4)	• Increased exposure, contrast and shadow (+) • Increased clarity and vibrance (+)

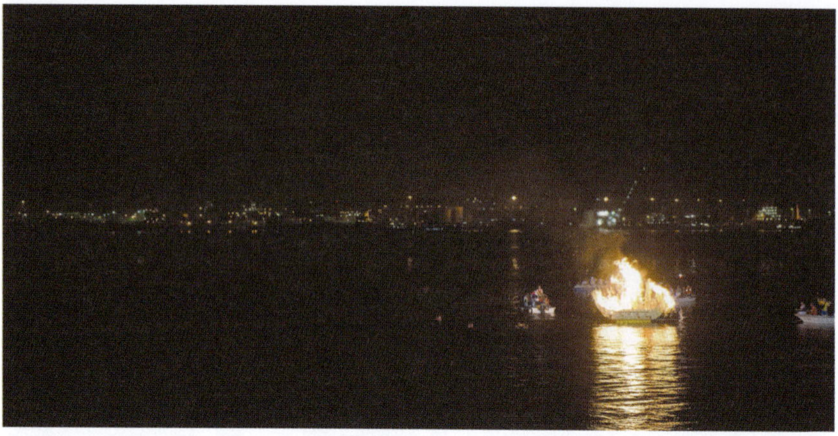

Figure 13.12 The final send-off involves setting fire to a paper effigy of a boat, loaded with devotees' petitions and prayers. Photographed through a wire-mesh fence.

Technical details	***Techniques used***	***Post-processing***
Aperture f/2.8 Shutter speed: 1/160 sec ISO: 3200 Metering: Matrix Exp comp: 0 Focal length: 62mm	Depth-of-field (Ch 7) Focus lock (Ch 5) Exposure lock (Ch 9) Rule-of-thirds (Ch 5) Level horizons (Ch 4)	• 16:9 Crop and straighten • Decreased highlights and whites (-)

References

Abbott, Berenice. 1939. "Changing New York." *New York Public Library Digital Collections*. http://digitalcollections.nypl.org/collections/changing-new-york#/?tab=about&scroll=39.

Allain, Rhett. 2012. "How to Make a Hobbit with Forced Perspective." http://www.wired.com/2012/12/how-to-make-a-hobbit-with-forced-perspective/.

Alper, M. 2013. "War on Instagram: Framing Conflict Photojournalism with Mobile Photography Apps." *New Media & Society* 16 (8) (September 18): 1233–1248. doi:10.1177/1461444813504265. http://nms.sagepub.com/content/early/2013/09/16/1461444813504265.

Anonymous. 2016. "Digital Camera Image Noise, Pt 2." *Cambridge in Colour*. Accessed February 19. http://www.cambridgeincolour.com/tutorials/image-noise-2.htm.

Avedon, Richard. 1963. "William Casby, Born in Slavery." http://www.christies.com/lotfinder/photographs/richard-avedon-william-casby-born-in-slavery-5379351-details.aspx.

Back, Les. 2007. *The Art of Listening*. Oxford and New York: Berg. https://books.google.com/books?id=tknuAAAAMAAJ&pgis=1.

Banks, Marcus. 2001. *Visual Methods in Social Research*. London: Sage.

Barthes, Roland. 1981. *Camera Lucida*. New York: Hill and Wang.

Bate, David. 2016. *Photography: The Key Concepts*. Bloomsbury Publishing. https://books.google.com/books?id=SoBUCwAAQBAJ&pgis=1.

Bates, Charlotte. 2014. *Video Methods: Social Science Research in Motion*. London: Routledge. https://books.google.com/books?id=ZXxsBAAAQBAJ&pgis=1.

Beasley, Douglas. 2015. "The Difference Between Taking a Snapshot & Making a Photograph." http://douglasbeasley.com/2015/04/02/the-difference-between-taking-a-snapshot-making-a-photograph/.

Beck, Jay, and Tony Grajeda. 2008. *Lowering the Boom: Critical Studies in Film Sound*. Illinois: University of Illinois Press. https://books.google.com/books?id=VoKROBFWuvoC&pgis=1.

Becker, Howard S. 2008. "Visual Sociology, Documentary Photography, and Photojournalism: It's (almost) All a Matter of Context" (July 3). http://www.tandfonline.com.libproxy1.nus.edu.sg/doi/abs/10.1080/14725869508583745#.UvI6mk3xtlU.

Benjamin, Walter. 2008. *The Work of Art in the Age of Mechanical Reproduction*. London: Penguin Books Limited. https://books.google.com/books?id=ZucuzeiI-24C&pgis=1.

Berger, John. 2008. *Ways of Seeing*. London: Penguin Books Limited. https://books.google.com/books?id=QxdperNq5R8C&pgis=1.

Bezner, Lili Corbus. 2002. "Wedding Photography: 'A Shining Language.'" *Visual Resources* 18 (1) (January 4): 1–16. doi:10.1080/01973760290026477. http://www.tandfonline.com/doi/abs/10.1080/01973760290026477.

Blaagaard, B. B. 2013. "Post-Human Viewing: A Discussion of the Ethics of Mobile Phone Imagery." *Visual Communication* 12 (3) (July 8): 359–374. doi:10.1177/1470357213483056. http://vcj.sagepub.com/content/12/3/359.abstract.

Bradley, Jason. 2015. *Creative Workflow in Lightroom: The Photographer's Guide to Managing, Developing, and Sharing Your Work*. New York: Taylor & Francis Group. https://books.google.com/books?id=2nvHsgEACAAJ&pgis=1.

Brady, Barry J. 2015. "How to Avoid and Reduce Noise in Your Images." *Digital Photography School*. http://digital-photography-school.com/how-to-avoid-and-reduce-noise-in-your-images/.

Buehl, Jonathan. 2014. "Toward an Ethical Rhetoric of the Digital Scientific Image: Learning From the Era When Science Met Photoshop." *Technical Communication Quarterly* 23 (3) (June 9): 184–206. doi:10.1080/10572252.2014.914783.http://www.tandfonline.com/doi/abs/10.1080/10572252.2014.914783.

Buse, Peter. 2010. "Polaroid into Digital: Technology, Cultural Form, and the Social Practices of Snapshot Photography." *Continuum: Journal of Media & Cultural Studies* (March 26). http://www.tandfonline.com/doi/abs/10.1080/10304310903363864.

Bush, Lewis. 2016. "Crystallisation or Simplification: World Press Photo 2015." http://www.disphotic.com/crystallization-or-simplification-world-press-photo-2015/.

Cade, D L. 2013. "Lewis Hine's Photography and the End of Child Labor in the United States." *PetaPixel*. http://petapixel.com/2013/09/07/lewis-hines-photography-end-child-labor-united-states/.

——. 2015. "Incredible Macro Photos Taken with a Smartphone & DIY Lens." https://iso.500px.com/incredible-macro-photos-taken-with-a-smartphone-diy-lens/.

Callon, Michel, John Law, and Arie Rip. 1986. *The Sociology of an Actor-Network: The Case of the Electric Vehicle*. Basingstoke: Macmillan.

Capa, Robert. 1944. "France. Normandy. June 6th, 1944. US Troops Assault Omaha Beach during the D-Day Landings." http://www.magnumphotos.com/Asset/-2S5RYD1KRDB1.html.

Carey, Peter West. 2010. "Lightroom's Clarity Slider – What Does It Do?" http://digital-photography-school.com/lightrooms-clarity-slider-what-does-it-do/.

Cartier-Bresson, Henri. 1948. "Final Days of the Kuomintang." http://www.magnumphotos.com/Asset/-2S5RYDZ7G9JU.html.

Chan, Kwok-bun, and Sai-shing Yung. 2005. "Chinese Entertainment, Ethnicity, and Pleasure." *Visual Anthropology* 18 (2–3) (March 1): 103–142. doi:10.1080/08949460590914813. http://www.tandfonline.com/doi/abs/10.1080/08949460590914813.

Chan, Margaret. 2006. *Ritual Is Theatre, Theatre Is Ritual: Spirit Medium Worship*. Singapore: Wee Kim Wee Centre, Singapore Management University.

Chappell, D., S. Chappell, and E. Margolis. 2010. "School as Ceremony and Ritual: How Photography Illuminates Performances of Ideological Transfer." *Qualitative Inquiry* 17 (1) (December 16): 56–73. doi:10.1177/1077800410389444. http://qix.sagepub.com/content/17/1/56.abstract.

Cheu, Hock Tong. 1993. "The Festival of the Nine Emperor Gods in Peninsular Southeast Asia." In *Studies on the Chinese Religion in Malaysia, Singapore and Indonesia: Chinese Beliefs and Practices in Southeast Asia*, edited by Hock Tong Cheu, 17–58. Malaysia: Pelanduk Publications.

Chia, Aik Beng. 2015a. "Singapore through an Instagrammer's Eyes." *The Guardian*. http://www.theguardian.com/travel/gallery/2015/mar/17/singapore-through-an-instagrammers-eyes.

——. 2015b. "Rochor Centre." http://www.aikbengchia.com/singkarpor#3.

Chong, Terence, and Yew-Foong Hui. 2013. *Different Under God: A Survey of Church-Going Protestants in Singapore*. Institute of Southeast Asian Studies. https://books.google.com/books?id=OEg8pmblkqUC&pgis=1.

Chopra, R. 1989. "Robert Gardner's 'Forest of Bliss' – A Review." *Visual Anthropology Review* 5 (1): 2–3.

Cicala, Roger. 2012. "The Camera Versus the Human Eye." *PetaPixel*. http://petapixel.com/2012/11/17/the-camera-versus-the-human-eye/.

Clark, Andrew, Jon Prosser, and Rose Wiles. 2010. "Ethical Issues in Image-Based Research." *Arts & Health* 2 (1) (March 22): 81–93. doi:10.1080/17533010903495298. http://www.tandfonline.com/doi/abs/10.1080/17533010903495298.

Clark, T. 2008. "'We're Over-Researched Here!': Exploring Accounts of Research Fatigue within Qualitative Research Engagements." *Sociology* 42 (5) (October 1): 953–970. doi:10.1177/0038038508094573. http://soc.sagepub.com/content/42/5/953.short.

Cobley, P., and N. Haeffner. 2009. "Digital Cameras and Domestic Photography: Communication, Agency and Structure." *Visual Communication* 8 (2) (April 22): 123–146. doi:10.1177/1470357209102110. http://vcj.sagepub.com/content/8/2/123.abstract.

Cohen, Robin. 1997. *Global Diasporas: An Introduction. Global Diasporas.* London: UCL Press.

Coleman, David. 2015. "Lightroom Alternative." http://havecamerawilltravel.com/photographer/lightroom-alternatives.

Collier, John, and Malcolm Collier. 1986. *Visual Anthropology: Photography as a Research Method.* Rev. and e. Albuquerque: University of New Mexico Press.

Comaroff, J. 2007. "Ghostly Topographies: Landscape and Biopower in Modern Singapore." *Cultural Geographies* 14 (1) (January 1): 56–73. doi:10.1177/1474474007072819. http://cgj.sagepub.com/content/14/1/56.short.

Crang, Mike. 1998. *Cultural Geography.* New York: Routledge.

Crawford, Adam. 2015. "Part I: Top 25 Famous Photographers and Their Cameras." *Precise Moment.* http://precise-moment.com/2015/02/09/top-25-famous-photographers-cameras/.

Cross, Karen. 2014. "Training the Eye of the Photographer: The Education of the Amateur." *Visual Studies* 29 (1) (January 27): 68–79. doi:10.1080/1472586X.2014.862996. http://www.tandfonline.com/doi/abs/10.1080/1472586X.2014.862996.

Dant, Tim, and David Bowles. 2003. "Dealing with Dirt: Servicing and Repairing Cars." *Sociological Research Online* 8 (2). http://www.socresonline.org.uk/8/2/dant.html.

Dean, Kenneth. 1995. *Taoist Ritual and Popular Cults of Southeast China.* Princeton NJ: Princeton University Press.

DeBernardi, Jean. 2004. *Rites of Belonging: Memory, Modernity, and Identity in a Malaysian Chinese Community.* Vol. 8. Stanford: Stanford University Press. https://books.google.com/books?id=vvR8TZB0dBUC&pgis=1.

DeBernardi, Jean Elizabeth. 2012. *The Way That Lives in the Heart: Chinese Popular Religion and Spirit Mediums in Penang, Malaysia.* Singapore: NUS Press. https://books.google.com.sg/books/about/The_Way_that_Lives_in_the_Heart.html?id=ao6DZwEACAAJ&pgis=1.

Di Bello, Patrizia. 2012. "Photographic Portraits." *Photography: The Whole Story.* London: Thames and Hudson.

Doisneau, Robert. 1950. "Kiss by the Hotel de Ville." http://masters-of-photography.com/D/doisneau/doisneau_kiss_full.html.

Edgerton, Harold. 1936. "Milk Drop Coronet." http://www.hrc.utexas.edu/exhibitions/permanent/windows/south/harold_edgerton.html.

Edwards, E. 1997. "Beyond the Boundary: A Consideration of the Expressive in Photography and Anthropology." In *Rethinking Visual Anthropology*, edited by Marcus Banks and Howard Morphy, 53–80. New Haven; London: Yale University Press.

Eliade, Mircea. 1961. *The Sacred and the Profane: The Nature of Religion.* New York: Harper & Brothers. https://books.google.com.sg/books/about/The_Sacred_and_the_Profane.html?id=uh4vAAAAYAAJ&pgis=1.

Elliott, Alan J.A. 1955. *Chinese Spirit-Medium Cults in Singapore*. London: London School of Economics and Political Science.

Evans, Grant. 1998. *The Politics of Ritual and Remembrance: Laos Since 1975*. Hawaii: University of Hawaii Press. https://books.google.com/books?id=YuFBztNY7akC&pgis=1.

Evans, Walker. 1936. "Alabama Tenant Farmer Wife." http://www.metmuseum.org/collection/the-collection-online/search/284685.

Evening, Martin. 2015. *Adobe Photoshop CC for Photographers, 2015 Release*. London: CRC Press. https://books.google.com/books?id=JrNmCgAAQBAJ&pgis=1.

Fellig, Arthur. 1939. "Tenement Fire." http://www.moma.org/collection/works/46198?locale=en.

——. 1941. "Brooklyn School Children See Gambler Murdered in Street." http://www.moma.org/collection/works/48156?locale=en.

Ford, Colin. 2005. "Portraiture." *The Oxford Companion to the Photograph*. Oxford: Oxford University Press.

Fox, Anna, and Richard Sawdon Smith. 2016. *Langford's Basic Photography: The Guide for Serious Photographers*. London: CRC Press. https://books.google.com/books?id=MJxYCwAAQBAJ&pgis=1.

Franklin, Stuart. 2016. "Undeceiving the World." *Harper's Magazine*, March. http://harpers.org/archive/2016/03/undeceiving-the-world/?single=1.

Freedman, Maurice. 1957. *Chinese Family and Marriage in Singapore*. London: Her Majesty's Stationery Office.

Gilroy, Paul. 1993. *The Black Atlantic: Modernity and Double Consciousness*. Cambridge, Mass.: Harvard University Press.

Goffman, Erving. 1969. *The Presentation of Self in Everyday Life*. London: Allen Lane The Penguin Press.

Gold, Steven J. 1997. "Visual Methods in Sociological Analysis – Introduction." *Qualitative Sociology* 20 (1): 3–6.

Gómez Cruz, Edgar, and Eric T. Meyer. 2012. "Creation and Control in the Photographic Process: iPhones and the Emerging Fifth Moment of Photography." *Photographies* 5 (2) (September 28): 203–221. doi:10.1080/17540763.2012.702123. http://www.tandfonline.com/doi/abs/10.1080/17540763.2012.702123?src=recsys.

Gomez, Rolando. 2010. "Cropping In Photography – An Element Of Composition." *Lens Diaries*. http://www.lensdiaries.com/photo-tips/cropping-photography-composition/.

Graburn, Nelson H H. 2001. "Secular Ritual: A General Theory of Tourism." In *Hosts and Guests Revisited: Tourism Issues of the 21st Century*, edited by Valene L. Smith and Maryann Brent, 42–50. Elmsford: Cognizant Communication.

Greer, Jennifer D., and Joseph D. Gosen. 2002. "How Much Is Too Much?" *Visual Communication Quarterly* 9 (3) (June 6): 4–13. doi:10.1080/15551390209363485. http://www.tandfonline.com/doi/abs/10.1080/15551390209363485?src=recsys.

Hall, Edward T. 1982. *The Hidden Dimension*. New York: Anchor Books. https://books.google.com/books?id=HP8-ngEACAAJ&pgis=1.

Hall, Kimberly. 2015. "Selfies and Self-Writing: Cue Card Confessions as Social Media Technologies of the Self." *Television & New Media* 17 (3) (June 22): 228–242. doi:10.1177/1527476415591221. http://tvn.sagepub.com/content/17/3/228.abstract.

Hall, Stuart, ed. 1997. *Representation*. London: Sage.

Hammersley, Martyn, and Paul Atkinson. 2007. *Ethnography: Principles in Practice*. New York: Routledge. https://books.google.com/books?id=QLY0h-_hdysC&pgis=1.

Harper, Douglas A. 2012. *Visual Sociology*. New York: Routledge.

Harper, D., C. Knowles, and P. Leonard. 2005. "Visually Narrating Post-Colonial Lives." *Visual Studies* 20 (1): 4–15.

Harris, Christopher R. 1991. "Digitization and Manipulation of News Photographs." *Journal of Mass Media Ethics* 6 (3) (September 17): 164–174. doi:10.1207/s15327728jmme0603_4. http://www.tandfonline.com/doi/abs/10.1207/s15327728jmme0603_4?src=recsys.

Harris, Tom. 2016. "How Cameras Work." Accessed February 22. http://electronics.howstuffworks.com/camera1.htm.

Hawkins, Marcus. 2015. "What Is Focal Length in Photography?" *Digital Camera World*. http://www.digitalcameraworld.com/2015/10/15/what-is-focal-length-camera-photography/.

Heng, Terence. 2011. "Making Chineseness in Transdiasporic Space: It's a Matter of Ethnic Taste." *Sociology*. London: Goldsmiths, University of London.

——. 2012. "A Wedding Photographer's Journey through the Chinese Singaporean Urban Landscape." *Cultural Geographies* 19 (2): 259–270.

——. 2014. "Hungry Ghosts in Urban Spaces: A Visual Study of Aesthetic Markers and Material Anchoring." *Visual Communication* 13 (2) (April 24): 147–162. doi:10.1177/1470357213496520. http://vcj.sagepub.com/content/13/2/147.abstract.

——. 2015. "An Appropriation of Ashes: Transient Aesthetic Markers and Spiritual Place-Making as Performances of Alternative Ethnic Identities." *The Sociological Review* 63 (1) (February 27): 57–78. doi:10.1111/1467-954X.12235. http://doi.wiley.com/10.1111/1467-954X.12235.

——. 2016. "Making 'Unofficial' Sacred Space: Spirit Mediums and House Temples in Singapore." *Geographical Review* 106 (2) (April 9): 215–234. doi:10.1111/j.1931-0846.2015.12156.x. http://doi.wiley.com/10.1111/j.1931-0846.2015.12156.x.

Hine, Lewis. 1912. "A Midnight Scene in More-Jonas Works." https://catalog.archives.gov/id/523234.

Hingley, Liz. 2011. "Photographer as Researcher in the Project 'Under Gods: Stories from Soho Road.'" *Visual Studies* 26 (3): 260–269.

Hjorth, L., and S. Pink. 2013. "New Visualities and the Digital Wayfarer: Reconceptualizing Camera Phone Photography and Locative Media." *Mobile Media & Communication* 2 (1) (December 24): 40–57. doi:10.1177/2050157913505257. http://mmc.sagepub.com/content/2/1/40.abstract.

Hochman, N. 2014. "The Social Media Image." *Big Data & Society* 1 (2) (August 29): 2053951714546645. doi:10.1177/2053951714546645. http://bds.sagepub.com/content/1/2/2053951714546645.abstract.

Hockings, Paul. 2010. "Visual Aspects of Ritual Behavior: The Funeral, for Instance." *Visual Anthropology* 23 (3): 175–185.

Hoffman, Daniel. 2012. "Corpus: Mining the Border." *Cultural Anthropology* 27. http://www.culanth.org/photo_essays/1-corpus-mining-the-border.

Houlihan, Kasia. 2004. "Annotation – Roland Barthes' Camera Lucida—Reflections on Photography." *Theories of Media Annotations.* http://csmt.uchicago.edu/annotations/barthescamera.htm.

Howlett, Robert. 1857. "Isambard Kingdom Brunel Standing Before the Launching Chains of the Great Eastern." http://www.metmuseum.org/collection/the-collection-online/search/283083.

Ingold, Tim. 2000. *The Perception of the Environment: Essays on Livelihood, Dwelling and Skill.* London: Routledge.

James, V. 1977. "Marriage Customs of Christian Son Kolis." *Asian Folklore Studies* 36 (2): 131–148.

Jarvis, Chase. 2009. "The Best Camera is the One That's with You: iPhone Photography by Chase Jarvis" (September 25). http://dl.acm.org/citation.cfm?id=1804566.

Jordan, Sara R. 2013. "Research Integrity, Image Manipulation, and Anonymizing Photographs in Visual Social Science Research." *International Journal of Social Research Methodology* 17 (4) (January 23): 441–454. doi:10.1080/13645579.2012.759333. http://www.tandfonline.com/doi/abs/10.1080/13645579.2012.759333.

Junker, Buford. 1960. *Field Work.* Chicago, Ill.: University of Chicago Press.

Keightley, E., and M. Pickering. 2014. "Technologies of Memory: Practices of Remembering in Analogue and Digital Photography." *New Media & Society* 16 (4) (May 15): 576–593. doi:10.1177/1461444814532062. http://nms.sagepub.com/content/16/4/576.short.

Keiller, Patrick. 2009. "Landscape and Cinematography." *Cultural Geographies* 16 (3) (June 25): 409–414. doi:10.1177/1474474009105056. http://cgj.sagepub.com/content/16/3/409.extract.

Keimig, Lance. 2010. *Night Photography: Finding Your Way in the Dark.* London: Taylor & Francis. https://books.google.com/books?hl=en&lr=&id=uSsZ5mxaU-kC&pgis=1.

Kelby, Scott. 2013. *The Adobe Photoshop Lightroom 5 Book for Digital Photographers.* San Francisco: Peachpit Press. https://books.google.com/books?id=0XEYAAAAQBAJ&pgis=1.

Kesting, Marietta. 2014. "Photographic Portraits of Migrants in South Africa: Framed between Identity Photographs and (self-)presentation." *Social Dynamics* 40 (3): 471–494. doi:10.1080/02533952.2014.989678. http://dx.doi.org/10.1080/02533952.2014.989678.

Kim, Eric. 2010. "How to Master 'The Decisive Moment.'" http://erickimphotography.com/blog/2010/07/01/%E2%80%9Chow-to-masterthe-decisive-moment%E2%80%9D/.

King, Elaine A, and Gail Levin. 2006. *Ethics and the Visual Arts*. New York: Allworth Press. https://books.google.com/books?id=gG3YMPiouEoC&pgis=1.

Knowles, Caroline. 2003. *Race and Social Analysis*. London: SAGE.

——. 2006. "Seeing Race Through the Lens." *Ethnic and Racial Studies* 29 (3).

——. 2014. *Flip-Flop: A Journey Through Globalisation's Backroads*. London: Pluto Press. https://books.google.com/books?id=L9V8ngEACAAJ&pgis=1.

Knowles, Caroline, and Douglas A Harper. 2009. *Hong Kong: Migrant Lives, Landscapes, and Journeys*. Chicago, Ill.: University of Chicago Press.

Knowles, Caroline, and Paul Sweetman. 2004. *Picturing the Social Landscape: Visual Methods and the Sociological Imagination*. London: Routledge.

Kobre, Kenneth, and Betsy Brill. 2004. *Photojournalism: The Professionals' Approach, Volume 1*. Oxford: Focal Press. https://books.google.com/books?id=UQ6gJMsiOJgC&pgis=1.

Kong, Lily. 1993. "Ideological Hegemony and the Political Symbolism of Religious Buildings in Singapore." *Environment and Planning D: Society and Space* 11 (1): 23–45. doi:10.1068/d110023. http://www.envplan.com/abstract.cgi?id=d110023.

Kong, Lily, and Brenda S A Yeoh. 2003. "Nation, Ethnicity and Identity." In *The Chinese Diaspora: Space, Place, Mobility, and Identity*, edited by Laurence J. C. Ma and Carolyn L. Cartier, 193–216. Lanham, Md.; Oxford: Rowman & Littlefield.

Kost, Julieanne. n.d. "LR – Using the Crop and Straighten Tools." http://tv.adobe.com/watch/adobe-evangelists-julieanne-kost/episode-1/.

la Grange, Ashley. 2005. *Basic Critical Theory for Photographers*. Oxford: Focal Press.

Lampe, Cliff A C, Nicole Ellison, and Charles Steinfield. 2007. "A Familiar Face(Book): Profile Elements As Signals in an Online Social Network." In *Proceedings of the SIGCHI Conference on Human Factors in Computing Systems*, 435–444. CHI '07. New York, NY, USA: ACM. doi:10.1145/1240624.1240695. http://doi.acm.org/10.1145/1240624.1240695.

Lange, Dorothea. 1936. "Migrant Mother, Nipomo, California." https://www.loc.gov/rr/print/list/128_migm.html.

Lange, Philip. 2006. "Toast." http://www.shutterstock.com/pic-3686512/stock-photo-five-pieces-of-toast-isolated-over-white-background-with-clipping-path.html?src=CNp3m7DtKQ2tXrH5XKVPJA-1-1.

Langmann, Sten, and David Pick. 2013. "Dignity and Ethics in Research Photography." *International Journal of Social Research Methodology* 17 (6) (August 9): 709–721. doi:10.1080/13645579.2013.825473. http://www.tandfonline.com/doi/abs/10.1080/13645579.2013.825473.

Lee, Raymond L. M. 1986. "Continuity and Change in Chinese Spirit Mediumship in Urban Malaysia." *Bijdragen Tot de Taal-, Land- En Volkenkunde*.

Leet, Sri-Kartini. 2013. "Nature as Construct: A Conservation Project in Singapore." *Photography and Culture* 6 (2): 235–244.

Lefebvre, Henri. 1991. *Critique of Everyday Life*. London: Verso.

——. 1996. *The Production of Space*. Oxford: Blackwell.

Lester, Paul Martin. 2015. *Photojournalism: An Ethical Approach*. Routledge. https://books.google.com/books?id=yegsCgAAQBAJ&pgis=1.

Ling, Richard Seyler. 2008. *New Tech, New Ties: How Mobile Communication Is Reshaping Social Cohesion*. Cambridge, MA: MIT Press. https://books.google.com/books?id=SZ24AAAAIAAJ&pgis=1.

Lockhart, Jordan. 2015. "Understanding Depth of Field: How Aperture Affects DOF, Visualized." *PetaPixel*. http://petapixel.com/2015/02/17/understanding-depth-field-aperture-affects-dof/.

Lomax, Helen, and Neil Casey. 1998. "Recording Social Life: Reflexivity and Video Methodology." *Sociological Research Online* 3 (2) (June 30). http://www.socresonline.org.uk/3/2/1.

Low, Bee Yin. 2014. "Google Study: Singapore Is World's Top Smartphone Market per Capita." *Mumbrella*. http://www.mumbrella.asia/2014/10/google-study-singapore-worlds-top-smartphone-market-per-capita/.

Lowrey, Wilson. 2003. "Normative Conflict in the Newsroom: The Case of Digital Photo Manipulation." *Journal of Mass Media Ethics* 18 (2) (June 17): 123–142. doi:10.1207/S15327728JMME1802_05. http://www.tandfonline.com/doi/abs/10.1207/S15327728JMME1802_05?src=recsys.

Lury, Celia. 1998. *Prosthetic Culture: Photography, Memory and Identity*. London: Routledge. https://books.google.com.sg/books/about/Prosthetic_Culture.html?id=-iFC3nzVIuwC&pgis=1.

Mabe, Michael A. 2010. "Scholarly Communication: A Long View." *New Review of Academic Librarianship* (October 20). http://www.tandfonline.com/doi/full/10.1080/13614533.2010.512242.

Malan, Francois. 2015. "Sensor Size, Perspective and Depth of Field." https://photographylife.com/sensor-size-perspective-and-depth-of-field.

Mandel, Jennifer L. 2003. "Negotiating Expectations in the Field: Gatekeepers, Research Fatigue and Cultural Biases." *Singapore Journal of Tropical Geography* 24 (2) (June 27): 198–210. doi:10.1111/1467-9493.00152. http://doi.wiley.com/10.1111/1467-9493.00152.

Mansurov, Nasim. 2010. "Understanding Metering and Metering Modes." https://photographylife.com/understanding-metering-modes.

——. 2012. "Focus and Recompose Technique." https://photographylife.com/focus-and-recompose-technique.

——. 2015. "What Is Reciprocal Rule in Photography?" https://photographylife.com/what-is-reciprocal-rule-in-photography.

Martin, Paul. 1895. "The Alhambra, London, by Night." http://www.moma.org/collection/works/52413?locale=en.

Matthews, David. 2005. "Ethics and Photography." *The Oxford Companion to the Photograph*. Oxford: Oxford University Press.

McLaren, Peter. 1999. *Schooling as a Ritual Performance: Toward a Political Economy of Educational Symbols and Gestures*. Rowman & Littlefield. https://books.google.com/books?id=4K3KzBfeSdAC&pgis=1.

Mead, Rebecca. 2007. *One Perfect Day: The Selling of the American Wedding*. New York: Penguin Press.

Menzel, Peter, and Faith D'Aluisio. 2010. *What I Eat: Around the World in 80 Diets*. Napa, California: Material World Books. https://books.google.com/books?id=shsgQAAACAAJ&pgis=1.

Menzel, Peter, and Charles C. Mann. 1994. *Material World: A Global Family Portrait*. Berkeley: University of California Press. https://books.google.com/books?id=NGQ7Ng2MDLIC&pgis=1.

Meyer, Jeff. 2012. "Free Portrait Photography Cropping Guide." *Digital Camera World*. http://www.digitalcameraworld.com/2012/03/30/free-portrait-photography-cropping-guide/.

——. 2013. "Histogram: Photography Cheat Sheets for Achieving Perfect Exposure." *Digital Camera World*. http://www.digitalcameraworld.com/2013/06/27/histogram-photography-cheat-sheets-for-achieving-perfect-exposure/.

Meyerowitz, Joel. 1963. "New York City." http://time.com/3793028/joel-meyerowitz-taking-his-time/.

Milicia, Gina. 2015. "Good Crop Bad Crop – How to Crop Portraits." *Digital Photography School*. http://digital-photography-school.com/good-crop-bad-crop-how-to-crop-portraits/.

Miller, Daniel. 2013. *The Comfort of Things*. John Wiley & Sons. https://books.google.com/books?id=qhVGrHGK65IC&pgis=1.

Mills, C. Wright. 2000. *The Sociological Imagination*. New York: Oxford University Press. https://books.google.com/books?id=UTQ6OkKwszoC&pgis=1.

Mitchell, Claudia. 2011. *Doing Visual Research*. London: SAGE.

Mitchell, William J. 1994. *The Reconfigured Eye: Visual Truth in the Post-Photographic Era*. MIT Press. https://books.google.com/books?id=2vtuJpdx5_gC&pgis=1.

Natchwey, James. 1994. "Rwanda." http://www.americansuburbx.com/2009/09/james-nachtwey-from-inferno-to-war-a-few-considerations-on-james-nachtwey-vii-and-war-photography%E2%80%9D-2004.html.

Newton, Julianne H. 1998. "The Burden of Visual Truth: The Role of Photojournalism in Mediating Reality." *Visual Communication Quarterly* 5 (4) (September 6): 4–9. doi:10.1080/15551399809363390. http://www.tandfonline.com/doi/abs/10.1080/15551399809363390.

Niépce, Joseph Nicéphore. 1826. "View from the Window at Le Gras." http://www.hrc.utexas.edu/exhibitions/permanent/windows/southeast/joseph_nicephore_niepce.html.

O'Neil Hughes, Bryan. 2015. "Introduction to Adobe Camera Raw: A Brief History." http://www.lynda.com/Lightroom-tutorials/short-history-Adobe-Camera-Raw-ACR/185329/412684-4.html.

Parr, Martin. 2009. *The Last Resort: Photographs of New Brighton*. Stockport: Dewi Lewis Publishing. https://books.google.com/books?id=391LAQAAIAAJ&pgis=1.

Peterson, Bryan. 2011. *Understanding Digital Photography*. Potter/TenSpeed/Harmony.https://books.google.com/books?id=FG4g-mEZcEMC&pgis=1.

Pinney, Christopher. 1997. *Camera Indica: The Social Life of Indian Photographs. Envisioning Asia*. London: Reaktion Books.

Pink, Sarah. 1997. *Women and Bullfighting: Gender, Sex and the Consumption of Tradition*. Vol. 1. London: Bloomsbury Academic. https://books.google.com/books?id=YyCCAAAAMAAJ&pgis=1.

——. 2007. *Doing Visual Ethnography: Images, Media and Representation in Research*. 2nd ed. London: SAGE Publications.

——. 2008. "An Urban Tour: The Sensory Sociality of Ethnographic Place-Making." *Ethnography* 9 (2): 175–196.

——. 2012a. *Situating Everyday Life: Practices and Places*. London: SAGE Publications. https://books.google.com/books?id=_qd08xcDVRcC&pgis=1.

——. 2012b. "The Visual in Ethnography: Photography, Video, Cultures and Individuals." In *SAGE Visual Methods*, edited by Jason Hughes, 123–144. London: SAGE.

Prakel, David. 2010. *Fundamentals of Creative Photography*. Lausanne, Switzerland: AVA Academic.

Prosser, Jon, and D Schwartz. 1998. "Photographs within the Sociological Research Process." In *Image-Based Research: A Sourcebook for Qualitative Researchers*, edited by Jon Prosser. London: Falmer Press.

PuruShotam, Nirmala. 1998. *Negotiating Language, Constructing Race: Disciplining Difference in Singapore*. Berlin: Mouton de Gruyter.

Reaves, Shiela, Jacqueline Bush Hitchon, Sung-Yeon Park, and Gi Woong Yun. 2004. "If Looks Could Kill: Digital Manipulation of Fashion Models." *Journal of Mass Media Ethics* 19 (1) (March 17): 56–71. doi:10.1207/s15327728jmme1901_5. http://www.tandfonline.com/doi/abs/10.1207/s15327728jmme1901_5.

Richardson, Warren. 2015. "A Man Passes a Baby through the Fence at the Hungarian-Serbian Border in Röszke, Hungary." http://www.worldpressphoto.org/collection/photo/2016/spot-news/warren-richardson.

Riis, Jacob. 1890. "Lodgers in a Crowded Bayard Street Tenement." http://herb.ashp.cuny.edu/items/show/1106.

Ritchin, Fred. 2010. *After Photography*. New York: W. W. Norton. https://books.google.com/books?id=DfFyPwAACAAJ&pgis=1.

Rockwell, Ken. 2012. "Fill Flash." http://www.kenrockwell.com/tech/fill-flash.htm.

Rodger, George. 1949. "The Champion of a Korongo Nuba Wrestling Match, Kordofan, Southern Sudan." http://www.georgerodgerphotographs.com/africa/xi5yle692npq6stff0lk5o9a2vqcn5.

Rorie, David. 1934. "Chamber-Pots Filled with Salt as Marriage Gifts." *Folklore* 45 (2): 162–163. http://links.jstor.org/sici?sici=0015-587X(193406)45:2<162:CFWSAM>2.0.CO;2-U.

Rose, Gillian. 2006. *Visual Methodologies: An Introduction to the Interpretation of Visual Materials*. 2nd ed. London: SAGE.

Rose, Gillian. 2012. *Doing Family Photography: The Domestic, the Public and the Politics of Sentiment*. Vol. 28. Surrey: Ashgate Publishing, Ltd. https://books.google.com/books?id=1uuU4Q4eiyMC&pgis=1.

Rowse, Darren. 2016. "Using Fill Flash." *Digital Photography School.* http://digital-photography-school.com/using-fill-flash/.

Russial, J., and W. Wanta. 1998. "Digital Imaging Skills and the Hiring and Training of Photojournalists." *Journalism & Mass Communication Quarterly* 75 (3) (September 1): 593–605. doi:10.1177/107769909807500312. http://jmq.sagepub.com/content/75/3/593.abstract.

Salgado, Sebastião, Eric Nepomuceno, Lélia Wanick Salgado, and Philadelphia Museum of Art. 1993. *Workers: An Archaeology of the Industrial Age.* New York: Aperture. https://books.google.com/books?id=iNCXQgAACAAJ&pgis=1.

Sassen-Koob, Saskia. 1990. *The Global City.* Princeton NJ: Princeton University Press.

Schiesser, Tim. 2016. "Know Your Smartphone: A Guide to Camera Hardware." *2014.* Accessed January 29. http://www.techspot.com/guides/850-smartphone-camera-hardware/page4.html.

Schwartz, Dona. 2009. *In the Kitchen.* Heidelberg: Kehrer.

SD Association. 2015. "Speed Class." Accessed August 7. https://www.sdcard.org/developers/overview/speed_class/.

Shapter, M J. 1993. "Image Manipulation and the Question of Ethics." *Journal of Audiovisual Media in Medicine* 16 (3): 130–132.

Sheppard, Rob. 2013. "The Importance of Blacks and Whites in Image Adjustment." http://www.natureandphotography.com/?p=1541.

Shu, Les. 2013. "Why Small Sensor Size May Leave Your Photos Feeling Inadequate." *Digital Trends.* http://www.digitaltrends.com/photography/image-sensor-size-matters/.

Sim, Chi Yin. 2014. "China's 'Rat Tribe.'" http://viiphoto.com/articles/chinas-rat-tribe/.

Simpson, P. 2012. "Apprehending Everyday Rhythms: Rhythm Analysis, Time-Lapse Photography, and the Space-Times of Street Performance." *Cultural Geographies* 19 (4) (June 21): 423–445. doi:10.1177/1474474012443201. http://cgj.sagepub.com/content/19/4/423.abstract.

Smith, Graham. 1983. "Thirty Eight Bastard Years on the Furnace Front. Mess Room for No.4 and No.5 Furnaces. Clay Lane, South Bank, Middlesbrough." http://theymadethislondon.com/photography/graham-smith.

Soh, Darren. 2014. "20 Geylang Lorong 3." http://theartling.com/artists/darren-soh/20-geylang-lorong-3-002/.

Soja, Edward W. 1989. *Postmodern Geographies: The Reassertion of Space in Critical Social Theory.* London: Verso.

——. 1996. *Thirdspace: Journeys to Los Angeles and Other Real-and-Imagined Places.* Oxford: Blackwell Publishers.

Sontag, Susan. 1977. *On Photography.* New York: Farrar, Straus and Giroux.

——. 2013. *Regarding the Pain of Others.* London: Penguin Books Limited. https://books.google.com/books?id=XYo3AAAAQBAJ&pgis=1.

Spencer, Stephen. 2011. *Visual Research Methods in the Social Sciences.* New York: Routledge.

Spinner, Jackie. 2013. "'Identity Crisis' in Photojournalism." *American Journalism Review.* http://ajr.org/2013/12/04/photojournalism-new-era/.

Sponaugle, Brittani. 2013. "How to Blur the Background of an Image in Photoshop Elements." https://blog.udemy.com/how-to-blur-background-in-photoshop/.

Stanton, Brandon. 2013. *Humans of New York.* New York: St. Martin's Press.

Steele, Colin. 2014. "Scholarly Communication, Scholarly Publishing and University Libraries. Plus Ça Change?" *Australian Academic & Research Libraries* 45 (4): 241–261.

Stieglitz, Alfred. 1898. "Icy Night, New York." http://www.moma.org/collection/works/51840?locale=en.

Suchar, Charles. 2004. "Amsterdam and Chicago: Seeing the Macro-Characteristics of Gentrification." In *Picturing the Social Landscape: Visual Methods and the Sociological Imagination*, edited by Caroline Knowles and Paul Sweetman, 147–165. London: Routledge.

Tagg, John. 1988. *The Burden of Representation: Essays on Photographies and Histories.* Minneapolis: University of Minnesota Press. https://books.google.com/books?id=jFiETIoAyZsC&pgis=1.

——. 2009. *The Disciplinary Frame: Photographic Truths and the Capture of Meaning.* U of Minnesota Press. https://books.google.com/books?id=tzR1iE_KLckC&pgis=1.

Tan, Khoon Yong. 2001. *Chinese Customs: Ways of Worship.* Singapore: Way Media.

Tan, Serene. 2012. "Serendipity by Serene." http://bukitbrown.com/main/?p=3028.

Taylor, John. 1998. *Body Horror: Photojournalism, Catastrophe and War.* Manchester: Manchester University Press. https://books.google.com/books?id=9aBTSTQoEQQC&pgis=1.

Teiser, Stephen. 1996. *The Ghost Festival in Medieval China.* New Jersey: Princeton University Press.

Tharoor, Ishaan. 2013. "David Guttenfelder Is TIME's Pick for Instagram Photographer of the Year 2013." *Time*, December. http://time.com/11618/david-guttenfelder-is-times-pick-for-instagram-photographer-of-the-year/.

Thomas, Gwen, and Janet Ibbotson. 2015. *Beyond the Lens.* London: Proving House LLP. https://books.google.com/books?id—krWBgAAQBAJ&pgis=1.

Tong, Chee Kiong. 2004. *Chinese Death Rituals in Singapore.* London: RoutledgeCurzon.

Tong, Chee Kiong, and Lily Kong. 2000. "Religion and Modernity: Ritual Transformations and the Reconstruction of Space and Time." *Social & Cultural Geography* 1 (1) (January 5): 29–44. doi:10.1080/14649369950133476. http://www.tandfonline.com/doi/abs/10.1080/14649369950133476#preview.

Van House, Nancy A. 2011. "Personal Photography, Digital Technologies and the Uses of the Visual." *Visual Studies* 26 (2) (June 9): 125–134. doi:10.1080

/1472586X.2011.571888. http://www.tandfonline.com/doi/abs/10.1080/1472586X.2011.571888?src=recsys.

Villi, Mikko. 2015. "'Hey, I'm Here Right Now': Camera Phone Photographs and Mediated Presence." *Photographies* 8 (1) (January 8): 3–22. doi:10.1080/17540763.2014.968937. http://www.tandfonline.com/doi/full/10.1080/17540763.2014.968937.

Wang, Gungwu. 1991. *China and the Chinese Overseas*. Singapore: Times Academic Press.

Wanyan, Shaoyuan. 2008. *Traditional Marriage Customs in China*. Singapore: McGraw-Hill.

Wells, Liz, ed. 2003. *The Photography Reader*. New York: Routledge. https://books.google.com/books?id=woFKAqh4XhoC&pgis=1.

West, Dave. 2012. "Photokina 2012: Hasselblad Shows off Ludicrously Expensive Lunar Mirrorless Camera." *Gadeget Helpline*. http://www.gadgethelpline.com/photokina-2012-hasselblad-shows-ludicrously-expensive-lunar-mirrorless-camera/.

Weston, Edward. 1965. "Seeing Photographically." *Encyclopedia of Photography*. New York: Greystone Press.

Wheeler, Thomas H. 2002. *Phototruth Or Photofiction: Ethics and Media Imagery in the Digital Age*. New York: Taylor & Francis. https://books.google.com.sg/books/about/Phototruth_Or_Photofiction.html?id=fgvdeX5fMvsC&pgis=1.

Wheeler, Tom, and Tim Gleason. 1995. "Photography Or Photofiction: An Ethical Protocol for the Digital Age." *Visual Communication Quarterly* 2 (1) (January 2): 8–12. doi:10.1080/15551393.1995.10387515. http://www.tandfonline.com/doi/abs/10.1080/15551393.1995.10387515.

Wiles, Rose, Amanda Coffey, Judy Robinson, and Sue Heath. 2012. "Anonymisation and Visual Images: Issues of Respect, 'voice' and Protection." *International Journal of Social Research Methodology* 15 (1) (January 13): 41–53. doi:10.1080/13645579.2011.564423. http://www.tandfonline.com/doi/abs/10.1080/13645579.2011.564423?src=recsys.

Wong, Deborah. 2001. *Sounding the Center: History and Aesthetics in Thai Buddhist Performance, Volume 1*. Chicago: University of Chicago Press. https://books.google.com/books?id=KbAk4rSmgxQC&pgis=1.

Yaschur, Carolyn. 2012. "Shooting the Shooter: How Experience Level Affects Photojournalistic Coverage of a Breaking News Event." *Visual Communication Quarterly* 19 (3) (July 13): 161–177. doi:10.1080/15551393.2012.706575. http://www.tandfonline.com/doi/abs/10.1080/15551393.2012.706575.

Zainal, Zakaria. 2012. *Our Gurkhas: Singapore Through Their Eyes*. Singapore: Epigram.

Zavoina, Susan, and Tom Reichert. 2000. "Media Convergence/Management Change: The Evolving Workflow for Visual Journalists." *Journal of Media Economics* 13 (2) (April 17): 143–151. doi:10.1207/S15327736ME1302_6. http://www.tandfonline.com/doi/abs/10.1207/S15327736ME1302_6.

Zhang, Michael. 2012. "Camera Synchronized to Chopper Blades Creates Amazing Illusion." http://petapixel.com/2012/10/19/camera-synchronized-to-chopper-blades-creates-amazing-illusion/.
——. 2016. "World Press Photo Disqualifies Winner." *2010.* Accessed February 12. http://petapixel.com/2010/03/03/world-press-photo-disqualifies-winner/.

Index